PRAISE

AUTISM UNCENSORED

"A spellbinding achievement. Startlingly lucid, magnificently honest, and written with a magic golden pen, this book is an act of personal deliverance, spiritual redemption and heroic citizenship. It will make you weep for the people inside of it but cheer for all humanity. The irrepressible Whitney Ellenby shows us that, even in our darkest hours, all is not lost, we can find a way to a personal light."

_CONGRESSMAN JAMiE RASKiN,
8th District, Maryland; Professor of Constitutional Law, American University, and Best-selling Author of *We the Students and Overruling Democracy: the Supreme Court vs. the American People*

"*Autism Uncensored* is an unflinching exploration of a mother's emotional—and, at times, physical—struggle for the dignity and humanity of her autistic son. A brave book."

—RON SUSKiND, Pulitzer-prize winning journalist and best-selling Author of *Life, Animated: A Story of Sidekicks, Heroes, and Autism (2014)*. Former senior national affairs writer for *The Wall Street Journal* from 1993 to 2000. Other books include *A Hope in the Unseen, The Price of Loyalty, The One Percent Doctrine, The Way of the World* and *Confidence Men*

"Whitney Ellenby's *Autism Uncensored* is not the Hallmark movie version of Autism. It is abrasively honest and often painful to read. But the story of her journey with Zack is one that needs to be told, and the triumphant ending feels earned precisely because of her candor about all that came before it. A truly inspiring read about a remarkable true story."

—BiLL TURQUE, former journalist for *The Washington Post* and Author of *Inventing Al Gore*

"Reading the story of Whitney and Zack is so real that I could visualize, feel, and smell the struggles, joys and emotions of their journey. I have worked with families and individuals with Autism Spectrum Disorder for over 30 years and never have I experienced the intimate depth of knowing what it takes to raise a child with Autism. The writing exposes a parent's vulnerability so that others can better learn and understand the true meaning of unconditional love and acceptance. This book is alive!"

—NANCY K. KELLY, MS Ed, NYS certified Special Education Teacher/Autism Spectrum Disorder Consultant and School District Administrator

"Whitney Ellenby has written a book of love, not just for her son Zack, but for every person who raises a child. Her story helps us comprehend the importance of balancing theory with the monumentally important component of following your gut."

—DONNA MEYER, First Grade Teacher, Bethesda Elementary School.

"What makes this book essential reading is its open and transparent nature. In telling both the darkest and the lightest of moments in raising Zack, Whitney Ellenby gives families dealing with similar situations the best gift of all; they are not alone."

—STEVEN OSHEROW,
Therapist and friend of Zack.

"She brilliantly shares how she went with her gut and used a strategy that ultimately was a success in bringing down the many, many walls that surround a child with autism often preventing them from functioning in our societies . . . The book is, at times, difficult to read, but even through the darkest chapters, the underlying love that is present between a mother and a child is what, I believe, Whitney wants all readers to feel. She is a mother, and she does what most mothers do, she loves! Whitney has taken the knowledge she has gained from her own personal experiences and is giving back to the autism community. *Autism Uncensored* ends with the story behind her priceless gift back to others in the form of service. Yes, not only was the curtain pulled back for Zack, but read the book and you will get the curtain pulled back for you as well!"

—ALLISON HERIN, CCC-SLP,
Waycross Magazine (2018)

"To quote Oprah at the Golden Globes, 'Speaking your truth is the most powerful tool we all have.' But when it comes to autism, agonizing truths are often buried under mounds of socially palatable euphemism, or locked inside homes where family members are barely able to survive, much less write a book. So when a work comes along that deftly shares agonizing scenes of a family besieged by severe autism we should all pay attention.

"In *Autism Uncensored: Pulling Back the Curtain*, author Whitney Ellenby throws the door wide open for all to see, in vivid detail served with layers of emotional turbulence shifting atop like clouds on a changeable day. We see the ripped up books, hear the tantrums, and feel the bites. She does not expose her family's narrative for any mean-spirited or weird voyeuristic purpose, but rather to explain the choices she's made with respect to her son Zack and to seek understanding and true acceptance based on lived experience rather than the sanitized autism fantasies trending in the media.

"In its truthiness, *Uncensored* offers several particularly satisfying messages . . . Because Ellenby does not get caught up in the artifice that is autism, she sees Zack for who he is, underneath and despite of the label. She accepts that he is permanently cognitively disabled, for sure, but she focuses on Zack as Zack, inviting fresh, out-of-the-box thinking about how to be the best parent she can be. That lesson alone is worth the price of the book.

"The book lucidly captures the dark interior monologues that flit through the heads of many an autism parent . . . An important message of Uncensored is this: if you have dark angels whispering in your ear, you are not alone.

"Ellenby seeks to dissolve the isolation endured by many individuals with autism and their families.

"The book contains a brilliant presentation to promote awareness and acceptance. Toward the end of the book, Ellenby has become a one-woman autism awareness and acceptance machine. I found her presentation to Zack's mainstream peers at school an instant classic. I won't repeat it here, but can only say I wish every schoolchild in America could hear it. It would make our autism world a much better place."

—JiLL ESCHER, President, Autism Society of San Francisco Bay Area, *Six Things to Love About 'Autism Uncensored', Cortical Chauvinism*

"THANK YOU WHITNEY ELLENBY for writing this book. I work as a therapist providing play-based therapy to children on the autism spectrum . . . I am so thankful that this book allows for a glimpse into the life of a parent dealing with a diagnosis and treatment. I get an uncensored peek into lives similar on a daily basis, but I feel as though this book gives me a better perspective on how the families could be feeling and what they could be thinking, but do not feel comfortable divulging. I feel like this insight will allow me to better serve my families, but most importantly, my kiddos. This mother decided to take a real-world approach to helping her son function in his world, and I must applaud her."

—GOODREADS REVIEW,
Slumbering Dragon

"I could not put it down and, when I did, I looked forward to getting right back into it. Extremely well-written, a non-fiction that reads like a novel and the vocabulary is wonderful. Her soul-sharing made it not only personal, but interesting . . . I now feel that I, too, am an expert having just learned from an expert . . . I have no doubt that those who read this book and are involved in the day to day caring for an autistic child, will have benefitted on so may levels. Again, it is beautifully written. I'm impressed."

—JOE BROWN, author of children's book series,
The Flights of Marceau

"I am a physician, advocate and most importantly a parent of a young adult with autism. This is a seminal work, outstanding and an absolute must read for every parent. This raw, real and uncensored personal account of raising a child with autism and severe behavioral issues will resonate with tens of thousands of parents who are struggling to help their sons and daughters. The reality is that, contrary to the popular media portrayal of autistic individuals with 'splinter skills,' this is not the reality for millions of families. The author details the incredible love and struggles she and her husband go through to give their son a life filled with respect and dignity. There is no other work like this, and to every parent and family struggling to provide for a son or daughter with autism you are not alone. The author's work is inspirational."

—MICHAEL D. GREENBERG, MD

"This book was not good, but truly excellent! Thank you for allowing me to hear your story. I too have a passion for 'anything Autism' but for different reasons. I truly believe your story has helped me as a clinician. I plan on asking my therapists to read it and definitely the PT, OT and Speech students we train. THANK YOU!"

—STACIE RUBIN SMITH,
Managing Director of the Child Development
Department, South Miami Hospital

"Whitney Ellenby holds nothing back and gives us a view into her reality and the life she and her family have been living since her child Zack was born. Her refreshing honesty forces the reader to face head on the challenges of living with a child with severe autism. Throughout the book she also conveys the love she has for Zack. She makes it clear that the story is her own and every family, every child, has different challenges - however there is a common thread that ties them to the greater community even when at times they feel isolated, especially when treatments and programs seem to fail. It is difficult to accept that your child is who they are and will never be neurotypical and will always have difficulties in a world not interested in catering to their needs and Whitney not only clears that hurdle she makes the effort to bring other families with her.

"The book ends with optimism and you know that her love and acceptance for her son means that she is going to make the world a better place for him and other families."

—SUSAN INGRAM, Executive Director, Community Support Services, non-profit provider of community-based support services to children andadults with Autism and other severe developmental disabilities

"Thank you Whitney Ellenby for writing *Autism Uncensored* and getting it out in the world. Ellenby is doing everything she can to help her son live in the world, and not in isolation. It's an important book, an honest look at severe autism. There is far too much media and questionable ideology attempting to normalize autism, ignoring those most severely challenged by developmental disability. *Autism Uncensored* needs to be read by politicians, policymakers, the public and especially the media, if we ever hope to solve the challenges faced by those most vulnerable among us. As Ellenby writes, '. . . I would have to be unflinchingly honest, providing unvarnished accounts of the brutality of autism both on the afflicted and those who love and care for them' . . . You have succeeded."

—BRUCE HALL, co-author & photographer, Immersed: Our Experience With Autism (2016)

"This book really does pull back the curtain on autism. From the gripping account of Zack's first plane ride to his mother's triumphant founding of "Autism Ambassadors," Autism Uncensored is a non-fiction book that reads like an engaging novel. Not only does the author allow us to invade her privacy, and eavesdrop on her innermost thoughts and emotions, but she also enables those of us lacking direct contact with autism to begin understanding the subtle effects that the spectrum can have on all of those who must confront it. The book's message is that persistence and perspective—as well as a healthy skepticism about prevailing conventions—are essential elements of an effective strategy for dealing with autism, and presumably other complex social problems. Ellenby's book will change the ways in which most of us think about the multidimensional people who are cursed and blessed with autism. And it may even end up changing the ways that we choose to treat their condition."

—GIRARDEAU A SPANN,
Georgetown University Law Professor

"Whitney does share some broadly applicable lessons from her story and you may draw your own from reading what she went through. I have heard that some find Whitney too honest. I am a biased audience as a friend of hers, but I find it brave and refreshing. Raising kids is always tough. It gets tougher when they had special needs. And I cannot imagine that anyone never has a negative thought about their child or situation. Kudos to Whitney for being willing to share what she and her family are living in print."

—MARYLAND DELEGATE MARC KORMAN,
District 16

AUTiSM UNCENSORED

HAS BEEN HONORED BY THE FOLLOWING:

WINNER, GOLD MEDAL PARENTING,
Independent Publisher Book Awards (IPPY) (2019)

WINNER, SILVER MEDAL, PARENTING,
Nautilis Book Awards (2019)

WINNER, GOLD MEDAL, NEW NONFICTION,
National Indie Excellence Awards (2019)

FINALIST, PARENTING NONFICTION,
Next Generation Indie Book Awards (2019)

WINNER, GOLD MEDAL,
Nonfiction Book Awards (2019)

Autism Uncensored:
Pulling Back the Curtain

by Whitney Ellenby

ISBN 978-1-63393-413-9

Published by

◥köehlerbooks™

210 60th Street
Virginia Beach, VA 23451
800-435-4811
www.koehlerbooks.com

AUTISM
UNCENSORED

PULLING BACK THE CURTAIN

WHITNEY ELLENBY

VIRGINIA BEACH
CAPE CHARLES

DEDICATION

*To Zack, the love of my life who took
everything away . . . and then
put it back in the right order.*

TABLE OF CONTENTS

FLASHBACK

By three methods we may learn wisdom: First, by reflection, which is noblest; second, by imitation, which is easiest; and third, by experience, which is the bitterest.

—CONFUCIUS

ZACK FURIOUSLY BEATS his head with both fists and begins to shriek loudly at a fever pitch. Some of the passengers are sensitive enough to grasp the crisis and turn away, studiously pretending to gaze out the airplane windows. But the spectacle is mounting. And my husband and I are too frantic—too humiliated—to care that we are adding to the scene by tearing into each other publicly, even as Zack starts coming out of his seat and lurching over the one in front of him. We're only in mid-flight, and there's no escaping this steel cabin.

"Goddamn it, we are *never* doing this again!" Keith hisses through clenched teeth.

It's our first plane trip in years with Zack, heading down to visit my family in Miami. I'm depleted and badly in need of the perennial sunshine from my youth.

"No, of course we won't do this again!" I snap back savagely, "We'll just keep him locked away at home his whole life and never go anywhere!"

"This isn't worth it!" Keith barks back. "Nothing is worth this! It's all about you, *your* need to make him do this. And it's selfish and wrong, he *cannot* do it, *HE CAN NOT DO IT!* This was a huge mistake . . . he's completely out of control!"

"SHUT UP!" I am screaming, trembling uncontrollably. "You don't deal with this crap every day like I do! I cannot fight you and him at the same time, so *SHUT THE HELL UP!*"

Once again, Zack's feral tantrum sets off a reactive chain whereby he erupts first and becomes the catalyst for further implosion. Hostility is contagious, as time and again it spreads like wildfire through my marriage, unhinging life partners into bitter rivals. Our combustible dissembling is as predictable as a lab experiment gone wrong.

Zack's shrieks are high-pitched and piercing, reaching passengers in the front rows who turn around with startled annoyance. And then, as always, comes that withering look, the unique tang of disapproval and disgust. *What the hell is wrong with that kid? Why would those parents even take him out in public?*

"I want 'bye-bye' plane! I want down! *I-WANT-DOWN!*" Zack screams, wholly terrorized.

As the tide of frustration floods Zack's body he begins savagely biting down on his wrist. His jaws clamp so ferociously that deep, red marks begin swelling along his forearm, the upper layers of skin ravaged and bursting into raw scraps of flesh. There is a swirling sickness in my stomach which heaves and grips my heart. I can barely breathe and I've been here before—far too many times.

I marvel at how, in these moments, Zack looks like a child who has not had even an ounce of behavioral therapy, when in fact he's had forty hours a week for over three years. But right now we are trapped inside a steel cabin, suspended thousands of feet in the air, where Zack's behavioral drills are bootless and his primal screams are sucking the very oxygen from the plane. My son has openly, violently lost control in a locked vessel with no ready exit, and I'm genuinely beginning to panic.

"Do you need us to land the plane?" asks an anxious flight attendant.

I cannot answer and am suddenly thrust into motion. Desperately, I try pinning Zack's legs to the cushy seat, but now his arms are flailing, smacking the man in the seat beside us who, with the utmost compassion, calmly readjusts and pretends to keep reading his book. A profound gesture of generosity—until his book is ruthlessly kicked from his hands and I am now wrestling my son to the ground in the narrow aisle, frantically pinning my entire body against his just to keep him contained.

I don't think that anyone believes this forty-pound child actually endangers their safety, but witnessing something so feral as a child completely losing all physical and emotional control must be terrorizing. I am rapidly losing my grip, too, over my son, my seizing heart, my sanity. I will remember this episode as one of the most terrifying of my life. My mind irrepressibly lurches towards darkness as I scream in silence, *I give up; I cannot take him anymore. He ruins everything and I don't give a damn anymore whether it's his fault. We can't go anywhere or do anything because of him!*

But I can no longer ignore Zack's impact on the other passengers. Gripping him in a tight vise between my thighs on the floor and then twisting to keep him locked in while gaining balance, I falteringly rise.

"I am so sorry," I announce as my body starts violently quaking. I think I can actually feel my heart searing open. "My son has autism. I didn't expect this and I'm doing the best I can. I *will* get him under control."

No one responds, just quiet smiles, appreciative nods, a silent chorus of compassion which spreads over me and nearly brings me to tears. They understand my agony, that I am disgraced, and their answer is kindness. I am not alone in this; they are on my side.

I inhale deeply and drop back down, heaving my full weight on top of Zack, which proves suddenly calming as he ceases screaming. I reach into his mind to inhabit his inner world: without warning he's been trapped inside a tight, locked steel vessel, suspended indefinitely, with no familiar visual markers to orient him. *Of course he's petrified,* I self-admonish, *I should have explained the experience of flight and temporary hiatus from the ground below, but maybe it's not too late.* I readjust myself and pivot directly behind him to physically wrap the entire length of my arms and legs firmly around his torso, squeezing tightly, radiating a sort of deep pressure chamber as I begin a slow and simple mantra.

"We're just moving forward, Zack, we're almost done. We're just moving forward, the plane will land down on the ground. We're almost there. Almost done, plane is almost done."

My hands instinctively begin moving down his little body to calm and further grasp his attention. First, I grip the top of his head with both hands sturdily in my clutches, stop, and squeeze. I then firmly cup both his ears, flattening them completely against his head, using my fleshy palms to block the ambient noise from his auditory canals. I steadily move my hands down and grip both his shoulders hard, applying deep pressure all the way down his arms, systematically, in rhythm to my voice; elbows, lower arms, clamping down securely over the bumpy terrain of riled skin from the deep bite wounds. Next, I clasp his small hands in mine, hold them tightly in a sealed grip, rub each finger consecutively, deeply, down its length.

"We're just moving forward, we're almost there. The plane will touch down, land on the ground, we're almost done." I whisper calmly over and over, speaking to his entire body with both my voice and hands, reordering the frenzy and letting him know he has nothing to fear.

Mesmerized by the deep pressure from my hands, Zack starts whimpering, but is no longer threatening to scream. He is dazed, his own hysteria having sent him into a trance, but he is also keenly concentrating on the orienting tactile sensation of calm. Although his face doesn't register comprehension, it's clear my words are penetrating as he slowly processes the joint messaging of words plus compression. My voice remains calm, controlled, a steady drumbeat of simple repeated assurances.

"We're almost there, almost done. You did it, Zack, you did it, you made it through the airplane flight, that's all you need to do. Just sit. Calm down and just sit here, there's nothing else, and you did it. Yes, my love, you did it, you just flew on an airplane! You're the best boy on earth."

A teenage girl shifts uncomfortably in her seat across the aisle and cannot stop staring. As she leans over to say something to me I stiffen in anticipation.

"I hope I can be as good a mother as you someday," she whispers. I smile and nod gratefully.

I exhale deeply as the plane begins its slow descent. Zack is now calm enough for me to lift him slowly from the aisle floor and back to his window seat where he sits contentedly, staring and wordless. He has just mastered the art of flight, of losing and regaining control, of allowing himself to be temporarily suspended in a strange space he does not fully understand but to which he just surrendered. He has captured something functional, crucial for navigating the world so filled with unpredictable departures.

I don't feel accomplished, just battered and wounded. But I

am composed and calm—and so is Zack. As the plane descends, familiar visuals slowly restore to sight—houses, oceans, trees, interstate highways—a welcome landscape for a child who decodes the world according to visual cues and becomes genuinely panicked when they suddenly and inexplicably disappear.

Finally, the plane touches down and as we taxi toward the gate Zack is wholly absorbed in the mechanics of returning to ground—the wheels' dismount and rotational grind as they strike the runway, the hinged metal flaps on the edges of the wings like fish gills seemingly breathing open and closed as the planes reduces speed. My husband's voice in my ear is decisive through angrily clenched teeth.

"We are *never* doing this again."

"No." I answer, shaken but clearheaded. "We will do it a hundred more times until he gets it right."

UGLY TRUTH

I utter what you would not dare think.

—FYODOR DOSTOYEVSKY

WHEN I CONSIDERED writing about the toll of autism I was determined to do so only if I had something new to say. To do so, I would have to be unflinchingly honest, providing unvarnished accounts of the brutality of autism both on the afflicted and those who love and care for them. Some experiences of the human condition are so serious and life-altering that only the unguarded truth can do them justice. People with autism, and those who care for them, are so precious and worthy that their lives must be lived without regard to the uninformed opinions or fears of others who have not walked in their shoes.

My story feels useful only if I reveal not just the unorthodox actions I chose to pursue with my son, but also the internal dialogue that provoked them. The portrait I paint involves dark thoughts and confessions some might find ugly, abhorrent or even excruciating, but an honest account of my journey demands that I reveal them. My goal in writing *Autism Uncensored* is to provide unguarded disclosures that might allow others in pain to know you are not alone, and that your situation can indeed improve.

Some experiences must be lived firsthand to be truly understood. My story is true and delivered in the first person, present tense, precisely to capture the reality I have lived. In telling my story I am talking directly to you, the reader, as if I am living the experience now––and placing you inside my head. You will not be hovering in the remote corners of these pages observing from a detached perspective: as I'm cobbled on the floor, you will be down on the floor with me. I am reliving the seminal moments of my life and so, through my writing, have reset my mind back in time. I attempt to conjure the emotions roiling inside me, actual inner dialogue, and exact conversations in their genuine, excruciating detail. My intent is to provide a verbatim account—what I actually felt, heard, smelled, thought and said at the time. If my recounting is imperfect, it's still overwhelmingly accurate.

Please know as you read that I am not speaking *for* other parents with autistic children, but rather *to* them, as well as to anyone sensitive enough to take the extraordinary ride. Autism is not easy; to pretend otherwise would betray what I and so many others experience on a daily basis. Revealing my innermost thoughts—and risk being publicly judged for them— is the price I pay for speaking my truth.

A more serious cost of being wholly uncensored is the betrayal of my son, Zack, whose limited verbal skills make it impossible for me to have the type of dialogue with him that would allow him to consent to such an intimate telling of our story. I may never know the breadth of his private feelings about me and what happened between us, just as he may never fully know mine. I've wrestled mightily with issues of disclosure and betrayal across many subjects in this book, but in the end I came down on the side of disclosure because Zack—the most unpretentious and courageous person I've ever known—is a living embodiment of "real-world" progress in the often inscrutable world of autism. In my heart I believe that he would approve of giving others what he has given me: an education that cannot be taught through words alone but through direct exposure to live situations. It is the immediacy of our experience which I seek to reproduce, and my hope is to impart unexpected truths and discoveries about autism worthy of the trust you have placed in me by reading my words.

So I start with a singular truth—that to live with an autistic child is to experience great joy and exquisite pain in equal measure.

Zack is a stunning, angel-faced child with the purest of hearts. But from the moment he was diagnosed with autism at nineteen months old, my world quite literally changed forever. There was an immediate and jolting disconnect between me and other parents that continues to this day and will remain for the rest of my life. As a toddler, it was *my* child who spun senselessly in circles, made conspicuous yelping noises and screeched loudly whenever I dared to redirect him. I was the only mother to shadow my toddler in every gym and music class, desperately pinning his legs to the floor to get him to follow the routines without spiraling off into his own world. If my son was mixed in with a group of children and there were sudden piercing shrieks, I knew without looking it was him, making me feel as isolated in my world as he was in his.

When your child is not typically developing, the reminders are ubiquitous. Every fairytale, TV commercial, and playground boasts a merciless tapestry of *normal*, that tightly woven fabric of children who are enchanting, imaginative, and *verbal*, smothering you at every turn with obvious reminders of what parenthood was supposed to mean. And so for me, parenting became an assault filled with relentless daily examples of all the ways my son was different; there was little joy, just a pervasive and haunting sense of *otherness*.

To have an autistic child is to view the world as an outsider. I watched as if from behind a wall of glass other children living life—playing "princess" and "cowboys," initiating shy introductions, negotiating ever-later bedtimes. Each taunt of *normal* delivered a swift punch to the gut because my son did not and might not ever do these things. Zack had none of the defining childlike characteristics about which parents habitually boast. *He was special in a bad way.*

When their normal children had explosive tantrums, my friends shrugged them off. They weren't terrified their child might still be throwing full-body tantrums when he turned eighteen. And all those cherished platitudes now curdled and sour: "Children say the darnedest things!" *Mine doesn't. He just yelps and screams in repetitious fits for no reason.* No, I could not gleefully chime in with friends about the outrageous statement my son just swiped me with today—my son could not even respond to his own name.

In truth, I have always been a jealous person. But I have never known a more bitter or corrosive envy than that coursing through my veins as I observed the world around me. Well-intended but foolish comments came at me constantly: *"A child is a blessing no matter what."* Really? Even if he bites and mutilates his own flesh for no apparent reason and walks past me with the same indifference he shows a piece of furniture? *"Even with all the challenges, you would never trade your child for any other."* Wouldn't I?

I watched numbly through a haze of tears as my son compulsively circled the perimeter of a playground in the identical pattern over and over, oblivious to the other children, to the swings and slides, to the notion of play itself. And beneath my frozen motherly façade I became lost in morbid fantasy—*if only I could slice open the skull of one of these other kids I could carve out my son's defective brain and exchange it with another child's, that one building castles in the sandbox, that one on the swing trading hysterical giggles with his father . . . I will take any child at this park regardless of personality and never look back. Just please, God, don't make me do this anymore.*

Outwardly, I appeared to handle my son's diagnosis well. Even my closest friends did not suspect the depth of my pain—shame and numbness masquerading as calm. Friends had no idea how much I had grown to despise their children, simply because they were normal. Today when I lecture young children about autism I assure them that it is not contagious. But indeed it is, spreading insidiously from child to parent so that like my son, I too experienced isolation, alienation, and the most profound loneliness I have ever known.

Autism assaults every facet of a parent's life—finances, emotional stability, siblings, the very future itself. It's no wonder statistics confirm that 85 percent of marriages collapse and disintegrate under its weight. A common pattern in couples takes hold—one spouse must immediately cease all other life functions to secure massive behavioral interventions for the newly diagnosed child, while the other becomes chained to never-ending work in order to finance the therapy, increasingly the only common thread which binds them together. Hovering over them both is the most ominous cloud of all: there is no proven remedy, no certain protocol, and no end in sight. I remember watching in horror as the fault lines between me and my husband cratered with each of Zack's explosive public tantrums, each vitriolic debate over how to handle them, and each clash over which one of us was *truly* sacrificing for this child. No matter, because the quicksand would envelop us both, pitting life partners against each other as bitter rivals in the desperate cause of rescuing our child. And as the money continued to hemorrhage on interventions, the gaping wounds of our marriage continued to bleed. As the earth kept shifting beneath our feet and our marriage began to crumble, one need only set foot in our house to know that a very real death had occurred.

There are no answers to autism and no clear causes. And there is no conventional wisdom for dealing with the pain. For many of life's tragedies there is redress, ritual and time to heal the wounds. But what was I to do with the grieving that never abated—the constant, renewed pain of watching my child struggle to learn the most basic of concepts; of realizing even the most innate developmental gestures required scripting; of watching him grow another year older but still function on the level of a child several years younger; of desperately fearing what the future brings for a child too compromised to defend himself?

Would my son *ever* experience what most parents blithely presume will belong to their children: romantic love, college, children of his own? Maybe, but probably not. And when in the grips of his public tantrum, amidst the horror and humiliation of him shrieking and splayed out fully on the ground while bystanders recoiled in shock, my mind lurched towards an inescapable truth—I want out from this nightmare. *I wanted out from this child.*

Until, one day, I discovered that there existed some unexplored territory which in my desperation I had overlooked. There was an untapped potential within Zack to overcome the debilitating fears that kept him from living a whole life. It was a potential discovered not in the closed room where he was drilled with intensive therapy but in the real world where our children must live. And so I plunged us both head-first into untested waters, powered only by desperation that our world was rapidly shrinking as Zack was increasingly unable to leave the house. I physically forced him into public situations that I had once fled at the first sound of his screams. I set higher standards for him than I thought he could reach.

It has not always been easy. I have publicly tackled my screaming child to the ground and pinned him down for the sake of allowing him to enter a movie theater for the first time. I have gripped my son's body in fierce restraint only to have him break loose long enough to ram his skull repeatedly into the floor in frantic protest. And I have overheard the baffled and cruel comments of bystanders who wondered aloud, "What is wrong with that child? They ought to just lock him up in a cage!"

I believe much of the public discourse on autism is saturated with confusion and false hope. The greatest promise that the mass media and consumer market for autism have offered parents thus far is the remote possibility of a "cure" or the "miraculous breakthrough" myth. Such stories are fed by the inextinguishable hope of parents that their own child might *recover* from autism, despite that such recoveries represent less than 10 percent of persons affected with the disability. It is indeed newsworthy when a nonverbal autistic child suddenly speaks after a particular intervention unlocks the key to his previous entrapment. But lurking beneath the celebratory headlines are legions of children for whom the identical methods have been tried and have failed. Thus media spotlighting of the "one-in-a-million recovery story" only further alienates those of us with *unrecovered* children who must endure the torment of knowing that someone else's child was cured but not ours, no matter how massive or dedicated our efforts.

Author Ron Suskind's remarkable novel, *Life, Animated*, is one of the most penetrating accounts of how his adult son with autism unexpectedly broke through language barriers to speak by indulging in his obsessive love for the dialogue and characters in Walt Disney movies. But even that extraordinary feat was not enough for some. In an otherwise glowing review of Suskind's book, one *New York Times* critic lamented that "Mr. Suskind's fealty to reality has another cost: We are denied the storybook ending we might expect from a Disney-infused tale." Indeed, millions of us wrestling with autism are similarly deprived of a fairytale ending.

I believe the population of parents who secretly or openly dread the future for their autistic children is the norm, and thus a parent whose story represents this norm must stand up and speak his or her truth. My truth is the not the story of a miraculous breakthrough or recovery from autism, but of an unorthodox way out of the shadow that autism had cast over my life, my marriage, and my son for so many years. I am not a clinician, a doctor or a scientist, and my story is not a prescription. I am simply a mother who found a way out of the darkness and despair who now wants to impart her discoveries along the way. My truths are the sort of raw and candid disclosures that I believe will resonate loudly with all parents of autistic children. I am uncensored out of respect for caretakers and children alike. We cannot grab hold of the ropes needed to climb out of the quicksand if they are coated in sugar. Neither we, nor our children, can afford pretense if we are to thrive in the ways we deserve.

Today my beloved son is still very much autistic, and I know he always will be. *Autism Uncensored* is the antidote to the recent swell of mainstream efforts to depict autism in movies and television. As the overwhelming majority of parents can attest, the scope of behaviors we confront daily bear little resemblance to trendy, popularized depictions in movies and on TV. Our children, by and large, are not engaging in quixotic romances or social gaffes, are not exceptional savants with doctor or espionage jobs, and not the locus of cool stories. Our children are not merely dusted by the disorder in socially awkward and amusing ways, but are wholly consumed. A true depiction of the average person with autism is anything but humorous—unpredictable tantrums, self-injurious behaviors, and a crippling lack of social awareness, which hardly makes for light entertainment.

My life has been defined by my journey with Zack, one which began as an accomplished US Department of Justice civil rights attorney who turned her back on disability rights law—ironically, due to lack of passion—at the very moment the life-altering "change" was gestating inside of me. *Autism Uncensored* is an unrestricted portal into the mind of someone who had no intention of sacrificing my life or career to a destructive force that ultimately became my reason for living. It is not, to my mind, a profile in courage, but rather the desperate measures I took to give Zack a life when nothing else was working and I had nothing left to lose. It's about what's possible when social mores are abandoned and professional directives are disobeyed in favor of raw parental instinct. Most critically, my true story is about how I learned to redefine accepted notions of *shame* and *conformity,* as strangers everywhere were transformed from foes to allies with a single, honest disclosure about my child.

I acknowledge that my experimental methods are controversial and highly individualized to Zack, thus I am not endorsing what I did for others to follow. My goal in writing *Autism Uncensored* is not to debate the efficacy of my methods but to provide unique insights about what happened along the way—receiving the autism diagnosis; feelings of disgrace and self-blame; the limitations of traditional behavioral interventions; a marriage crippled by chronic strain; and ultimately, unexpected discovery about the true potential of our children to navigate the world *regardless of whether or not they recover or overcome the limitations of their disability.*

I also hope to impart to the general public crucial discoveries I made about the role strangers can play in the true inclusion of a child with autism in his community. This message goes out to all of you compassionate bystanders who witness a public tantrum by one of our children and feel helpless about how to help your embittered compatriots. It serves as a reminder to pause before leaping to conclusions about a ragingly inappropriate outburst, and consider that you may be witnessing a parent trapped in the darkest nightmare she's ever known.

Finally, I hope to spark a new conversation, which goes beyond simply accepting persons with autism for who they are, but considers pushing them beyond their comfort zones to learn who they are capable of becoming.

I dedicate this book to my muse, Zack. I also dedicate it to the hundreds of families who attend my recreational "Autism Ambassadors" events to take refuge in the glory of a judgment-free "room of our own" where our children all along the spectrum play on their own terms. *Autism Uncensored* goes out to the legions of parents working exhaustively with their children to turn back the tide of autism, to those who feel demoralized by the supposed *failure* of their children, and to those who in their bleakest hours may even wish that their autistic child had never been born. I know because I have been there too.

Although my messages may not be embraced by all parents who struggle with autism, this book nonetheless goes out to all of you. Along with this are my wishes for a better life for you and your child than you may be able to envision at this moment. I share your challenge and I stand with you.

And this is my answer to all who ask, "What's it really like to have a child with autism?"

iRONiC GESTATiON

We plan, God laughs.

—YIDDISH PROVERB

FROM THE MOMENT of my birth I was destined for adulthood. Preternaturally precocious, in high school I preferred the company of my teachers over my peers, often sequestering them during recess and after school to engage in prolonged explanations about academics. Far from ridiculing them, I wanted to join them. I didn't fear the burdens of growing up and assuming full-time work. To the contrary, the most brutal wall to scale during school years was assimilating with peers.

As I grew to adolescence in the 1980s in the Miami heat, the seductive beckoning of the beaches and uninhibited partying at South Beach held no interest for me. At a time when oats were being wildly sowed, my focus was soberly plotting my professional future. First, nail a flawless grade point average that glides me into a prestigious college, then amplify the intensity again to earn admission to the highest level law school possible.

Then graduate to coveted adulthood, one filled with penetrating conversations over dinner and enjoying movies.

My recreational aspirations were highly divergent for my age. No parties, no sororities or other frivolous popularity contests; no time and no need for such unproductive endeavors. My unyielding sense of urgency about becoming an adult was so consuming that even I didn't understand where exactly it came from. All I knew was a sort of inbred, humming reminder that I was never to take my foot off the gas, or I would risk being derailed.

As president of my junior and senior high school classes, I was understood by teachers and students alike to be talented, but more than that, exceptionally driven, the kind of person for whom everyone predicts outstanding achievements in later life.

I had no intention of letting them down. By my senior year in high school I'd adopted study habits so intense that friends had to physically pry my fingers off books to get me to go out at night. My parents expressed concern at my intensity, pleading with me to dial it down and take my future *less* seriously. But that propulsive sense of urgency just roared louder, angry that no one seemed to grasp that my punishing work ethic was mandatory if I was to become a professional. What no one understood, including me, was that I was genuinely incapable of modulating my drive to excel.

As far back as I can remember, I had an affinity for *losers*— those unfortunate peers branded as strange and unworthy of friendship because they were too introverted, unattractive or unusual. I felt instantly comfortable in their presence, relieved of the pretense of appearing hip or cool. *Unpopulars* were treated as damaged, but it was precisely that social disadvantage which made them the kindest, coolest and most accessible people I knew. On those occasions where popular friends scolded me for befriending those whom they believed lacked value, I bit back ferociously; that type of social scouring was shortsighted and immature. No one was going to prescribe whom I should value, nor would they shame me into rejecting the quiet and extraordinary intellectuals. Most memorable from my high school experience was an indelible impression that everyone should know first-hand what it's like to inhabit both camps—the privileges of being popular and the ostracism of being a loser.

College at Barnard University and the University of Michigan was in many ways an extension of high school, another trial to be endured more than enjoyed. As I staked out in the graduate school law library, studying into the wee hours of the morning, dutiful friends once again pried my grip from the books and forced me out. As the only one who didn't belong to a sorority, I was forcefully dragged into fraternity parties where I stood confounded at what these young people considered amusing— girls holding back each other's hair while each vomited violently into toilets; boys leering seductively behind them ready to take advantage; everyone so drunk they could barely string a sentence together. I was never lonelier than when surrounded by inebriated peers. It was too discordant, I was too afraid, too intimated to ever belong. Scarcely able to mask my discomfort, I would steal away from wild parties, unnoticed, back to my dorm room, and longingly plot the coordinates of my future as a well-adjusted adult who had finally come into her own.

By the time I hit Georgetown University Law School, I was finally on my way to realizing a major milestone. Ever the insatiable worker, I competed and earned the main position on Georgetown's venerated National Moot Court team which traveled across the country to compete with other students in the art of oral argument before judges. My distinction on the team was lofty. I assumed the role as the *Swing Oralist*, charged with alternately arguing competing sides of the same legal issue in back-to-back trials. Fear of incompetence stoked my nightmares. Being anything less than over-prepared was not an option. I studied and rehearsed assiduously, so frightened of being caught off guard by an unanticipated question that my every waking hour was devoted to practice. I would sooner forego food and water than walk into an arena unprepared. I routinely lost a dramatic amount of weight leading up to competitions.

During competition, I moved fluidly between opposing positions like a well-oiled pendulum, arguing different sides before different sets of judges. The pain of my intense preparation was both mitigated and validated by being awarded the distinction of *Best Oralist* for the Northeastern Moot Court region. The engraved gavel I was awarded seemed almost fatalistic proof that I was both destined and designed for oral advocacy. I was referred to around law school as "the girl with the weight of the world on her shoulders," nice enough but inaccessible, as if distracted by some overriding mission. So it was that my relentless drive, coupled with my affinity for outcasts, led me to stake out the one judicial institution that could tap my passion and mobilize my advocacy—I would become a civil rights lawyer with the Department of Justice.

There can be no more prestigious job for an aspiring lawyer who wants to topple the apple cart of social norms in favor of the disadvantaged. So, I pursued Justice with a single-minded intensity that was almost frightening.

I reached out to division heads of each section with a fervor and persistence that would have qualified me as a stalker, had I pursued them as private citizens. I spent over a year engaged in ferocious networking, consumed gallons of coffee over quick-meets, and spent countless hours lying in wait for a single job opening, a chance to break through just ahead of the thousands of other résumés competing for a single slot. Once selected for an interview, the grilling interrogation by department heads as to why I pursued the Civil Rights division, my personal connection to their mission, and what I in particular had to offer to advance their purpose were weighted with the gravity of becoming a public servant. Once chosen, the scrupulous criminal background checks, fingerprinting, taking a sacred oath to defend the DOJ, all building towards the crescendo of finally being handed the DOJ badge—a police-like sterling star within a pouch to be carried with me at all times, proof of the gravitas of safeguarding the public trust with which I was now charged.

I landed in the Disability Rights Section where I stood proudly on the side of persons with cognitive and physical impairments, checking off my lifelong ambition to fight for those most vulnerable and in need of a voice. But I've never been friends with anyone with a disability or had any personal connection to the subject—I'm just someone who wanted "in" so badly that at the age of twenty-nine, I was knighted as one of the select, vaunted guardians of the American with Disabilities Act that protects millions of disabled people nationwide from being unjustly denied access to public places of recreation, or deprived of employment due to their need to be accommodated.

Yet deep down, where the unspeakable lives, I felt no genuine nexus to any of it. No inner connection with my clients or to the intricate content of the ADA statute itself. I couldn't fully grasp the myriad complexities of the language, so bogged down by minutiae and exclusions, so many legal hurdles to clear just to determine the seminal issue of whether a person even qualifies as "an individual with a disability." It never dawned on me that the notion of whether a person is disabled could itself be contested; nor that unscrupulous complainants might attempt to masquerade difficulties as disabilities in order to seek legal shelter under specifically crafted protections to which they are not entitled. To the extent I considered it at all, the term "disabled" always triggered within me an automatic binary response—the disabled were models of extraordinary courage but also, inescapably, objects of pity. To be disabled is to be jilted of the full range of human experience; I could never find any way around that conclusion.

***

Here at Justice, I'm now assaulted by a multitude of disabilities, so many I never knew existed, some congenital deficits I'm afraid to know because it makes my heart ache to think that an infant should arrive into the world so severely comprised that even basic functions of breathing and swallowing are dangerously labored. Intellectually, I grasp the letter of the law; emotionally, I am clueless and floundering.

Upon meeting some of my disabled clients I am visibly unhinged by the sight of them, so much that I have trouble maintaining eye contact, which is the very least of my moral duties. I can't look some of my severely disfigured clients in the eye when transcribing the facts of their grievances because my own body language is a jangly toss of confusion, embarrassment and inexorable pity. Pity, which oozes as conspicuously as the perspiration welling from my pores and stains the armpits of my blouse. In my heart, I acknowledge that nothing noble has been ignited inside of me. No divine spark has been lit. None of the passionate anger I know I'm capable of channeling for the right cause. So, I confess that I'm not nearly as competent an attorney as I know I'm capable of being.

I've spent years training for complex litigation, but at Justice I spend my days on my hands and knees measuring bathroom stalls to ensure that all sized wheelchairs can be accommodated. These are mechanical matters of mere inches upon which many lives depend, but to me they are tediously unrewarding. No courtroom appearances in sight. No opportunity for me to flaunt my oratory heft in the manner I envisioned on behalf of the government's most muscular division. Not much original writing either, because the basic arguments on behalf of complainants fit within a mold that was crafted long before I arrived.

My legal briefs are comprised largely of paragraphs grafted from previous briefs. Worst of all, I have no autonomy about whether to accept a case or pursue an intriguing argument to the end. Every probative decision at DOJ must be run up the bureaucratic chain of command where time-sensitive matters often languish for weeks. I'm wildly impatient and frustrated by the stagnation, often worried that a particularly despondent client might take matters into her own hands, or even injure herself in despair, while left languishing. Far from feeling divinely anointed, I'm a toothless cog spinning furiously within a sluggish, rusty wheel.

It's become abundantly clear that for my own sense of purpose—and sanity—the DOJ cannot be my final destination. Intuitively I've known from the start that I do not belong, like so many times before in my life.

So I grab a far quieter plum, a less celebrated, but infinitely more gratifying, position with a tiny boutique adoption law firm for which I once did free legal work many years ago. The pay is considerably lower but the glory of the work far more palpable, even exhilarating. I will change lives by facilitating the transfer of urgently wanted children into the arms of childless parents. Desperate parents I can handle. Finally a chance to practice law as I was meant to, complete with bold writing, persuasive oral arguments and fiery closing statements before juries. Only then will I fulfill my professional purpose.

My deepest wish has always been to advocate on behalf of others who for some reason cannot argue for themselves—this was the sole reason I went to law school: to give voice to an impassioned true story which alters the outcome for someone in pain who might not otherwise find justice without me. I freely admit that my very self-esteem and self-definition depend on having a successful advocacy career. I make no apologies; that's just who I am.

The decision of how best to exit DOJ, what precise words to offer my department head to justify my unforeseen departure, has badly roiled my insides for weeks. I've set aside time to obsess, staked out on my home toilet where all great existential decisions are made. I've become sanguine about the chronic constipation that been plaguing me: it's as though my body is frantically absorbing every morsel of food and storing it away in preparation for some major event. I'm used to intestinal distress but this feels distinct from anything I've felt before, and abruptly it dawns on me that it's *possible* there's something more to the blockage. Incredibly remote, but possible that my body is stubbornly refusing output to harvest nutrients for a nascent human being.

My husband and I rarely see each other, both our lives consumed lately by practicing law and self-preoccupation. Indeed, the only time we even crossed paths recently for a unplanned conjugal visit occurred during a hasty, feverish fusion I affectionately dubbed our "practice run" for future conception, which would be scheduled. Conception is not happening any time soon. It stands in line far behind the year or so I'll need to get fully entrenched in my new job. Not to mention that I haven't weaned myself off those nightly sleeping pills, and am still leaning heavily on them to ease my anxious transition out of DOJ. Out of curiosity, I did actually buy one of those kits a few months back, stashed it away in the tumble jammed under the bathroom sink. Let's just see, let's be absolutely sure there's nothing behind this intestinal jam apart from extreme stress and chronically poor diet and—

Oh Dear God. This is not happening—this cannot be happening, this stick cannot be turning a different color so fast.

The gauzy white portion is practically sprinting towards a hot pink hue like this is some kind of sick game of its own! Not now, please God, I'm nowhere near ready for this, I don't want this, please God no, are my compulsively looping thoughts.

A brittle, icy shock rips up my spine, breaks open and radiates through my limbs, which are quivering convulsively in jagged, involuntary spasms. My entire body is literally quaking in disbelief, totally aghast and unprepared. And now suddenly I'm on fire and drenched in perspiration, every single pore erupting with prickly stings as my heart gallops uncontrollably in a defiant, irregular drumbeat. My throat clenches and is badly parched as I manage a single strangled sob: "*KEITH, help me! Come right now, please help!*"

"Can't!" he fires back impatiently. "Riding the bike! Just deal with it, whatever it is, I'll come when I'm done!" A fair reply, since I'm the one who dogged him to use our recumbent bike as something other than an extended towel rod.

"NO! STOP! I'm not kidding! *GET IN HERE NOW!*"

Irritated and panting heavily, he abruptly dismounts while scolding me, "You know you're going to have to start killing these damn cricket spiders yourself! You can't just start screaming and interrupt me every time you see a . . . " He immediately halts, his entire body stiffens at the sight of my trembling outstretched hand.

"It was just supposed to be a 'practice run,'" I whisper almost inaudibly, my head bowed as a raucous wave of anxiety grabs hold of my abdomen and releases, forcing liquid shocks of waste to come spurting out in a defiant cascade. I feel light-headed and queasy enough to topple off the seat. I quickly set my arms on the counter to steady myself as I cradle my head in despair, panting heavily, lobbing it down between my knees to catch breath. A sour acid rises in my throat as I whisper miserably, "I haven't even changed my diet yet, I didn't stop the sleeping pills . . . "

The clinical stick is indifferent, its sole function to measure fluctuating hormones. Having completed its task, it boasts an unmistakable hot pink plus sign. Positive for *pregnancy*, case closed. But something about this feels unnatural and wrong, a rude surprise: this is no way to begin what was meant to be a planned and auspicious occasion.

"*Oh my God!*" Keith exhales slowly, his eyes glued to the stick. "*Oh my God . . . !*" but then he breaks into a huge whooping laugh and exclaims, "This is FANTASTIC! On our first try, and we weren't even really trying, I can't believe it! Good for us, this is absolutely terrific!"

I stare up at him uncomprehendingly, then quickly duck back down to brace for another convulsive wave of spurting liquid. It's as though someone released a fire hose valve which is rapidly draining my insides, as if my body itself is in rebellious dissent of the results. My body is now excavating my insides so painfully it seems threatening to evict the pregnancy as quickly as it started. *NO*, is my silent internal roar. *I'm not ready for this, I don't want this yet*. I'm sick with regret over my capricious act. I plan everything.

But there's no unwinding the clock, and despite the gushing geysers I sense an irreversible fate that this pregnancy will stick. Disbelief slowly yields to awe at the sheer improbability of such a swift conception on the heels of such a messy "practice run," an encounter so unmemorable I never even glanced back to consider that it might result in pregnancy. And now, I'm going to be a mother, ready or not. My every choice from this very moment forward feels grave.

Inhaling in deliberately calibrated breaths, I steady myself with a dose of reality. First and foremost, I'm an attorney, on my way to studied mastery in my field with no intent of slowing down or relinquishing my grip. I've spent my entire adolescent and adult life readying myself to become an expert in something, and I've just now settled upon the chosen legal field in which I'm rolling. No way am I loosening the reins on my ambition because of a twist of fate. I will grant myself the traditional three months maternity hiatus, then return promptly to work to pick up where I left off. Meanwhile, I'll research the most competent nanny agencies and daycare providers, since it was never my intent to be a full-time, stay-at-home parent even under the best planned circumstances.

I am meant to be a mother; I always wanted to be one. I adore children in all their enchantment and never imagined the stretch of my life without them. Once I calm down I will eventually embrace motherhood with the same uninhibited zeal that powers all my major life choices—even if I'm not ready, even if I feel tricked, even if it's not fitting into my master plan.

I just won't be the kind of parent who surrenders *everything* for her children, or prioritizes her children's everyday needs and wants at the expense of my own hard-fought goals. Doing so doesn't make me a selfish mother, just an exceptionally committed worker. Which is all I've ever been my whole life; that's just who I am.

THOROUGHLY VETTED

There's the progress we have found
A way to talk around the problem
Building towered foresight
Isn't anything at all

—*FALL ON ME*, LYRICS BY R.E.M.

I RARELY LEAVE important matters to chance; my instincts are to control anything of serious consequence. Being out of control, physically or emotionally, has always been my greatest unspoken fear. So petrified of exposing myself to danger or losing it, that I've never been drunk, stoned, or under the influence of anything but my insatiable need to remain focused. Vomiting, inebriation and panic attacks are still horrors to be avoided at all costs. So intense is my fear that I keep prescription medication on hand to manage the unexpected.

It's not surprising, then, that I'm not enjoying this pregnancy filled with so many unpredictable jolts and queasy fluctuations. For most women these symptoms are merely unpleasant, but for me they are terrifying. My pulse quickens at the sight of an occasional blood spotting on my underwear, or sudden swells of nausea. My thoughts chronically fix on the fragile interdependence between me and this developing fetus whose very existence and health rests upon my daily choices. So, I carefully consider everything I ingest, inhale and do, which feels compromised and unnatural. I mourn my former physical autonomy but can't possibly share my irrational fears with anyone else because I know how selfish it sounds. I should be grateful for this precious gift; how lucky I was to get pregnant on the very first try, compared to friends who have suffered through chronic infertility. And the truth is, my pregnancy thus far is by-the-book and without complication.

But at ten weeks along, stripped of my usual habit of medicating away heart palpitations, the only outlet for my acute sense of helplessness is maniacal pacing. Desperate to pass the queasy hours, I pace the streets every chance I get—before work, during my lunch break and on the long, lonely walk home. No one at my new adoption job dares ask about my condition as I'm new to the practice; everyone's just bewildered by how often I sprint from meetings to the bathroom. My belly is already beginning to distend and I'm astounded at how often well-wishing strangers boldly take it upon themselves to smile and mouth "congratulations." I nod quickly to acknowledge their kindness while hurriedly brushing past, avoiding eye contact for fear of bursting into tears. *I'm not as strong as other women, I'm just not cut out for this.* Walking briskly, under the guise of "healthy exercise" for the baby, I furtively wipe away tears.

Just as I'm convinced I cannot survive this constant state of nausea one moment longer, it mercifully breaks. Rounding out thirteen weeks, the sickness abates and I slowly get my bearings, grateful that the worst has passed. A reassuring calm spreads over me. I'm once again in control: the danger of early miscarriage is gone, and my eating and exercise are fully restored to choice rather than desperation. Buoyed by feelings of wellness, my appetite suddenly explodes! Until now, I've only felt food aversions, no cravings, so I gleefully jump-start the process by devouring large, soft-baked, gooey chocolate chip cookies, which I infuse *to the baby* roughly every hour on the hour. I'm not one for pleasure deprivation that's been earned. And what difference does it make? Any discernible waistline or crusade to zip my pants went missing weeks ago. But I must strike a healthy balance, so I opt for tofu and brown rice daily as I envision my baby born with bones of steel.

Not only am I taking scrupulously good care of myself, but I'm finding that I'm remarkably protective of my unborn child. Despite being a newly minted attorney in my tiny firm, I boldly assert myself about a hazardous workplace situation. Our offices are being refurbished and the paint and glue fumes feel intolerable. I'm breathing just fine, which my doctor assures me is all that matters, but I'm not taking any chances of exposing my developing baby to noxious fumes. So, my willingness to continue working in my exposed cubicle versus working from home hinges on my employer's willingness to move me to another office floor. Done.

As headstrong winds blow me into my second trimester, I'm happier and more in control than I could have imagined possible in pregnancy, my excitement building towards the final act. I no longer maniacally pace the streets; I virtually bounce, proudly ensconced in my sexy new adoption practice and on my way to joining the ranks of resplendent earth mother. I bound into work, vigorously shaking hands and initiating high-fives with total strangers along the way with the assurance of a politician just informed of a landslide win.

All this boundless joy is due in part to my well-preserved secret—*I'm having a boy*. I don't actually know this for sure, and I won't until the baby is born because Keith and I opted to be surprised. But, indescribably, I already know I'm carrying a little prince. From the moment that pregnancy stick turned pink I knew, gut instinct, something in the way I feel, the elevated shape of my stomach, even the wholly unencumbered way I move. Pregnancy has not slowed my stride nor my baby's, even the faintest flutters from within bespeak a vigorous linebacker. Or maybe it's that I so desperately want a boy, breaking the mold of many expectant mothers who yearn for a precious daughter. And for the most unexpectedly romantic reason—Keith.

***

From the first instant I laid eyes on Keith through the peephole of my apartment door, I had an overwhelming feeling of familiarity. Fixed up on a blind date with no soaring expectations on either side, we'd spent weeks chatting on the phone without any burning desire to actually meet. Both of us had been recently burned by fixed meets, so neither wanted to implode our burgeoning friendship by risking the likelihood that we'd lose the chemistry by meeting in person. I was initially wary of his Ivy League pedigree. A Maryland native, he was recruited from high school to Yale University, followed by the University of Pennsylvania law school and a steady stream of prestigious, nationally venerated employers. I braced myself for signs of a condescending, bloated ego, but was delighted when he informed me we had better meet soon, and get along, because his current job at his posh D.C. firm was in such peril he would likely quit and need a friendly couch to sleep upon. Time and again I marveled at how humble and self-effacing this "Yalie" was despite his heady streak of achievements.

Upon entering my apartment for our first greet, we were so instantly at ease that his casual suggestion that I change into something less dressy (he wasn't taking me anywhere fancy) felt perfectly natural. Just as natural as his offhand observation, upon sizing up the filthy stack in my kitchen sink, that I seemed to be a slob. Just one hour into the dinner conversation I knew we'd marry. And that he'd do the cooking and cleaning.

Unbeknownst to me, the single quality Keith held in highest esteem was a dedication to being equitable, by which he meant being sensitive to another person's needs, willing to assume equal responsibility in all matters without any lopsided sense of entitlement. So when I absentmindedly offered to split the dinner check, he virtually levitated from his seat with beaming admiration so transparent I had to laugh. When I plucked a rose from the carefully arranged bowl in the lobby and handed it to him, he blushed just as crimson a hue at my emotional outspokenness. He had a magnetic aura of goodness, an earnestness that drew me to him instantly, and when he made casual reference to calling me after our date, I believed him.

Keith didn't wear his heart on his sleeve. Instead, he was regulated in his emotions and calibrated with revealing intimacies. But as the unspooling of our previous romances was laid bare, he explained a fascinating commitment he'd made to himself amidst the turmoil of a past romance gone sour—a dedication to maintaining emotional equilibrium. His priority was to never swing too high or too low, regardless of what life threw at him. That I had not learned this lesson, nor ever considered it, struck him as refreshing. Far from being jolted by my impulsive candor and wicked humor, Keith seemed delighted by my lack of inhibition in which he sought refuge to confess aloud certain truths he might not otherwise have shared. Whereas I was the professional gladiator for justice, he was far more comfortable operating at detached arm's length within the legal field of health care finance. While his professional interests struck me as bland and lacking in drama, he himself was not. As we grew closer, we leaned more heavily upon each other to fill in our own gaps. He reveled in enlisting me to "represent" him in awkward social confrontations, I sought his wisdom on how to relinquish my lifelong tendency to overreact and hold personal grudges. He wouldn't allow it, demanding in most loving fashion that no matter how wounded I was, I grudgingly keep the door of forgiveness open.

In other ways we were so similar it was almost scary—virtually identical idiosyncrasies and peeves, even a similar habit of chewing body parts. An unrepentant nail-biter since childhood, I gnawed my fingernails down to the nub; he voraciously chewed at his lips so mercilessly the top layers of flesh chronically erupted to expose new flesh, waiting to be ravaged. Both headstrong, neither of us prone to shy away from vehement disagreement, we had fights that were epic and earth-shattering, like two titans clashing in thunderous rage, but always aware of our mutual respect at having met an equal on all fronts.

Keith was passionately certain that what he wanted most in life, apart from his career, was a wife and children. He made no secret of his desire to start a family, and while I was impressed with his straightforwardness, in this respect he was less ambivalent than I was. No doubt he would make an excellent father. His easy assurance, good humor and natural optimism were a healthy foil to my tendency towards protective cynicism and fear. He was dazzlingly *mature*, a quality I held in great esteem, and in him I'd finally found a trusted friend and partner with whom I could safely lose control—a man of his word, intoxicatingly reliable, an adult.

My own notions of marriage were not embedded in romance so much as being part of an indestructible pact, a sturdy corporation between compatible partners committed to union but still retaining vestiges of autonomy. I was determined to remain financially independent and self-reliant no matter how deeply in love, and in that vein kept my last name so my identity didn't blend into his. I would not settle for anything less than true partnership: I had worked too hard in my life developing my own ambition to dissolve into his. Keith's own affinity for equity, together with my lack of any presumptive entitlement, only buttressed his certainty that I was "the one." Paramount to me was that the merger provide a bedrock foundation from which we would maintain a unified front, a shared worldview from which we would stand up for and defend one another, and thus act as bulwark and refuge from a cruel world. My vision of marriage was a protective shield from the vagaries of life to which I had never become accustomed, badly wishing for a true ally. Even more than children, what I wanted most in my adult life was someone to stand beside me in coping with life.

Even as Keith made clear he was falling in love, I privately questioned whether this eligible man fully understood what he was getting into, who exactly he was linking himself to for life. He seemed the embodiment of mental health. Taken together with his indiscriminate kindness towards others, legions of close friends, and princely good looks, he was a magnificent catch. Alongside my joy during our courtship was a distinct unease that once he discovered the *real* me—my ambitious yet querulous nature—he'd walk away in search of someone sunnier and less complex. Because Keith was the sort of winsome, gregarious, handsomely dimpled man that I'd only ever met on the arms of other women, I never imagined I'd truly attract him for myself. After a lifetime of toil in exchange for each and every gain, for the first time ever I believed myself to be truly lucky.

During our engagement, I couldn't help but envision our future children, which caught me by surprise: I'd never before conjured actual images. I was inspired by Keith, both his own enthusiasm for children, and my growing appreciation that passing along his integrity and brilliance, combined with his set of spectacularly defined dimples, dark wavy hair, sparkling brown eyes and symmetrical features, felt like the greatest gift I could give my child. Sounds absurd, I know. I wanted to create another Keith.

But at twenty weeks along in my unplanned pregnancy, my doctor blind-sides me with a terrifying prospect I hadn't anticipated—an alpha-fetoprotein (AFP) screening test to detect abnormalities. The *triple screen* measures hormone levels which, combined with the mother's age, weight, ethnicity and gestation of pregnancy, are used to assess probabilities of potential genetic disorders.

Part of routine prenatal screening, my blood is drawn into three tubes to be tested with results expected in a week. The doctor senses my rising panic and patiently explains that my AFP numbers will indicate whether I have an elevated risk for certain chromosomal abnormalities such as Down's syndrome, Edwards' Syndrome, spina bifida or anencephaly. An AFP test can also help find an omphalocele, a congenital problem in which some of the baby's intestines stick out through the belly wall, a prospect that has me literally gagging with fear.

He reassures me that these abnormalities are statistically improbable given my clean genetic background and relatively young age, but I'm stopped in my tracks, my blood gone cold about the gravity of what's at stake. I realize that until just now I hadn't even considered an abnormality or how I might cope with difficult news this far along in the pregnancy when I'd assumed we were out of the woods. My head spins with paranoia, a rolodex of everything that could go wrong. Our presumably healthy baby could have a grave disability that might require immediate and ongoing surgeries. He could have health-related emergencies that persist throughout his life; the thought of a heart irregularity and cardiac surgery is enough to make mine gallop in terror. I've never been good with physical illness, it's always been my Achilles' heel, and there would be equally grave cognitive issues, irreversible and incurable. Losing breath and perspective, I immediately enlist Keith in my ordeal as my speech is garbled by panic.

"So we'll know soon, next week soon. But if it looks like the baby has an elevated risk of one of these abnormalities, I don't know if I can cope, we'll just—" I stop abruptly, letting my voice drop off so he can finish the sentence as I'm expecting he will.

"Then we learn all we can about the disability and figure out how to get him everything he needs," Keith completes the dangling hypothetical without equivocation. I'm amazed by his resolve and the certainty he's ready to rise to the challenge. But I'm also somewhat skeptical. This was nothing we'd ever discussed. I'd assumed we shared the same outlook, yet I have not arrived at the same destination. After all, I wasn't the one desperate to have children so soon. I needed to be forcibly nudged by an impatient husband at a time when my career was finally taking off.

And if there's one unequivocal truth, it's that I cannot handle the pain and lifelong commitment of a seriously disabled child. I'm not made of that mettle; I don't have the innate goodness, selflessness and perseverance that others seem to naturally possess. Or maybe I simply don't want children badly enough to make the sacrifices necessary to care for a seriously compromised child for the rest of my life. Like everyone, I've seen those saintly parents in the shopping mall who lovingly assist their disabled child with a walker or wheelchair, and I take a second, privately, to salute them for their selfless courage before carrying on with my own business. But these are extraordinary parents destined to step up to meet extraordinary circumstances—this is not me. The thought of walking in their shoes for even one day is unimaginable, the thought of enduring it for a lifetime, unbearable. So, I decide to do something wholly uncharacteristic, which is not to decide, remain in limbo unless and until a decision is forced upon me by test results. Deep down in places I don't discuss, I don't need to take the social temperature or seek counsel on this most personal issue. Deep down, I'm quite certain of my limitations.

Days later while absorbed in my work, I absentmindedly check my home voicemail. Even before he delivers the news, the cheerful cadence of my doctor's voice betrays the results. "Hey Whitney, just calling to confirm the great news. Your AFP numbers are good on all counts, right where they should be, everything looks fine . . ."

I exhale deeply, caught off guard but grateful not to have known beforehand exactly when or how the results would be delivered. *Thank God.* I slowly rise from my chair and walk over to the plush couch in the firm's lobby for a few moments, collecting myself. *That was truly harrowing.* I ponder the situation of mothers who right now are receiving entirely different news from their doctors, and I can feel my heart searing open at the thought of being hit with such devastating news at this juncture, when a mother is already so deeply bonded to the unborn child growing inside her. But I best not dwell here—I'm virtually gulping for air and it's not healthy for me or the baby. But I need to stop absorbing problems that aren't mine, that distract me from staying steady and healthy. Out of respect for the courage exhibited by parents of disabled children, I'll donate to a charity in the spirit of having been briefly suspended in uncertainty about the terrifying possibility of having my own child severely compromised. *Yes, I'll look into a worthy cause tomorrow . . .*

But for now, wow, so much still to do on my checklist now restored to sharp focus. More tofu, refill prenatal vitamins, another round of maternity shopping for my dangerously expanding waistline—maybe a few less cookies are in order as my doctor admonished last time I stepped off the scale—I need not enjoy pregnancy this heavily. But these are just trifles against the larger backdrop of ushering in a glorious and sturdy newborn, an eventuality I now appreciate with even greater force. The happy chatter continues like a babbling brook as I reach for a ballpoint and begin scribbling my list on an errant paper. But wait, my prince is restive, jabbing an insistent elbow into my ribs in a rousing ploy to get my attention.

I set down the pen and ease back into the deep couch, then audibly gasp as, even beneath my clothes, the tight, rounded surface of my belly suddenly rips into a lumpy wave, which spreads in diameter as my prince readjusts himself. I gasp again as a sudden swift kick to the uterine wall actually dislodges the paper from my stomach, sending it swaying to the floor. I didn't know it was possible for a fetus to produce such conspicuous results from within. Despite the confines of my womb, he's moving dexterously and often. I watch in awe as the lumps rise, swell and subside like muscular, slow-moving ocean waves crashing ashore. Smilingly I telepath a message to my line-backer: *I cannot wait to meet you, I've imagined it a hundred times and I already love you more than I even knew possible. We are one now and even after we divide at birth, you and I will still be one.*

It's all coming together. I grin uncontrollably as I rest my head and begin quietly dozing off—then quickly catch myself, remembering I'm still at work and lucky to have stolen these moments alone. Time to get back to it. I still have a burgeoning profession to tend to and clients in great need who are depending on me to help make their own dreams come true. But I am the most fortunate parent, thoroughly vetted and abundantly prepared. I'm on my way.

NEW BEGINNINGS

Fortune smiles at some and laughs at others.

—13 CONVERSATIONS ABOUT ONE THING,
MOVIE QUOTE (2002)

I FEEL ALMOST guilty about my good luck. Although adoptions are still new to me, facilitating them is unlike anything I've known, wholly engrossing and at times even thrilling, the most rewarding legal experience thus far by all measures. When I describe to Keith the drama inherent in the process, he winces at the baring intimacy of it all—despondent birth mothers, anxious prospective parents, tense and often distrustful exchanges between them, despite their mutual dependency.

In my profession, when an adoption falls through and the birth mother revokes her consent, it provides me an opportunity to use my worldly perspective and remind my clients to never surrender. Nothing great was ever achieved easily, and even as they weep, still they must still soldier forward, hanging flyers and reaching out to new birth mothers, because no disappointment is too grave ever to make them give up on their dream of a child. Through this work, I've gained insight on the depth of grief that accompanies failed adoptions. Adoptive parents have often endured unimaginable ordeals and loss before they even arrive at the lawyer's door, and then are subjected to the twists and turns of the adoption process—months of breath-holding throughout the pregnancy for which they can offer support but no control. Then the emotional birth, and what follows in the immediate aftermath is a state of surrealism during which the birth mother can revoke consent. On those rare occasions when she does revoke, prospective parents do not merely forfeit money or time invested, they are also literally deprived of the child they thought was theirs, the same as if the baby had been stillborn.

I've come to feel quite changed in aligning myself with their life-altering journey. It's taken on a new dimension, precisely because the discordant pieces of my own life are finally aligned. I don't take my fortune for granted. I buckle down and study harder about all the varying adoption laws from state to state. I intend to become a virtuoso so dedicated and experienced that desperate parents everywhere can rely upon me in their darkest and most vulnerable hours of need. After so long a search I've arrived at my destiny. This is what I want most: to matter to others in pain.

The electricity of my professional passion is amplified by the crescendo of my own pregnancy, striking a balance for me between motherhood with a venerated career.

The birth was arduous but glorious, labor extended nearly eight hours with four spent strenuously pushing every ten minutes in a state of crippling exhaustion. Never in my life have I been so breathlessly consumed; nothing has ever commanded this degree of concentration and endurance—not a law school exam, taking the odious bar entrance test, nor any courtroom argument. Natural delivery proved the most arduous feat of my life.

When the baby became lodged in the birth canal, a group of male nurses placed eight hands on my engorged belly and provided the final collective shove. The force finally dislodged the baby, and now at last we meet: he's breathtaking. His head circumference, balanced features, dark hair and ruby lips are perfection. He is Zack Hunter, with a bountiful size and strength just as I'd strived for during pregnancy. His Apgar birth scores are off the charts, a superlative score just shy of a perfect ten, the numeric indication he's as healthy as a newborn can be. "Zack" because the pithy masculine punch feels right, and "Hunter," befitting his *in utero* and now externalized athletic prowess. "*Hit it out of the park, Zack!*" his teammates will yell. Even those early hospital days as I recuperated from the battery of a prolonged birth were bliss because he was an uncommonly easygoing newborn. I remember once hearing that the personality a newborn exhibits in those very first days is surprisingly predictive, and Zack was almost preternaturally calm.

Babies are inscrutable creatures and at three months, Zack is no exception. He's amazingly voracious, though perhaps unsurprisingly since he did indirectly receive hourly infusions of large chocolate chip cookies during gestation to which he and I both had become accustomed. But it's genuinely hard to keep up with his insatiable appetite. He sucks down breast milk, then an entire bottle of formula, more breast milk, another bottle. This baby is one passionate eater. Not much of a sleeper, though. There's a restlessness about him, and some nights he's so discontented and inconsolable that passing the stretched hours from midnight until dawn feels achingly lonely, surreal and depleting. But when those intensely dark eyes lock on mine, we are the only two people in the entire world, reunited by wordless communication and spinning in orbit around one another as everyone else fades into the distance. When he's not staring off into space, he's carefully tracking my every move. Even when I hand him off to a trusted family member or friend, his little head instantly turns away from their adoring gaze and towards me longingly, as if he's comfortable only in my embrace.

One peculiar observation is that his vigorous nursing isn't so much about hunger as direct contact: he seems more interested in the physical sensations of mouthing than in eating. Oral fixation is common in babies, but it seems he needs constant oral stimulation even after he's been fed, and he becomes amazingly fretful if he's deprived. It's also a little strange that at three months he still doesn't know his own name, even though he's heard it spoken incessantly. On those occasions when he's not visually fixed on me, I call out to him from across the room. But he never turns towards me in acknowledgement or responds in the slightest way—no sign of identification with his moniker whatsoever. I guess he's so accustomed to people talking over him and about him that he doesn't realize that sometimes it's him I'm talking to. *It'll come,* I tell myself.

Despite my maternity leave I'm still contributing remotely on select cases as often as I can, in part to remind my colleagues that I'm still very much in the game. While also balancing Zack, I have the faintest echoes that he should be more expressive, more responsive, no longer swaddled in newborn exhaustion. But kids grow at their own pace, and even twins or siblings with virtually identical upbringings often develop differently. Of course, since Zack is our first child, I don't have any comparative yardstick. Never one to value abject conformity, I don't pore over parenting books to ensure that Zack is sleeping on austere regimen or rising to precise milestones. Besides, I would have been alerted to anything urgent by Zack's pediatrician on our regular visits, and thus far Zack is measuring squarely within normal physical bounds on height and weight.

The issue of greatest discussion actually involves me: my inability to satiate Zack by breastfeeding. I simply can't make enough milk so I'm forced to supplement with formula, which feels like a failure. And it's not for lack of trying—I literally drink liters of water every day in my fervor to provide the gold standard, and I barely leave my house because I need a toilet within sprinting distance every ten minutes. I've consulted his pediatrician, breastfeeding experts, used breast pumps to stimulate production, but I recently gave up after chastising my body for insufficient output. I shouldn't be so hard on myself, a point the pediatrician confirmed by jokingly reminding me of the old adage that as a mother, there will be plenty of bigger problems down the road about which I can torment myself . . . !

As my maternity leave winds down at just over three months, much as I've come to cherish the symbiotic rhythms with Zack, I'm eager to return to work and the office atmosphere. I can't seem find enough ways to entertain and amuse Zack all day long, particularly given his restive nature and inability to sleep for long periods. And I confess, there have even been some unexpectedly dark moments when I feel suffocated and caged by caring for this demanding newborn at virtually all hours, so returning to work actually feels like somewhat of a hiatus.

And thrillingly, I'm now certain my quest for professional meaning has arrived in this legal niche of adoption law. Looking back at DOJ, I'm still keenly aware of the disconnect between my expectations and personal fulfillment, between the prestige of the sterling DOJ badge and the uninspiring tedium of the job itself. It's odd that no part of disability rights law ever resonated with me. But I'm ready to resume my rightful part of the legal apparatus that delivers children to childless couples; in the end we must go where we're most needed.

TOUGH AUDIENCE

I thought that I heard you laughing
I thought that I heard you sing
I think I thought I saw you try
But that was just a dream, try, cry, why, try
That was just a dream, just a dream, just a dream
Dream

—*LOSING MY RELIGION*, LYRICS BY R.E.M.

IT SEEMS EVERYONE has an opinion on Zack, who has just cleared his first year of life. Family members boldly take it upon themselves to share unsolicited advice and openly ruminate about him. Zack's initial homecoming from the hospital inspired a unanimous shower of approval that he was one of the most breathtaking newborns, expert at breastfeeding, a mass producer of excrement. I took these plaudits in stride since Zack, like every newborn, was expected to do little else. But now it seems both he and I are under constant scrutiny for his every move, or lack thereof.

It's true that Zack seems developmentally sluggish in certain areas, but not alarmingly so. My mother opined out loud whether Zack's head circumference was disproportionately large compared to his body, and asked if I had inquired about this to his pediatrician? Another expressed concern that Zack seems capable of only of babbling and vocalizing, but has not yet acquired any distinctive words. I pointedly remind everyone of common lore that boys are often less verbal than girls at the outset, and that sometimes language doesn't fully come in until they are age two or even three. An obliging aunt notified me, after babysitting for one hour, that Zack was so preoccupied and self-absorbed that he refused her repeated efforts to enlist him in a rousing "pat-a-cake." He turned his face away abruptly as if offended, withdrawing his hands angrily from her enthusiastic grasp. Didn't this strike me as strange? she asked. *Perhaps, like his mom, Zack resents intrusion into his personal space, forced intimacy and violating his boundaries,* I thought, *much as I resent the obligatory kiss on the mouth you force on me at our every greet.*

Lately I've been working long hours on a bitterly contested adoption, so I'm weary of the open forum on Zack, the almost conspiratorial hunt for shortcomings by family members far too invested in Zack emulating his "brilliant" parents.

Keith is not remotely concerned, which is reassuring. As the more magnanimous one when it comes to intrusive poking, he more easily tolerates the comments. And dismisses all concerns raised about Zack's behavior as "just allergies," which has become our inside joke for deflecting unsolicited remarks.

I'm tired of everyone weighing in, especially since Zack's pediatrician belongs to a highly reputable group. Each of the milestone visits, at three months, six months, nine months and now one year, took place with different doctors in the practice, none of whom mentioned any irregularities. To the contrary, Zack's head circumference, height and weight are perfectly within range, his eyes properly track movement. His eye contact with the doctors was brief but present, his hearing intact, and his muscle tone solid. That he wasn't yet talking or walking was only briefly touched upon in this recent one-year visit, but as they reiterated, babies catch on at wildly different rates along the developmental timeline, thus competitive comparisons are not useful.

On this past milestone visit, I did raise some mild concerns I have regarding Zack's seemingly flat affect and lack of animation when others try to engage him playfully. I was reassured that not all babies are indiscriminately kind to strangers. That struck me as apt because, although Zack meets my gaze and voice with tangible enthusiasm, he doesn't automatically turn on the charm for just anyone. *Zack has very discriminating taste.* Reinforcing the point, Zack's main pediatrician who tracks his development most closely, offered up a cheerful metaphor: like an orchestral symphony where each instrument takes its turn, as different parts bob up and down, babies likewise erupt and settle in their growth at different times, each at his or her own pace until eventually, usually by kindergarten, they have all caught up in harmonious tandem behind the same starting line. So I made a point of relaying Zack's most recent bill of health in a single e-mail to all family members. This was intended both to update them on Zack's progress and more importantly, get them collectively off our backs. I'm becoming downright hostile if any of them persist with invasive observations, particularly given everything else I had on my plate, work-wise. My clients caught in contested adoptions have real problems.

Although our families have been silenced, I must admit I'm actually now noticing some confounding behavior. Zack is not at all interested in attempting different bodily positions, he never grabs hold of the rails of his crib or corners of low tables to pull himself upright. He has no proclivity for standing nor any interest in trying to walk. As a baby, I was myself a very late walker, so Zack likely inherited my sense of leisure. He's certainly not lacking in physical agility; his crawling has reached Olympic speed as he jettisons across floors on all fours; everyone remarks they've never seen anything like it.

But there's something alarming about his abject refusal to stand. He's not just disinterested, he's ragingly defiant. Whenever I prop him up onto his little legs, he refuses to bear weight, immediately recoiling and retracting his legs into fetal posture. When I once dared to untangle his legs and deliberately plant his feet on the floor, he let out a shriek so scalding it blindsided me, literally toppling me over in shock. He screams as if I'm exposing live, raw nerves simply by placing his feet down flat on the floor. A sense is creeping inside me that Zack's extreme reaction is not physical but behavioral, that what he abhors is being physically manipulated and made to do things he disfavors.

***

I've seen enough babies his age seated in high chairs at restaurants and I know that they regularly adjust their fingers in a pincher grasp to seize and lift pieces of food to their mouths. But despite his insatiable appetite, Zack has ruled out even trying, instead glaring at the spread of food on his tray with querulous frustration while he waits for me to relent and feed him. What's curious is that his refusal seems less a matter of will than genuine inability to execute the simple pincher grasp. Watching his fingers flutter and wave furiously at the food, without ever organizing into a grasp, makes me wonder whether Zack lacks the dexterity to form a pinch. Even when I sit beside him and model the maneuver, he will not imitate; he just sits screaming at me, enraged, until I give up and deliver the food to his mouth.

I finally got so fed up that I force-taught him. In exasperation, I placed an oblong teething biscuit into his palm and forced his little fingers to wrap around it, which they did. But he steadfastly refused to lift his arm, and held it so rigidly straight and rod-like that I grabbed it impatiently, forcibly bent his elbow and shoved his arm upwards while he let out a blood-curdling screech. His resistance was so extreme, so outrageous, I paused to consider whether I literally hurt him. But he *must* learn. This is basic feeding, and I'm tired of him refusing to help himself and wearing me down, so I overrode his screams. It was not until the biscuit actually grazed his lips several times did he finally taste the crumbs and catch on to the purpose behind my forceful maneuvering. From that point on he's executed self-feeding flawlessly, but I'm dumbfounded why such an instinctively self-gratifying activity was initially so lost on him.

Zack is proving to be a tough audience. And not just to strangers, but for me as well. He doesn't emulate Keith's easygoing nature, nor my robust sense of humor. He rarely laughs at all, which strikes me as odd for so young an infant. He has nothing but antipathy for books when I open one to read: he angrily swats it closed. The only feature of books that intrigues him is the spine; he's fascinated by the hinging mechanism by which books open and close. In checking with close friends on this I'm reassured to hear that several of their boys are similarly hostile about being read to. *Okay, it can wait.*

Getting Zack to actually laugh out loud is no easy feat. I'm having to resort to ever more exaggerated stunts and props to get him to even smile. I engage in major flourishes like exaggerated faux falls down the staircase, complete with dramatic screams, but even when he laughs it erupts in a brief spurt which abruptly turns off, as he quickly resorts to his humorless affect. Sometimes it feels hostile, like a movie critic perennially unimpressed with my best efforts, not even trying to conceal his laconic reaction. I'm working every bit as hard at home with Zack as at work with demanding clients. Trying to capture and hold his attention, desperately seeking his approval, feels unnatural. *I shouldn't have to work this hard to engage my own baby.*

But when he does ignite and grin widely, nothing is more rewarding than the shimmer in his intensely dark eyes, a reflexive glint of adoration he reserves especially for me. As I relay these brief episodes to Keith, we joke that the enormous difficulty in entertaining Zack is just further proof of his astute, discerning nature. *Zack is a delightful snob who responds only to the highest caliber entertainment.*

On a bright note, Zack's remarkably independent. Unlike other babies, he doesn't fret when Keith or I exit the room; he scarcely seems to notice. We're both relieved to see that Zack isn't tormented by the separation anxiety we've observed so often in other babies who whine and cry within seconds of their parents' disappearance. But privately, I can't help but feel sort of jilted. I just wish he cared more, was more demonstrative in his affection for me. I wish I didn't have to compete so hard to intrigue him. I love that he's so discriminating, but honestly, I just wish he was easier.

When I ask Keith whether Zack's indifference bothers him, he's characteristically unconcerned and nonchalant. He reminds me that Zack has a unique personality and displays of affection can't be forced: he is who he is. But when I once asked, "Do you think he truly loves us?" Keith was brought up short pondering Zack's behavior, then responded, "Well, I think he feels very *attached* to us . . . " *Attached?!* Frantic and bereft, I thought, *I would take a bullet for this child and his own father thinks Zack simply feels attached?* But when I've been away for many consecutive hours at a time, upon my return Zack is almost apoplectic with glee! He doesn't light up exactly, though he has this peculiar but endearing gesture of rapidly balling up and releasing both fists over and over, like bursting fireworks. He loves me for sure; the sparks are entirely mutual. I was foolish to ever question it.

Interestingly, there is actually one stimulant guaranteed to elicit a head turn from Zack every time—music. Music in any form—singing, television shows, even the tinkling prelude to the popping puppet in his jack-in-the-box—unfailingly intrigues Zack. He immediately pivots his head and body towards music and permanently affixes his gaze. No wonder he's so enraptured by those famous "Baby Einstein" videos, where melodies play throughout as various toys and objects are constantly spinning and twirling. Zack is positively transfixed for the entire forty-minute stretch, which is terrific since the videos provide my only real respite. He's not a great sleeper so, absent any enthusiasm for most toys or books, the musical videos offer a brief but uninterrupted chance for me to exercise or focus on work-related issues. I confess that sometimes I even play two videos back-to-back to buy more time to myself.

Amidst all of Zack's curious traits, one stands loudly apart from the rest and now truly alarms me. Well over a year old, Zack is still not responding to his name—at all. Not identifying with the word nor registering any comprehension that he is *Zack*. He's so unresponsive I even wonder whether he actually dislikes his name. It suddenly hits me that the answer might lie in a serious hearing impairment. That would explain the selective attention to music but not his own name. Hearing loss might explain the other delays, too. Frightening as it is to contemplate, for his sake and mine I must investigate immediately. I bypass any pediatric recommendation and make the soonest possible appointment with a renowned local "Treatment and Learning Center" which specializes in hearing evaluations.

The testing apparatus is far more elaborate than I expected, conducted with Zack sitting on my lap inside a large red booth adorned with flashing bulbs, animated characters and popping doors. The stimulation is designed to track Zack's auditory perception, and while at first he looks totally baffled and dumbstruck, he eventually catches on and begins responding to the drills. Zack ultimately sails through with ease, pivoting correctly towards alternating birds popping through windows, sudden light flashes, and friendly characters which leap out from either side of the booth. Watching him succeed is exhilarating: I knew Zack couldn't have anything profoundly wrong. I still have no explanation for why he's so immune to his name, and watching his responses I have this strange feeling that what Zack is alerted to is the visuals. He's tracking the sudden sights more than sounds, and reacts much more quickly when errant sounds are paired with visual props, especially when sounds are musical.

The test results are unambiguous. Zack has no auditory impairment whatsoever. I exhale a grateful sigh of relief as the technician delivers this bottom line, then follows up by dissecting the specific results into finite categories.

I'm so overwhelmingly relieved I lose track of the categorical specifics. But I'm perplexed by the technician's own flat, serious affect. *Isn't this fantastic news that Zack just passed with flying colors?* I wonder. *Why isn't she more cheerful in delivering the results? What's her problem?* I wish she'd stop stealing furtive, darting glances at Zack. Zack is wholly disinterested in the litany of results and not paying the slightest attention to her, unsurprising since he's a one-year-old who just endured a battery of tests. The technician's posture is wooden and her cadence forced, as if she's restraining herself from saying something unpleasant, which feels incredibly rude since it's her medical responsibility to be fulsome about what she's observed.

"You know, we don't actually provide a diagnosis outside of a hearing loss or other issues related to auditory processing," she declares inexplicably. In response to my baffled expression she continues, "You might want to get further evaluations for Zack. Again, we don't provide a full development assessment apart from hearing tests . . . " *Why on earth would I do that?* I think defensively. We've just ruled out hearing loss, and everything else has been checked, so why would I expend more time and money investigating something that doesn't exist? Spend thousands of dollars just to give Zack a comprehensive infant evaluation to rule out absolutely every possibility?

I'm almost offended by what feels like an opportunistic ploy to get "overactive" parents to lay out money not just to investigate a concrete concern, but to affirmatively rule out everything else in existence. But then I remember where we live, and her presumptive recommendation makes sense, given our particular demographic. We are city dwellers in what has been nationally calculated to be one of the most educated populations in the entire country. Statistically, our city is a haven for enlightened intellectuals and graduate school elites—chronic overachievers, affluent and fastidious, who presume any destination short of the Ivy League for their offspring reflects badly on the parents themselves. Exhaustive and expensive evaluations are common in these parts; testing infants as young as Zack, just to be completely and absolutely certain of no learning defect or other imperceptible issue, is routine.

But I'm not about to waste money confirming what we already know: that Zack has a distinctive personality but is otherwise fine. His regularly scheduled *health insurance-covered* pediatric visits are more than sufficient. Come to think of it, it's actually reassuring that Zack's delays cut across a variety of developmental traits that seem totally unrelated to each other. A concentration of dysfunction in a single area—like vision or hearing—would more likely signify something serious. The shortcomings with Zack's growth are random, with no distinct pattern or cluster to indicate a syndrome of some kind. He's just generally lagging in development, typical of baby boys, and he'll eventually catch up just as the pediatrician said.

Later that evening, Keith is unsurprised to hear the good news that Zack has no hearing problem; he was never worried in the first place. Then again, Keith is ever the sanguine optimist. But he's also especially preoccupied by work these days, even more than usual because he took a new job right as Zack was born. He was recruited, along with a fleet of other disaffected attorneys, by a genius entrepreneur who focuses on the business side of healthcare finance. For Keith, who had always leaned more towards business than law, this was a welcome draft into the transactional side of his field where he's now an executive. Though I've never grasped the particulars of his new healthcare finance job, I'm thrilled to see him so much happier. The new job carries a significant increase in income, but also exacts a price—Keith works far longer hours well into the night, arriving home as late as 11 p.m., long after I've already fed, bathed and put Zack to bed. The uptick in his responsibilities also involves major travel nationwide to close lending deals, which keeps him away for days at a time, every week.

Over this past year, I've had my share of resentful and exasperated moments dealing with Zack on my own, not to mention some incredibly lonely nights. I didn't get married and have a child only to raise him by myself. But then I remember I agreed to the job change, and for the right reasons. When Keith first consulted me, he laid out how this was precisely the type of work for which he's suited, and I understood his disenchantment with practicing law only too well. He'd been wholly supportive of my defection from the stale DOJ to a juicier, but lower-paying, job at my boutique firm. The opportunities for Keith to rise dramatically within the new company are visible, and his excitement about joining the new venture was so palpable I was not about to block his ambition. Just as, given my philosophy of our marital pact, he would never thwart mine.

THANK YOU, DOCTOR

I hear my silence talked of in every lane;
The suppression of a cry is itself a cry of pain.

—DARSHAN SINGH

"ARE YOU CERTAIN he can hear?"

"Yes, I had his hearing checked, it's fine."

"But he doesn't respond to his name at all, no turning of his head . . . other gestures of recognition?"

"No," I say placidly. Zack is nineteen months old and still has no words. Silently, I recall the many times when Zack's back was to me and I stood directly behind him, testing. I literally shouted out his name, and he barely flinched.

"How's his eye contact?"

"Good with me—but no one else. And even with me it's fleeting. He can't seem to stay with me for any length of time." My voice drops off at the end.

I avert my gaze towards a small window while I struggle to absorb the reality of who I suddenly am—a first-time mother, seated in a sterile hospital room across from a pediatric neurologist, about to learn whether something is wrong with my son. Even as I scheduled the appointment I still expected to leave with a bland reassurance that Zack is merely delayed, so I didn't insist that Keith join me today. Here at the pediatric neurology division of Georgetown University Hospital, alone with Zack, I'm expecting to report back to Keith the unspectacular results of this consult. But the doctor's tone is austere, sending shivers up my spine. I'm clamping down hard to control myself. This is nuts, I should have insisted that Keith come. But it's too late now, his work has him out of town, I don't even remember where at this point.

And now I'm watching in shock through a clinical glass window as an entire team of developmental therapists—occupational, speech, physical—repeatedly prompt and prod Zack to perform the simplest task of pinning facial features to a blank doll. Zack is confounded, his flailing gestures signaling that he hasn't even the slightest comprehension of what he's being asked to do. I watch as he fails early level motor and language assessments, shuffling across the floor with his peculiar crawl, refusing to bear weight on his feet, slapping away books and turning his indifferent nose up at educational toys. The glass begins to dampen and fog from my labored breath as the nurses nearby keep close watch, at one point nearly having to restrain me from bursting through the door in sheer humiliation to supply Zack an answer—just once.

Forced to watch his consecutive mounting failures, I'm trying to decode the quick head shakes and knowing glances between experts. I watch as they do their very best to help Zack succeed, going so far as to physically assist Zack by placing their hands over his to cue him how to perform certain tasks, only to give up several trials later. Something about the way this is unfolding is chillingly embarrassing, I'm his mother, the one who apparently failed to teach him properly about basic skills.

And now suddenly it is my turn to be glued to a seat, to be probed and interrogated against my will.

"Does he line up objects, or seem fascinated by spinning objects?" the doctor inquires soberly.

"Yes." I answer succinctly. I should elaborate, there's more to it than my truncated answer implies, but there's a distinct tremor to my voice that I don't want him to notice. "Um, yes, Zack sometimes gets *caught* on spinning objects. We have these little round stacking cups and he actually takes my wrist and directs my hand to spin them over and over while he watches." I can picture Zack now, crouched on the floor, immobilized by the sight of the twirling cups, riveted and spellbound, as if nothing else in the world existed other than that rapidly spinning disc. And then his disappointment as the cups slowly wobble and tumble to a stop, his hand anxiously darting towards mine as he forcibly takes my wrist and directs it to the cups to start the spinning process over. I always cooperate, the idea never once having crossed my mind that his obsession might signify something deeper and more serious.

I quickly snap back to the present. I've been lost and absorbed in thought. But the doctor is also preoccupied, vigorously scrawling all over his notepad. He didn't seem to notice my absence, and barely looks up at me as he continues the interrogation.

"Anything unusual about the way he stands? Do his feet seem firmly and flatly planted to the floor or is there bobbing or bouncing?" *What on earth does that have to do with anything?* My throat is so parched from fear I can't answer. He looks up abruptly from his note-taking and assesses my quizzical gaze. "Does he stand mainly on the balls of his feet?"

"*Y-e-s,*" I answer haltingly. The air in the room is still and stale, and I can feel sweat pooling up in my armpits and slowly streaming down the backs of my arm. I want to readjust in my chair, give some vent to my armpits, but suddenly I cannot move. Or breathe. My breath is shallow and tight in my throat, my body taking in only the barest sips of air necessary to keep it going.

"Does he point to direct your attention to favored items?"

"No," I whisper miserably, staring down at my feet.

"Pointing is a form of shared communication, or as we call it behaviorally, joint attention. An infant instinctively points to a desired object because he comprehends that his perspective differs from that of the person he is communicating with. He points to whatever is it he wants because he understands others can't read his mind."

I look down at Zack. We have been talking about him as if he is not in the room, when in fact he's right here at my feet, so silent it's as if he's absent. He's contentedly playing with his shoelaces, quietly rearranging them over and under one another.

"Zack has never pointed, not once," I mumble, and realize that I've begun to bow my head, as if ready to take a blow. "Doctor, this is very bad, isn't it?"

"Not just yet." He abruptly holds out his hand in a sort of stop sign. "I need to ask a few more questions. How is his general affect, his overall demeanor day to day?" A bitterness begins rising in my throat. I may vomit.

"Flat," I barely whisper, finally making a connection that had eluded and disturbed me for so long. With his porcelain complexion and captivatingly dark eyes, Zack has always been an uncommonly beautiful child. Strangers are routinely drawn to him, unable to restrain themselves from thrusting their faces up close to his in an effort to engage and enchant him, showing their desire for proximity to this beautiful creature. But always the opposite occurs, with Zack abruptly turning his face away as if revolted. This habit had always bothered me as oddly rude and so uncharacteristic of babies who, other than Zack, always seem naturally delighted by a sincere show of warmth and attention.

"Does Zack brighten or laugh at interactive games?" I recall the first time I raised this question with Keith, and was so crushed: "I mean, of course we'll love him no matter what, but he just seems so aloof, so humorless, so unimpressed no matter what I do . . . "

At the time, imagining that Zack had a cold and unwelcoming personality was disappointment enough. But now, suddenly, the flat affect and lack of humor have become discernible pieces of a much larger, more horrifying puzzle. I am actually starting to feel petrified; something terrible is happening in this room. We are gaining momentum, this doctor and I, galloping towards something sinister. A slow shiver runs up my spine as I realize how intensely vulnerable I have just become, steadily disarmed of any illusions or excuses for Zack's behaviors. *Dear God, there is something seriously wrong with my child.*

"Is Zack ever excited to see you when you come into his room, let's say first thing in the morning?"

"Yes!" I practically shout, relieved finally to offer something positive about Zack. The doctor looks up, also surprised by the unexpected break in the pattern, and my heart rebounds with excitement. "That's good, right? Yes! Yes he's definitely happy to see me when I come in, and also if I've been gone during the day for many hours he's visibly excited when I come back."

But suddenly the doctor is distracted, looking down sternly at Zack moving on the floor. "Does he often do that?"

I look over at Zack who is sort of half-walking, half-crawling in what seems to be a distinctive pattern across the floor. Silently, we watch as he shuffles over to a low cabinet door which he swings open once, staring with fascination at the hinges as they interlock and slide back and forth. He then abruptly abandons the door to shuffle back over to his shoe to rearrange the laces, and then moves back to the cabinet door. Back and forth. Back and forth. Zack repeats the identical routine as if he has been bound to a track. The doctor is glaring at Zack now with harsh disapproval, as a cord of urgency rips through me.

"Does that mean something, that he does it exactly the same way every time?" I know now that it does. "Doctor, I can't take this anymore. I need to know what you're thinking, what all these questions are adding up to—there's something seriously wrong with him, isn't there?"

"Yes," he answers simply, "yes, there is."

My blood turns cold as my stomach bottoms out, and he gingerly places his pen on the desk to indicate no further inquiry is needed. "I was hoping not to have to tell you this but it's pretty clear, especially with what he's doing right now. Zack meets the medical criteria for Autism Spectrum Disorder. Zack has autism."

The doctor takes a moment to allow this to sink in, and for the first time he is looking directly at me, trying to access my comprehension. But I cannot face him. I look away, humiliated, as the horrible realization begins to sweep over me. *Zack is not just delayed, he is disabled. This is not temporary. This is who he is.*

The doctor's voice quickly turns soft. "You see, there are many indicators of a developmental delay, but there's a certain constellation of symptoms that warrant a diagnosis of autism. They present in what we've classified as three categories: social deficits, language delay and perseverative behaviors, which is what he's doing right now, that going back and forth in the identical pattern. It's an almost ritualistic mode of behavior, what we call 'self-stimulating,' which children with autism tend to engage in because it gives them a sense of comfort and predictability."

I have long since stopped listening. A frantic alarm is going off inside my head, the ringing in my ears has exploded into a deafening scream. *AUTISM! This is not happening! Autism, like "Rain Man" autism?* Something in my body has broken loose. I cannot tell what, but I can feel it. Someone has just reached inside and ripped it down and it's dangling by a thread, bleeding profusely. *It can't be, it cannot be this serious; my child is NOT disabled! Or diseased. Is that what he's telling me...that Zack has some kind of cognitive disease that went undetected all this time? No—my son is normal, he is normal!* A horrid voice is bellowing deep inside me. *This cannot be happening, I cannot have a cognitively disabled child. This cannot be my life!*

The doctor never stops talking as he studies me intently, and it suddenly dawns on me that this is a man accustomed to delivering bad news. It feels eerily rehearsed: the detached clinician who looks on as the poor mother goes to pieces before his eyes. As huge, uncontrollable tears begin coursing down my cheeks and I begin gasping for air, it's suddenly the doctor who cannot bear to maintain eye contact, as his eyes begin darting anxiously to avoid mine.

"Ultimately, of course, what all parents want to know is 'Will my child ever recover from this, go on to lead a typical life? Will he ever go to high school or college?'" I look up desperately and start heavily panting with fear. *Yes, I want to know that . . .*

"The truth is, we just don't know." I am very still. "It all depends on the child and we never know how a particular child will respond to behavioral therapy, which is what I am recommending: intensive applied behavioral therapy." He reaches over his desk and hands me several papers from neatly stacked piles, papers thoughtfully pre-arranged with the foresight that they will be handed out often. I glance down and see the phrase *"ABA, applied behavioral analysis for children on the Autism Spectrum"* printed boldly throughout the papers in mockingly cheerful text, as if the service being offered is highly desirable and sought-after rather than sickening. Something else printed here about a minimum of *"40 hours of intensive one-to-one therapy"* per week. My breath catches in my throat. *Forty hours per week? How am I supposed to manage that with my job? I'm going to have to quit my job.* I can't possibly meet Zack's urgent needs and still be the professional I'm climbing towards.

"So, we just never know how far a particular child will go but—" The doctor pauses, bracing himself to deliver the next blow, "but the truth is, when the symptoms present so strongly in the manner they appear to with Zack the prognosis is, well, it's not quite as good."

Not as good as what? As children who are only mildly autistic? Do you mean he'll be living with us forever? Will he never be normal? Not even a chance? Just what the hell are you telling me here? Hideous questions bombard me, crashing angrily into one another, but I ask none of them because I have lost my voice. I cannot will my mouth to speak or my limbs to move; they are sickly withered and drained of hope. Through a dizzying haze of tears I can feel that I am moving, but I cannot see where. I can feel my legs beginning to buckle under me as I begin spiraling downwards. I am stumbling down the hospital hallway, tripping over my feet, drunk with grief.

It seems I cannot stand, so someone has seated me in a sturdy chair in front of the receptionist's desk. Someone has seized Zack and is drawing blood from his arm in another room, having first had to forcibly restrain him. I can hear his screams as my heart lurches out to rescue him, but I'm so hobbled I cannot move. I'm briskly told by the receptionist that I need to make more appointments, that further tests are needed to rule out the possibility that Zack may be having seizures associated with autism, or that he may have further chromosomal or other cognitive abnormalities. *You mean there may be even more wrong with him?* Zack will need a comprehensive brain scan and EEG that will require multiple electrodes to be fastened to his head while electrode observation takes place over twenty-four hours with an overnight hospital stay. What are my available dates to schedule the EEG?

"Ms. Ellenby, I'm going to need some dates from you," she urges.

I manage to form one question, which I whisper, barely coherent, "When will I get the blood test results back?" With that I am down, broken and sobbing, on the floor. I have slipped from the chair and am on my hands and knees, sucking for air in desperate yelps. I have never in my life publicly lost control but I'm doing it now. I scold myself to get back up. *Hold it together, just long enough to schedule the appointments and get out the door. Just get up.*

But my body is divorced from reason, and as it surrenders fully to the grief, I can hear myself wailing loudly. This is surreal as I dissociate and, as if hovering from above, watch from a distance as this pitiful woman is hobbled and writhing on the hospital floor while others witness with frozen shock. Strange, guttural sobs, almost inhuman, like an animal caught in a trap, emanate from my mouth. Several doctors drop their clipboards and lurch toward me in alarm, as the receptionist immediately races out from behind her desk and kneels before me anxiously.

"Oh my God, oh my dear God!" She grabs me and holds me tightly in her embrace as I continue sobbing uncontrollably. "It's going to be okay," she whispers gently and again, "It's going to be okay." As she wraps her arms around me and several strangers lift me to my feet, she steadies me and focuses my eyes upon hers.

"I'm going to pray for you," she says gravely. I look back at her in bewilderment. *Pray for me?* It is of no comfort, but as I look into her kind eyes I can see that she means it. As I wobble to the hallway to retrieve Zack, I glance back at her one last time and see that she has not moved an inch from where she is standing: she is determined to see that I make it out safely. Her eyes are different now, steely and concentrated with an almost mechanical gaze beneath which she seems to be carrying on a silent conversation: she has already begun praying for me.

Dazed and disoriented, I don't remember how I made it to my car and strapped Zack in. I look down moments later to see

I'm steering us by habit, but my watery vision is badly blurred. I know this is dangerous, but I don't care. *Go ahead, let me smash head-on into a tree. I welcome the impact, a merciful exit. Because I've just learned I have nothing to live for anymore and nothing to lose. My child is gone, you see, he's just nineteen months old but his life is already over. He is gone.*

Through my rearview mirror I squint in an attempt to focus on Zack. He is the picture of serenity, gazing contentedly out the window as always, completely unaware of the wreckage of his life. Senselessly, I become angry at him for not comprehending the tragedy. He's just sitting there; he doesn't even get it! He's not even a boy really, but the *shell* of a boy, an exquisite cutout of a child with no actual stuffing. He is damaged . . . deformed . . . *disgraced.* And his disgrace is my own.

This is what my glorious womb has produced, a profoundly dysfunctional child even despite my most scrupulous attempt to shield him from harm during my pregnancy. That's the cruelest irony of all, that I was *careful* during my pregnancy, deeply cautious in refusing exposure to any toxic fumes, and yet at this very moment there are babies being born addicted to crack cocaine whose brains stand a better chance of recovery than my son's.

And am I expected to single-handedly rescue this child from this oppressive blanket that's suffocating his brain? Am I expected to surrender my entire life and career in pursuit of some remote chance, years down the road, of recovery from an incurable disease? For the first time in my life, I have no master plan, no discernible path forward. I cannot see my future.

And already I am failing the immediate task at hand. I should be interacting with Zack in a meaningful and engaging way as often as possible to keep him from withdrawing even more. That bit of doctor's advice which I managed to capture through the bleary haze:

"Zack is a child who can go either way. It's possible he can be drawn out socially, but he's showing an equal potential to retreat entirely into own world. You must make every effort to engage him. Do not let him slip into self-stimulating or perseverative behaviors, keep interrupting and engaging him at all times."

Bitterly I consider the irony of expecting a parent to meaningfully engage her child after having just received news of a lifelong deficit so devastating the parent can barely speak. *Forgive me, doctor, but I've just learned that my child has an incurable brain disorder, I'm a bit too numb to engage and enthrall.*

I swerve over to the side of the road. Against my better judgment I decide to call Keith. This is unfair, I know. This is not the right time or way to deliver the news, and I should wait until he returns home. But I'm volatile and desperate and not about to carry this grief alone.

"Well, I've been to the neurologist, I just left." My tone is dead.

"And?" Keith asks. I stop suddenly to consider where my husband is—he's likely driving on unfamiliar interstate roads— and the danger of what I'm about to do to him.

"And, we'll talk about it when you get home. We'll talk then."

But of course now the door has been opened and he must know. And he would have pressured me anyway because he knew I was taking Zack to the neurologist this morning where there was a chance we would leave with some explanation and prescription to address his delays.

"Zack has autism," I blurt. "This isn't just a developmental delay, this isn't just delayed speech, this is really serious . . . and he's really got it. They tested him and he's only functioning on the level of a six-month-old in so many areas and he failed all the tests and—" The shrill emotion in my voice rises swiftly.

"Oh," my husband answers in a quiet, contemplative voice. "Okay, it's okay."

Enraged, I immediately fire back, "NO it's NOT ok! Do you get what this means? HE'S GOT AUTISM! He may never talk, he may never go to high school or live on his own! DO YOU GET THAT?" I bite back through fiercely clenched teeth. "DO YOU GET HOW SERIOUS THIS IS?"

Of course he does. But he is only just this second digesting the news, which I'm not even allowing him to interpret his own way. And this is a man who has already met with true tragedy and loss, the loss of his beloved older brother only one year ago. And Keith meets adversity with an equanimity that is both rare and astonishing.

In the past I've admired Keith's remarkable capacity to stay even, but right now I just need Keith to explode right along with me. Because right now I am insane with possibilities and spiraling towards darkness—debilitating seizures, further brain damage, institutionalization, physical assault by unscrupulous aides. So right now I just want Keith, for once, to be as unhinged as I am at the tragic news.

And sensing all of this, my husband refuses to engage me.

"STOP," he instructs me forcefully. "Just stop! I'm not going to do this with you now. I need time to think, I need some distance, we'll talk when I get home." And with that he abruptly hangs up. And even in my enraged state, I understand the wisdom of his refusal to go down the dark path I am laying before him.

As I continue slowly driving home, I realize I must now perform the unbearable task of notifying *everyone* who's waiting to learn of Zack's fate. I foolishly told everyone beforehand that today was the day we would find out what's really going on with Zack. It's a story I'll have to recite over and over to concerned friends, all the while knowing deep down that each one will hang up the phone with a profound sense of sorrow—and pity—and *relief* that this isn't happening to their child. I know because that's precisely how I would feel if I was not me. And right now I just can't take it. I cannot even fathom interacting with friends whose lives are intact, whose children are healthy and normal, when my son's future has just been irreversibly shattered. If I'm going to be cut off from the ordinary dreams and joy of having children, then I might as well cut ties now.

I call my closest friend, Heather. We became close friends as DOJ attorneys working in close proximity, our offices next door to each other. We shared the identical time frame for having children, and similar attitudes towards retaining our careers. We were delighted that we got pregnant with our children at the same time and shared all the vicissitudes of pregnancy and postpartum challenges. Her daughter's birth was just three weeks after Zack's and we've remained the closest confidantes ever since. But mercifully I just got her voicemail because I can barely form the words:

> *Hey, Heather, um, well, so we did get a diagnosis today and uh, it's pretty bad. Zack has autism. And I'm just now digesting all of this, dealing with all of this and there's a lot I'm going to have to do. So, if I'm unavailable for a while and I don't pick up the phone, that's why. And also I'll be really busy getting things lined up for Zack because he's going to need tons of intervention, so please don't call me back. I just—I'll get back in touch when I'm able."*

And with that, I hang up. *There. All alone. Much better.*

A TOXiC WOMB

The perpetration of a crime is accompanied by illness.

−CRIME AND PUNISHMENT,
F. DOSTOYEVSKY

OUR HOUSE IS a tomb and we are walking cadavers. No matter how vigorously I shake my head I can't expel the fog of disorientation and disbelief. It's as if we've been suddenly tossed out into an alternate universe light years away from friends and family where nothing is predictable, no rules fit, and there are no inhabitants but the three of us in a galaxy of silence spinning helplessly in space. As the initial shock of Zack's diagnosis wears off, a funereal dread has replaced it. Everything we understood about the past, present and future is entirely wrong. Stripped of our bearings, Keith and I must revise our prior interpretations of Zack's odd behaviors and face them as clinical symptoms rather than idiosyncrasies.

Zack's stoicism is not deliberate; it's textbook autism. His personality is not his personality, but the shallow reflection of a disorder that snuffed out whatever giggling, animated affect he was meant to have. And Zack, staring vacantly into the distance, is a constant reminder that, while the physical child is still present, his very essence is not. It feels both strange and surreal as we move about the house, mechanically performing the same perfunctory tasks of feeding, changing diapers, bathing. Ashen and grey, we move in a zombie-like trance that propels us forward, powered only by habit while any sense of achievement stands still. It's the fault lines of *before* and *after* and we are living in the *after* world.

Before, operating under the presumption that Zack was just delayed but otherwise thriving, our childcare chores felt frivolous and fun, even the most exhausting were light-hearted compared to the awe of having delivered this spectacular new creature into the world. That Zack was physically breathtaking only added to the intoxicating mix of wonder and beaming pride at having joined the ranks of the sleep-deprived, delirious, bragging cult of new parents. As we passed our bundle from friend to friend, Keith and I locked eyes appreciatively as each adoring gazer extolled, the gasps were real, reinforcing our private conspiratorial delight at having made such an exquisitely raven-haired, ruby-lipped infant.

But we are not smiling now; we are barely breathing and the house is silent. No more visitors for now. We are still not sleeping, but now our insomnia is the stuff of nightmares as we lie awake at night, side by side, in silence. I rise on command to the sound of crying and move silently through Zack's feed until there is silence again, grateful to be relieved of my duties so I can longingly retreat back to my bed, my tomb. I have never known anything like this, this feeling of being so completely hollowed out inside that I cannot even summon tears. And there are those moments when I'm seized by an icy shock that rips through my abdomen, constricting my muscles and wracking my insides with involuntary spasms and jerks. I'm forced to my knees and doubled-over in pain, I clutch my insides with both forearms while gagging on air. Just as suddenly, the spasm breaks and gives way to an abject numbness that renders me flat and incapable of feeling, a zombie. It's as if the chemical beakers in my brain are being flippantly tossed back and forth, sloshing and spilling uncontrollably to knock me sideways and keep me permanently off balance. Terrified by my constantly shifting mental states, I pray for stability. But in those rare moments when the dense fog lifts, what replaces it is far worse—a clenched fist is gripping my heart, clamping down and tightening like a vise that causes a stabbing pain. It's the kind of psychosomatic symptom I would have dismissed as phantom if I wasn't actually experiencing it, but the physical pain is real and breathtaking. It's incomprehensible to me that a chemical imbalance in the brain can unleash such physical sensations.

Zack, as we knew him, is gone and a very real death has taken place. Death of our expectations. Death of our future. Death of the child we thought we knew. As I stare at the inscrutable stranger who has replaced him, it's dawning on me how much of those early months of parenting depend upon illusion. An infant, unable to demonstrate any truly unique capabilities, exists mostly as a projection of the parents' expectations. So a new parent simultaneously inhabits two worlds—the joy of the present, which consists of gazing and adoring exchanges with the newborn, and the joy of the future, which is the projection of personality traits you presume your baby possesses. Into a faint smile we read contentment, into the eye contact we infer deep connection. But in truth we know nothing in those early months. Not until those crucial developmental milestone are met, or missed, do we begin to apprehend who this person is apart from who we've imagined. Only now can I appreciate how the initial rapture is predicated on the single, unproven assumption that the child is healthy.

For the vast majority this is so taken for granted as to be scarcely acknowledged. But for the parent who is suddenly handed a grave diagnosis, there is the immediate and jolting chasm between herself and all other parents from this moment on. There exists a divide between her child and all others who will forever surround him, an amputation real and irreversible.

Mother and child are cut off from the cult of normal to which everyone else belongs, and she knows she will never experience life quite the same way again. She realizes she must rediscover her own child with whom she imagined she shared the most intimate understanding. Because he is changed now. Therein lies the cruelest casualty of all; robbed of my illusions about my child nearly two years after he was born, I'm left with the vacant cavity of expectations that Zack is incapable of filling. Was there any reciprocity during our supposedly mutual encounters? I want desperately to believe he possesses intent, that deep down in ways he can't outwardly demonstrate he truly cares about his surroundings and deeply loves me. But his vacuous expression is so fixed, so immutable, it's impossible to believe in an inner depth or dimensions to him beneath what hits the surface. My beautiful, lobotomized child.

A diagnosis is not just a diagnosis, but an entirely new identity. Zack seems so much smaller now, visibly shrunken by the diagnosis. Now that he's assumed a new status—*disabled*— it feels fraudulently incomplete to refer to him simply as Zack because it leaves out his defining characteristic. Zack is a child with autism, a child so cognitively compromised, who requires medical intervention so intense, he cannot fairly be ranked as healthy. No, Zack is not healthy; we are not healthy. It is a contagious illness, a sickness which has spread throughout the entire house and left me too enervated to make even the simplest decisions. *Should I take him for a walk or read a book to him? Does it even matter?*

We're on the clock: every day he's not meaningfully engaged we risk losing him further to the void, that hideous doctor's observation. "Zack is showing some traces of social skill but he's a child who could go either way. He can be pulling out more if you intervene early and aggressively, but he could also retreat further into his own world . . . "

There are decisive steps I should be taking, clearly spelled out on that cheerful ABA flyer about early behavioral intervention, emphasis on *early*. But the thought of all the work I have to do just to get started—so much research, so much time spent reciting the litany of symptoms over and over—and I'm just so depleted. The enormity of what's at stake if I wait is precisely why I cannot bear to start. My arms are so weak and drained that even the simple act of lifting the phone causes them to ache. *No calls yet, not now . . . maybe later.*

I look to Keith, but he's lost in his own world, seemingly preoccupied with figuring something out but he's not sharing. And so it goes, living day by day with the barest communications between us, just enough to get by, until one day Keith unexpectedly breaks the silence.

He knows what happened to Zack. With tears brimming and eyes full of sorrow he recounts to me that once when he and Zack were bathing together, he lifted Zack from the tub so hastily that Zack slammed his head hard into the metal shower rod. Really hard, maybe even hard enough to cause permanent brain damage. Zack looked woozy and out of sorts for several minutes after he sustained the blow. I'm deeply moved by Keith's confession as he recounts the incident. I can tell from his pained grimace that he's been tormenting himself privately for some time. But I'm also amazed that he's assumed blame, believing that such an accident could cause this type of brain anomaly. But as he speaks, I see how the absence of any rational explanation, the absence of genetic markers to explain Zack's disability, can drive a parent mad. Like me, Keith is groping in the dark for answers and desperately grasping at straws.

"No, sweetheart," I reassure him tenderly, cradling his own wounded head in my arms. "Babies' skulls are much sturdier than that. They can withstand hard blows to the head, some even fall and hit their heads on concrete without having serious brain injury. Zack didn't get a concussion from hitting the shower rod, just a shock. What Zack has is innate and developmental. It was there all along, but we didn't know it. It probably happened *in utero*, maybe something I ate or inhaled during gestation, but he was born with this and it's finally surfacing. His autism is in no way your fault." Keith still looks miserable and unconvinced, so deep is his pain.

No, of course, this is not Keith's fault. A man so decent, so imbued with honesty and integrity I spent much of our courtship disbelieving that I was the one he had chosen to spend his life with. Dating him felt like a cleansing for my own sordid past. Keith was the reason I wanted the little raven-haired prince in the first place.

There's no mystery why this is happening, but unlike Keith I can't speak my confession aloud. My past has not been perfect, far from it, and in my soul I knew that a life of transgressions would catch up with me. Growing up I was not always the most scrupulous person. I engaged in ruthless bullying of others in childhood without any comprehension of how badly I was scarring them. As a teen I was so romantically insecure and fearful that I might lose a boyfriend to infidelity that I always kept someone else waiting in the wings, dishonorable and distrusting.

Even as a young adult I behaved badly. I shoplifted regularly and behaved unscrupulously out of my own loneliness. I once inserted myself into a stable relationship that I had no business being in nor any right to disrupt, but I did it anyway, selfishly, and with devastating consequences. I walked away from the wreckage mostly unscathed and determined never again to repeat my destructive behaviors. And I delivered on that promise when Keith entered the picture: dating him felt like immersing myself in a cleansing, regenerating shower. But I was still selfish, and still put my needs first. Why else would I have continued taking that nightly sleeping pill even after we began trying for a baby? As a lifetime insomniac I was desperate for sleep and planned to wean myself off them well before we started trying to get pregnant, but foolishly figured we wouldn't conceive right away—*how could I possibly take that chance? What the hell was I thinking?*

In my panic upon first learning of the pregnancy, I drilled specialists about the potential harm to the fetus from those few pills which overlapped with conception, but was reassured that the low dose would do no harm to my baby. But serious harm has come.

Maybe it was the steady stream of music videos I subjected Zack to as an infant. All those times I stuck Zack in front of the TV so I could steal an hour to myself to exercise, to study the law, again: what was I thinking? Because looking back, I remember vividly how transfixed he was by the music and incessantly spinning objects, and think that a more astute mother would have realized his fascination signaled something very wrong. Maybe if I hadn't eschewed all those parenting books I would have been alert to the fact that Zack wasn't hitting critical developmental milestones, but I never read them. Granted, Zack's pediatrician didn't catch his symptoms either, but I am his mother, the one charged with knowing him and who spent more time observing him than anyone else, so I should have identified the idiosyncrasies as red flags and insisted upon a comprehensive evaluation across all areas. And if I had done so sooner, if I hadn't been so damned eager to restart my own career, maybe we could have caught his disability at nine months rather than nineteen.

Had I started behavioral intervention a year earlier maybe he'd be in a different place. But now we've lost precious months that allowed the autism to flourish and more fully consume him. All while I remained ignorant of the danger growing right before my eyes that I continued to rationalize away.

After weeks of being entombed by numbness, my heart is finally giving way to the realization that I'm being justly punished. Weeks of sleep deprivation has given rise to fugue states during which I believe I've located the demons. I know this is logically absurd, but my emotions are divorced from reason and in a very real way this injustice feels like absolute justice. There is something rotten inside me, a badness so endemic it allowed me to break up relationships. Now, my own most intimate and lifelong relationship is broken for good. Zack's autism is collateral damage for a life poorly lived. I just never imagined the punishment for my bad deeds would be inflicted on my innocent child, or be so brutal, so permanent.

Ruefully, I must admit the punishment fits the crime. The morally ambiguous woman has just been nailed down for good; the disrupter just got disrupted. It took an infant son to finally make an honest woman of me, and I will be incarcerated and tied to him for the rest of my life, a prison sentence where cheating isn't an option and shortcuts don't exist. I'm shackled to the house, as all my vaunted accomplishments come crashing down on my head, a stay-at-home parent for eternity. The universe is having its way with me, and deep down I know I deserve it.

My guilt is wracking me with hysterical sobs. Kneeling alone in my closet, I can finally unleash the unbearable tension that's been building for so long as I thrust my wet face into my pillow to muffle the wailing until finally it's run its course, and I emerge wearily. Time to pull myself together and get to work, steady myself and start making calls. Sobbing and sleep deprivation have left me confused, but my resolve is clear. I must steel my spine and do right by this child, which means setting aside my own needs and devoting myself entirely to his. I will resign my job to begin a new one, and do everything in my power to rescue my child from the beast that is smothering his brain. I will peel back the layers one by one no matter how long it takes. I will devote all of our finances, all of my emotional resources, and bring all my skills to bear on this project that feels very much like life and death. The best therapists, best programs, best intervention our money can buy. After all I've done, it's the least I can do.

PICTURE A STAIRCASE

ABA Lovaas Experimental Group*: The children in this group received 40-hours-per-week, and the treatment lasted two-to six-years. The outcomes indicated 47% of the children (i.e., 9/19) became indistinguishable from their peers or "best outcome," many were able to have their "autism" label removed.*

[By contrast] the children in this group received 10-hours per week with special education, and the treatment lasted two-to six-years. The outcomes indicated none of the children achieved best outcome.

Following this study, many people started implementing "Lovaas Therapy."

—THE "87" STUDY, IVAR LOVAAS LOVAAS TREATMENT CENTER, PROVEN METHODS FOR MANAGING AUTISM

I'VE NEVER LOBBIED in my entire career for anything as vigorously as I've done to recruit one of the most esteemed Lovaas ABA experts to lead my home therapy program. A young virtuoso named Cara (not her actual name) is heralded in local autism circles for running a tight ship and rescuing the most kids. Hailing from New York City, she's a Columbia University-degreed Lovaas adherent, a career professional who reportedly was personal friends with progenitor Ivar Lovaas himself. Her recruitment is contingent upon a group of local families who jointly retain Cara to run their respective programs, thereby allowing us to divide the costs of her airline travel and hotel reservations when she commutes from New York on a monthly basis to assess the children's progress. Cara's been running ABA home programs for more than ten years and her outcomes are legendary. So, I stop at nothing to campaign and win her over to Zack's team.

Over the phone, Cara lays out the therapy protocol that requires a series of rotating in-house therapists who each assume two-hour shifts mornings and afternoons daily for a total intensity of forty hours per week. Unfortunately, there's a dearth of professionals trained to administer Lovaas, so I must recruit students from local colleges and graduate schools by whatever means necessary—flyers, emails, phone calls—all baited with pay incentives and job description designed to induce ambitious students to pad their resumes with special-needs credentials.

It's not just Zack's brain we strive to rewire. The students themselves will be coached and molded into bona fide ABA therapists, a distinction usually sought by those pursuing a career in special education. Anyone can administer the rote drills, Cara preaches. The key is the "wow" factor, those competent cheerleaders who possess the spark needed to excite children and capture their attention, especially kids with cognitive deficits who approach therapy with disdain, even venom.

I'm competing with a host of area parents all fishing in the same pond for these vaunted yet inexperienced students. Aim for those enrolled in autism behavior graduate courses, Cara instructs, and prepare to offer a competitive hourly fee to lure them away from other families in need. Call Cara back once I've retained at least four team members.

But what exactly are the particulars they will be drilling into Zack? What precisely is meant by *intensive therapy*? Cara deftly punts my myriad questions as topics to be discussed later at our first intensive training. There is an unmistakable urgency to her voice, an impatience coursing through our conversation that *Zack is already twenty months old* and we need to get him going.

Early egress to Zack's brain is imperative, and recruitment of a high caliber team takes time and scrupulous vetting. So does purchasing the vast assortment of ABA paraphernalia of flashcards, binders, ABA data and program sheets, 2D and 3D objects and manipulatives, all of which must be organized into at least twenty separate therapy bins. Get my checkbook out because, between Cara's consulting fees, travel and hotel expenses, all four therapists' hourly rates at $20 per hour each, and the myriad materials, I'm about to wade into deeply expensive waters. Expenses upwards of $80,000 a year, none of it reimbursed nor covered by any health insurance regardless of Zack's diagnostic code or medical necessity.

I feel in over my head in more ways than one, but there's no time to question. I need to start sprinting ahead of other families with identical needs. I'm already agitated by the logistical burdens and feeling perilously behind in the race: the starter pistol fired at Zack's initial diagnosis. In response to my repeated questions about the particulars of the programs, I'm met with a brisk cheer, "Don't worry, we'll get Zack going strong!" And with that reassurance, Cara's phone clicks off, the introduction is over.

I studiously begin crafting cheerful, highlighter-bright flyers which I plan to blanket the walls of a local graduate special needs program. I wonder whether it's exploitative to affix a photo of Zack's gorgeous face to the flyer. But I'm not playing games here. My son's brain is at stake. The position for hire is not a babysitter but a dedicated technician charged with the most intricate rewiring. My flyer must stand out, I must employ whatever advantages are at my disposal. So Zack's face is in.

With sickening knots in my stomach I set about layering the flyers over every conceivable space, marketing Zack's face in numbers too great to ignore. I also send emails—with Zack's photo attached—to the special education department head and every graduate instructor, with messages coyly worded to entice ambitious students seeking "excellent remuneration and hands-on training," for an unparalleled opportunity. I will match or exceed others' rates, which again feels revolting simply because I'm fortunate enough to afford it. Cheap tactics I would never consider if I was pursuing employment for myself are suddenly fair game. This is a rescue mission; no manipulative expense can be spared. The flyers and emails detail every feature of the job, beguilingly imprecise on the actual duties since they have not been shared with me yet. The chase begins.

Even before I arrive home from the flyer blanket, my cell phone starts ringing incessantly. Zack's face did indeed stand out and courted a slew of intrigued and anxious applicants tripping over each other for the position. Male and female students excited by the enticing position are calling so often I can barely keep track of names, gender, qualifications. I do my best to make initial assessments simply by the carriage of their voices. Some sound so listless and enervated it's not worth the meet. Others seem titillated in ways that feel wary. Others articulate upfront that the hourly fee is decisive; these folks are immediately disqualified from consideration for their callousness. But within the week-long courting process and dizzying morass, there emerges a handful of candidates who strike the balance I'm seeking: excited but principled, those candidates sensitive enough to inquire about Zack himself, his needs and preferences. It's an alarmingly shrunken number from the original stampede, but it's enough to start interviewing.

The interviews resemble speed-dating at its worst. Consecutive probing meets take place at my house at all hours of the day and night, each side desperately seeking mutual attraction. I'm stunned to discover a frequent disconnect between those who sounded assured and qualified over the phone but in person are oddly detached, barely able to speak or sustain eye contact with me, and not remotely animated in greeting Zack for the first time. Over the following weeks the list is whittled down to the final four who've survived the reality contest, though much about them still remains unknown. They are still total strangers with whom I have virtually nothing in common, who I would not otherwise have any reason to interact with except for my total dependence upon them to rescue my son's brain. Strangers are enlisted into Zack's regimen, who I hope don't have a serious criminal record because I'm overwhelmed just checking references. The initial training meeting is set to last five consecutive days—Cara, four students and me locked in a tiny sunroom-turned-therapy room, our only available space for therapy.

As Cara enters the house she wholly meets my expectations of a crisp, intelligent, well-groomed salesperson ready to extol the virtues of intensive ABA. There's a confident spring to her step, borne of years of swooping in during parents' darkest hours to execute with surgical precision the most critical operation of their young child's life.

"Welcome everyone! I'm Cara, and we all know why we're here: to administer intensive daily therapy to Whitney's son, Zack! We in the trade affectionately refer to ABA as 'baby boot camp' because the obligations are so stringent and very real."

Beneath her upbeat tone is a soberness that bespeaks the gravity involved in altering the very circuitry and synapses of Zack's developing brain, every bit as consequential if he were undergoing actual surgery. Right now, the prospect of a finite procedure feels preferable to the sickening stretch of daily therapy about to saturate every aspect of my life for several years. I rebuke myself. I mustn't allow my face to betray any doubt or dread. No transparency, the façade of gracious and grateful optimist must remain fixed on my face and voice for the sake of my young soldiers.

My lapsed concentration refocused, I catch Cara's stern warning that consistency in administering drills and recording data is imperative. Each session builds on the one before, so therapists must always be recording which targets to repeat, hit next, and hit hardest. *Oh God, Zack will be hit hardest by the monotony hour after hour,* I think mournfully. But then, *Stop it now; pull it together; sit up straight and smile if it kills you.*

ABA etiquette is spelled out in authoritative pieces:

- There are at least twenty separate behavioral programs, each targeting a sequential list of skills such as identifying emotions, objects, people or colors via flashcards and manipulative objects. Happy, sad, man, lady, purple.

- Prompting is hierarchical and intended to fade. We begin by coupling a verbal demand with a physical prompt, such as telling Zack to "touch red" while simultaneously grasping his hand and placing it squarely on the red card in a field of three colors. Do not wait for Zack to hesitate or get it wrong, but steer him physically to the correct answer until he catches on enough to hit it independently on command. Physical prompts are faded until Zack responds to a singular verbal demand.

- Positive reinforcement for correct answers is supplied to Zack continuously throughout the sessions in the form of food—M&Ms, Doritos, anything Zack loves and is willing to work for— though portions must be kept tiny so he is always motivated, never satiated.

- Drills are repeated both within and across sessions until the target is mastered. Mastery is achieved only when Zack correctly answers, without prompting, a drill over three consecutive sessions, with three different therapists. Answers are recorded as either prompted, correct or incorrect, and only an unprompted correct answer across three sessions proves that Zack has mastered a concept. Each of the twenty programs contains its own target list, and data must be scrupulously taken for every drill, with attendant notes if needed.

Certain behaviors will not be tolerated. Cara grabs a flashcard and mimics a characteristic autistic habit of hand-flapping, then rocks her body back and forth in the chair: these are examples of behavior that contaminate answers. If Zack is instructed to "touch red" and does so accurately, his answer is nonetheless incorrect if his hand flaps on the way down to red. The only correct response is a determined, straight hit. Rewiring Zack's brain is not just for epistemic accuracy, but also for the behavioral appearance of normalcy. Typical children don't flap, bounce or yelp when they answer a question, thus neither may Zack.

As I peruse the programs and targets for each, I'm sickened by the enormous swipe of autism on the nascent brain;

absolutely nothing is taken for granted, even the most basic skills like clapping or pointing must be meticulously scripted. Natural impulses that derive organically within other children are tediously choreographed, broken down into concrete steps, and force-fed to the autistic child through an intensive diet of repeat demands, supplying or withholding reinforcement, and stringent data collection. I must quickly avert my eyes and stifle a sob because it's difficult to envision anything more heartbreaking, or a disorder more cruel than one which erases the most innate reflexes of birth. Humans are equipped to perform rudimentary tasks for survival—sucking, eye contact, smiling. But some humans have brains so thoroughly muted into uncommunicative parts they must be drilled and drilled, bit by agonizing bit, to perform "natural" behaviors, like impulses as primitive as turning one's head in response to one's name.

Cara announces a final cardinal rule we must all observe from this moment forward. Forty hours per week is an inflexible mandate: it shall not be truncated for any reason short of severe illness. Back in the 1950s, when Dr. Lovaas first crafted ABA, he discovered that forty hours was the dedicated floor below which therapy hours could not fall even the slightest. Even thirty-five hours compared to forty is insufficient for recovery; don't bother with just ten hours per week, it's the equivalent of none. Therapists' reliable attendance is a scientific imperative.

All of this information is loaded on us in the first few hours of boot camp training. The following days are a kaleidoscope of demonstrations so dizzying the days begin bleeding into each other as we fight emotional anemia—blank stares all around. No one dares complain, we are in professional territory as each therapist is subjected in turn to the potentially humiliating ritual of being called to the therapy table to demonstrate proper execution of drills before the entire group. They did not knowingly sign on for this. I'm growing more restive every hour from watching demands being layered onto the therapists who were not prepared for this stringency. I wasn't prepared either.

It dawns on me, as we sit dripping with sweat, too cowed to ask for a break, that this is perhaps why Cara's explanations were so abbreviated on our first phone call. Had she been fulsome about the duration and force of initial training I might have objected. But now we are planted here, unable to escape for fear of each other's, and Cara's, reaction. I silently tally up the total hours for which I will have to pay every therapist separately, along with Cara's fees, for this days-long ordeal. Sensing agitation hanging in the air, Cara chirps that once we are "trained up," it will never be this bad again! We can look forward to monthly progress meetings, which take only five or six uninterrupted hours, and the emotional and financial price feels staggering.

As Cara finally winds down the interminable lecture, she offers a parting shot: *"Each of you is part of Zack's family now.* You are in their house on a regular basis, practically living with them. You may overhear parental fights. You'll likely see Whitney and Keith at their very worst and most vulnerable. Please be mindful that you are now genuinely inhabiting their world. And they are counting on you."

I swallow hard and my stomach plummets at this forced intimacy. I despise intrusions on my privacy, invasions of my boundaries, and the idea of being forced to keep up appearances even within the sanctuary of my own house is repellent. But these therapists are now part of my interior life, witnessing my domestic turmoil like voyeurs, as adhesive to my private dwelling as the wallpaper itself. Strangers are taking up residence, squatters' rights, privy to all the outbursts. This feels so invasive I must silently remind myself that I chose this protocol because of my a determination to give Zack the absolute best—though with no comprehension of all the ways it would cost me.

As I inhale Cara's words I silently marvel at the trap into which we've all just been ensnared. Having just spent so many hours training together in this room, a sort of educational hazing, we're bonded in tribal allegiance. Only now, after the training is complete—now that we know how steep the learning curve, how grave the obligation, down to the very hours—can we each silently consider how treasonous it would feel to back out, to defect from our comrades at the onset of a battle which has only just begun. The obligation weighs more heavily on me than anyone. I can't possibly insist on exemplary performance by them as a prerequisite for keeping their jobs. No way can I fire them after what I just put them through, nor can I fathom starting the training process over again with someone new. So we're collectively entrapped into fulfilling the very mandate ABA requires: unflinching loyalty to the 40-hours-per-week. It would be wise to pay the newly minted therapists immediately so, checkbook in hand to pay each in full as I walk them apologetically to the door, I promise it will get better.

I now assert my right to pin Cara down on a specific point: assuming all ABA conditions are met, what are the real chances for Zack's recovery? Cara guides me gently to the couch and unfolds the metaphor:

> "Picture a staircase with all the autistic kids standing at the bottom. There are no handrails on either side. Now, all the kids start ascending the staircase. Each step represents progress to more advanced, higher-level programs. Some of the most severely impacted kids won't even make it to that first step; it will be a giant struggle just to get them to sit at the table for drills. But the majority will make it past the step to the next ones. As ABA treatment continue to advance, more and

more kids will begin dropping off the sides of the
staircase or else get stuck on one of the stairs,
unable to climb any higher. Fewer and fewer
children keep steadily ascending until, finally, a
select group of kids make it all the way to the very
top step. These are the kids who recover, who are
mainstreamed in general education by age five
and from then on require only minimal support."

Those children who make it to that vaunted apex of the
staircase will be fully included by kindergarten age with their
neurotypical peers. Sure, these kids might still need some
tweaking or background support, like an after-school tutor or
small-group instruction in school. Some may need educational
supports like extra time for taking tests. But fundamentally
they are mainstreamed, wholly included with, and indiscernible
from, their same-aged peers.

"And how many kids really do make it to the top?" I ask
haltingly.

"We rescue about 50 percent of the kids."

Half the kids—50 percent! I had no idea it was that high! That's
squarely within reach, far more optimistic than the prognosis
implied by that pediatric neurologist who first diagnosed Zack.
Keith and I are intelligent, surely Zack has our genes and with me
pushing him from behind, of course Zack will be in that upper
half! I'm actually excited now to lead this dedicated team, proud
of myself for campaigning so hard to recruit Cara. Smiling and
somewhat giddy from exhaustion, I now know for sure we're
giving Zack the best means to succeed and overcome his autism.
He's not even two yet: he'll surely shed his disorder by age five.

I've never shied away from hard work and now I'm primed
to win, even if it means years of unrelenting sacrifice. Then I,
too, can get back on track, and this will all have been worth it.

40 HOURS

Nobody realizes that some people expend tremendous energy merely to be normal.

—*THE STRANGER*, ALBERT CAMUS

LIVING HOUR BY hour. Entire existence predicated on single rule—forty-hours-per-week rescue mission. Reverberating and bouncing on a violent streak against all sides of my brain—*Zack* must *have 40 hours, no less. Falling below 40 hours is tantamount to ten hours, which is the same as if he has none.*

Therapists rotate in and out of house until I confuse their names. I'm dizzy, sorry, which one are you? Wake Zack up, drag him into room, both of us still groggy from incomplete sleep. No matter, start drilling, every hour counts. Racing against hazy deadline of "too late to save him," quotidian haze governed by single fact—*Zack must have 40 hours, no less.* Don't think about anything else.

No time to consider my own fractured life. Haven't seen Keith in a while. *Where's he gone? Oh right, he's traveling for work, alone, again.*

We're slipping, back-sliding: Zack got several drills wrong! One step forward and two back. I'm emotionally schizoid. One minute Zack slaps his hand down decisively to identify "red" and I'm elated. *Yes, this kid's going to make it!* But the next minute he's scrabbling on the floor screaming and won't even come to therapy table. I'm struck down. *He's not going to make it.*

In between two-hour sessions take Zack out to sample real life, but time is brief. I long to give him reprieve from tedious work schedule. He's only two years old.

Zack must have 40 hours, no less. Dart to local mall indoor playground. Rubberized structures to leap from with other kids, tactile beads on rods, play! It's all we have time for before afternoon session, so make it count. Zack nestles to floor to spin beads, spin beads on rods, over and over, fixated, totally ignoring, and ignored by, peers. Invisible, inanimate, like beads he spins on that fixture. Zack is a fixture. No happy scurrying or rambling; no pretend fencing with imaginary swords; no other kids exist; no bounding off rubber structures in glee; no movement—just spinning.

Other kids read Zack as not worth engaging, kid in corner, twisting fingers in front of face, spinning beads. Not remotely part of fabric of play, not present, not here.

Time to move, get him home.

Back to work. *What's this now?* Therapist is a no-show, again. Damn her! Okay. Jump in myself, seize Zack and drag him weeping and kicking into room. Zack no want mommy as therapist, neither do I. *Zack must have 40 hours, no less.* I swear all this drilling day and night is just making him hate it worse. But I'm a faithful disciple, tick-tock, tick-tock, clock is ticking. Keep him engaged, drill deeper, get on your knees, set up flash cards, start prompting. Go!

NO! he screams, *No Mommy!*

Too bad, Zack, I'm way too invested in your recovery to

tolerate resistance. OK, do easier drill. *"Do This"* program. The "do this" verbal prompt coupled with act he can copy, drill designed to teach imitation. Imitation is foundation of higher learning for all kids, but doesn't come naturally to ours. Even learning to imitate is itself taught.

Grab rubber ball and place at feet. "Zack, do this, kick the ball." I kick first, then replace at his foot.

NO! He drops defiantly to floor. *No Mommy, no!* he shouts.

Grab him hard and yank him upright; losing patience. *You need this, Zack, I'm doing this for you so get up!*

"Zack, kick the ball, 'do this.'" I kick and replace again.

NO! sobbing hysterically now. *Get up, not giving in. Damn therapist is no-show, I hate this, too. No choice for either of us, GET UP!*

"Zack! Kick the ball!" Angrily, I reach over and aggressively seize his little calf with both hands hard, force them into forward-swinging motion. My grasp is too angry, too tight.

"Kick it! KICK it! KICK THE BALL!" Raving now, scared of his defiance, he scared of me. Drill must be administered calmly. This is self-defeating, Zack defeating. *Stop it, you're far too emotional, get a grip and take a deep breath.* "OK. PLEASE, Mommy is so sorry. Please just show Mommy you can do it. I know you can do it, my sweetheart. Kick . . .The . . . Ball."

Zack miserable now and dissolving fast, crumpling to floor in disheveled heap. This has to stop. But no session equals two hours lost, two lost from *40*. It matters, every single hour matters, each adds up to the magic *40*. Anything less than 40 equals ten, which equals failure to recover.

Okay, Zack, it's all right. "You didn't like Mommy's tone; my fault." Get down on floor with him now, pivot to gentle. "Sweetheart, you can do this! I know you can do this, just show Mommy how strong you are!"

"OUCH!" I roar blind-sided as hard sting rips across my

cheek. "My GOD!"

Zack just smacked me incredibly hard in the face. I didn't even see his hand raising. He's never hit me before. This is not recalcitrance but desperation. Only way to make his voice heard is by physical delivery to Mommy—his one true love egregiously violating his boundaries. My force is a betrayal. I fall to carpet, stunned. *He hit me, hit me hard, actually struck me in the face. He's that miserable.*

He's long gone now, fled therapy room, wailing and sprinting to other side of basement, traumatized. So this is what I've become: someone he needs to escape from. I stay on floor on my back, broken and weeping from our brutal failed encounter. My fault, I totally lost my cool. I'm too invested. I can't be his therapist. Too hinged on him answering every single question right, performing every drill right, too frantic he won't recover if he doesn't move fast enough. So desperate to save him that I'm actually hurting him.

I stay on the carpet for hours, no idea what time it is, or where Zack is. Finally I rise, climb stairs, and find him sitting on floor spinning stacking cups. He hears my gait and looks up, terrified, afraid Mommy will drag him back down. *Zack, let me join you here on floor and I'll even flick my wrist to keep those cups spinning, anything to make you trust me again. Because I'm on your side, even if you can't tell. Mommy is just so very afraid, you see.* I won't hurt him for any endgame. Screw *40* hours.

I bend down and scoop little prince gently into tight embrace, stroke his sweaty little head. Bedtime awaits. I carry him upstairs. I sing softly and caress his matted hair, stroke his back as he drifts calmly off to sleep. *Please don't stop trusting me, Zack, I'm as new to this as you are, and I will make mistakes. I'm just desperate for you to heal, get all better. For your sake and mine.*

No sleep for me yet, much work to do still. Update therapy program book, I'm at least good at that. Insert new data sheets, detail additional program steps, organize bins and manipulatives, rearrange flash cards, line up books all along wall, rearrange furniture and desk to make room feel different, erase dark memory of today. Insert weekly hours sheets, glance at the number of hours each therapist worked so far, and my own hours. I fudge mine. Two hours with Zack today, goals hit. Some therapists have been paid, some are owed pay. I calculate hours plus fees, and write checks. It's 2:13 AM. Almost done. Program book and bins are great-looking, arranged to perfection for drills.

God, I'm tired. Just for one second, I gingerly place my head on notebook.

NO! I awake with startled gasp. What time is it? Where's Keith? Oh right, traveling for work. I squint hard; it's bleary 3:27 AM. Need to get Zack up in a few hours for morning session.

Zack must have 40 hours, no less. Research is clear, fall below 40-hour floor might as well be ten hours of therapy, and ten might as well be none. *Less than 40 is tantamount to quitting. Tantamount to failing to recover your son's brain. Early intervention is key, keep drilling or dive over the edge and lose him to darkness.*

> *Tick-tock*
> > *Tick-tock*
> > > *Tick-tock*

Don't lose him, Mom, keep him engaged every single waking hour of every single day. Shame on you if you don't! Keep up, jump in, it's on you.

Most days I'm struggling to breathe. Even when therapists show there's just too much at stake. Panting, sucking for air because time is of the essence; we can't lose, we can't lose Zack.

I can't hold a thought in my head; I can't hold two thoughts at once. Tripping on stairs on way down to therapy room, fumbling on the way back up, so clumsy and scared I'm falling down everywhere. If only I could get more oxygen into my lungs and slow careening heart of mine.

Eat, chew, swallow, breathe. Ignore thick lump in your throat and force feed if you have to, just get it down, keep it down. Digest, breathe, sleep—basic functions so innate even a newborn can do them are labored for me in this state of constant emergency. I can hear therapists straining to drag him to table, force hands down on objects, clutch to restrain him to read same book again. I cover my ears and try to block out the screams. I can't sit still, can't intervene or escape, overhearing yelps and wails. Get out of the house, pace the streets, then return to sound of screams. Go pace some more. *Breathe, damnit! You're no good to Zack unconscious.*

Swooning and under siege, I dragoon my young son to forced child labor for *40* hours. Day and night, night into day into night into hour upon hour. At this rate I'm the one losing my grip. I'm gonna be the one outstretched on the hospital gurney. Need to get these heart palpitations checked, they are wreaking havoc on my body. I'm going to have a heart attack.

POSITIVE REINFORCEMENT

If punishment is the bad guy of ABA, who is often misunderstood... Then reinforcement is the hero of ABA, who is loved by all!

—"THE GREATEST AMERICAN HERO: REINFORCEMENT—I LOVE ABA!" WWW.ILOVEABA.COM. (2012)

HALLELUJAH! ZACK IS finally getting it! He's caught on to ABA methods and is hitting his academic stride, fully in sync with the twenty-plus programs now. As he should, he's been doing this for six months straight, four hours every morning and night, poor child. But he is the greatest, bravest and smartest of children. I can see that now, thanks to ABA.

The time-honored method is taking hold and shaping Zack into what we all want, a child whose brain is cognitively rewired and reprogrammed by massive early intervention. The glowing data sheets filled out by the therapists after every drill validate his ascension. He is consistently scoring "correct" in answers the first time asked, and without prompting. He's completing tasks accurately across three consecutive sessions with three different therapists, which means mastery of the skill taught, mastery sufficient to keep moving down the list of targets as he keeps climbing up that staircase! There's nothing more thrilling than hearing from enthusiastic therapists how quickly they're now moving. My boy is on a roll!

Zack now comes willingly to the table to sit for drills, wholly compliant in line with our aspirations. The resistance is over, he even seems to be enjoying his newfound ability to concentrate and succeed on discrete tasks. His compliance will serve him well in school, his future job, his entire life. Because it takes some children with autism as many as six months of profound physical struggle just to get them to come obediently to the table. So, Zack is already way ahead of the game! I am beaming proud of him and beholden to each and every diligent member of my rotating team who nobly escort him through gain after gain of skills, identifying colors, letters, numbers, understanding how to "go get" and retrieve an item, learning prepositions such as whether the shoe is "on top" or "under" the couch. None of these hard-fought conquests is taken for granted because of the tedious repetition required to solidify them. Into mastery.

I owe these therapists far more than their hourly pay. I may end up owing them Zack's life. I tell them every chance I get how indescribably grateful I am, but words can't capture my reverence for this most difficult job they've undertaken on my disabled child's behalf.

I feel confident for the first time about the end goal I've longed for since my initial meet with Cara: Zack will clearly be among the fifty percent who mainstream by age 5! Technically speaking, there is no cure or recovery from autism. I remind myself, constantly—it's permanent and irreversible. But I can hope for the next best outcome. If a child acquires enough academic and functional skills, enough compensating behaviors to mitigate the perseveration, he can effectively lose his autism diagnosis.

Cara has buoyed my spirits. She says it's looking very good. So, I should know I can ultimately have Zack's diagnosis court-sealed and expunged from any public records. His diagnosis will be tucked away by court order so it cannot be discovered by public schools he attends down the road. Success means autism remains a private family matter.

Cara assures me that the prognosis for kids who reach the highest rungs of ABA is full inclusion with peers in general education. Zack will likely need minor curriculum modifications and special educational supports to keep pace, but he will belong. Best-case scenario, Zack will function like other children, able to participate in class, comprehend the lessons oral and written, and benefit from being in smaller learning groups designated for kids with mild learning disabilities. Extra focus supplied in small group instruction is common, and particularly well-suited to a child like Zack already accustomed to attending to tasks one-to-one from his years of ABA.

At age three, Zack's language is still nonexistent, but now there's reason to hope. Even in typical kids, verbal expression sometimes lags developmentally and is the last milestone to emerge. Just when a typical child's parents begin to worry that something serious might be wrong, the child suddenly begins speaking. I've heard anecdotes from countless parents long before I had Zack. He will speak too, in time, I'm sure of it.

"Compensating behaviors" in ABA-speak refers to functioning which allows the child to stifle his autistic tendencies in favor of conventional behaviors. Expressive language, suppression of tics, cluing in to social cues, all allow the child to function enough to "pass for normal." The child has been successfully rewired and thus capable of assimilating.

Personally, Zack is giving me more than enough compensation to sustain me. The spontaneous bursts of warmth, connectedness and sustained, smiling eye contact with me means the good easily outweighs the bad. His burgeoning displays of affection towards me, manifested by gripping bear hugs the second he emerges from the therapy room, are incredibly nourishing. His new habit of spying me across a room and charging at me like an ardent athlete to tackle me to the ground and begin pecking my neck with kisses, remind me of those early musings during pregnancy about my vigorous linebacker. At just over thirty pounds now, sinewy and muscular, his tackle has the force to knock me sideways, but I adore being swiped! I devour these precious moments when we cling tightly to each another, the deep bond born of our mutual struggle, knowing we are both coming out the other side. He feels it down to his precious fingers and toes how truly impressed I am at the disciplined worker he's become. Zack is mitigating the early anguish. He has made me whole again.

On a particularly contented evening, Keith and I are cozily nestled in our tight basement with Zack who is busying himself on the floor, beyond thrilled about our recent purchase of a huge inflated yellow bouncy castle. It's bigger than we expected, barely fits the space, but is in full bloom and overflowing with colorful balls. After every therapy session Zack torpedoes into the castle, headfirst, a thirty-pound missile ready to rock the yellow inflatable to its core! The castle is undaunted and unafraid, made of resilient anti-burst latex. It retains its vigor despite the enormous impact of Zack's full-body blows. This kid is a live wire who devours things body and soul, hungrily diving in, rolling rowdily side to side and smashing into the supple boundaries, then bounding vigorously up and down with full force. And the castle is our sturdy partner, faithfully absorbing the hits and jolts, rebounding upright, impervious to the physical insults it endures day after day.

But tonight Zack seems captivated not by the castle but by one of the lightweight colored balls, studiously examining it with a very serious expression. His stillness is almost alarming. It would be fascinating to know what he's thinking this very moment. He's rapidly spinning the ball over and over before and holding it strangely close to his face, not frustrated or amused, just intensely inquisitive.

What was that sound? He's murmuring something indiscernible as he twirls the ball up close to his enlarged eyes. I silently kneel and lean in to listen but can't make out the garble. The gurgling continues as Zack remains transfixed, clearly working something out in his busy little mind.

"*Pur*" comes the utterance. Then *"pup"* . . . *"pur"* . . . *"pup."*

"*Pur-pup,*" it's broken, but now discernible. "*Pur-pel. Pur-pel. Purple.*"

I sit up, riveted in disbelief.

"Keith!" I startle him from his relaxed stupor and he looks annoyed. "Keith, he's saying something!"

"What's he saying? I don't hear anything but sounds, good sounds, but not actual words." He's incredulous, but I've become a virtuoso in Zack's garbled utterances, and I know this is intentional.

"No, no, he's trying to say something! Listen, listen quietly, don't break his concentration."

Zack is suddenly ready to prove mommy right.

"*Purple.*" There it is! He states it clearly, having rolled the consonants on his tongue long enough to orient his mouth for proper enunciation. And it's irrefutably, brilliantly clear. "*Purple,*" he states again declaratively, this time turning his face towards mine for confirmation whether he has correctly identified the ball's hue, fully aware that he's provoked a strong reaction in me as I lie on the floor beside him. Absorbing my bottled-up energy, he unleashes it fully, shouting decisively: "PURPLE!"

YES! That glorious fusion of red and blue just formed my child's first word! Too elated to speak, I raucously swoop his entire body into my arms and bury my face in his tender neck, whooping and laughing and rolling us over and over each other on the carpet in giddy celebration. "ZACK, YOU DID IT! You are a genius! Yes, the ball is purple! You are brilliant, my love!"

I sincerely doubt that in its entire history, even though it's the symbolic color of royalty, that the color purple has ever know a more enthusiastic fan than me in this moment. PURPLE ROCKS! No wonder royals don purple robes to indicate sartorial nobility! Purple should become our country's official color, too—why struggle with the onerous red, white and blue when we could cut to the chase by celebrating their glorious fusion: PURPLE!

Panting heavily, coming down off my high, I'm laughing hysterically with Zack in my embrace, who is equally delirious. My son comprehends that he has just done something spectacular, as Keith sits back in awe at the sight of us. In the erupting celebration, I'd forgotten Keith was in the room. But he heard it, the skeptic turned believer, he stares astonished but appreciatively at both of us, stunned to have heard his autistic son speak his first word. He hangs back as if to honor the moment he feels belongs to Zack and me who have toiled so hard, daily, to earn it. The culmination of so many arduous hours just erupted into an accomplishment so profound that I'm the one left speechless in joy.

While much about Zack still remains a mystery to me, more and more is coming into focus. His zesty appetite, culinary affinities and aversions, are virtually identical to mine. He loves tofu and mounds of pasta with butter, just like me; he hates citrus or grape-flavored anything, just like me. But what he loves most in this world is the pure and unadulterated flavor of vanilla bean ice cream. Okay, not exactly like me but close enough. Of all the myriad tastings of 31 flavors at Baskin-Robbins that we sample regularly, introducing to Zack each and every flavor, it's vanilla that speaks loudest. So, pints of gourmet vanilla ice cream are surreptitiously stored in the remote regions of the freezer from which they miraculously appear to reward Zack for anything and everything he does correctly. And sometimes, for no particular reason at all. Now seems like a good time to break open a pint.

I am bursting with glee to email Cara and the team about Zack's first spoken word, but I don't want to jinx it. I don't want to chase it back under by having them pummel him with requests for a repeat performance before it's fully grown in. Not yet. I'll keep this little gem to myself for now; other words will surely follow and they can witness the impending stream, but for now this one is all mine.

Oh, I almost forgot that tomorrow is another monthly program meet. Cara's flying in bright and early from New York. We should get some sleep. She'll be scrawling copious notes as she observes the therapists run through the twenty programs with Zack dutifully performing, and the wearing meeting will last at least five hours straight. But given Zack's progress, no one is complaining. Zack will have trouble coming down off the vanilla sugar high I just infused, but no matter if he's a little groggy tomorrow. It was well worth it.

Before I know it, it's already tomorrow. I didn't sleep a wink, too excited about Zack's breakthrough to care. I'm surprisingly alert and refreshed—here we are again, with Zack seated obediently ready to proving his ABA mettle, not just his mastery of targeted skills, but his sheer stamina in pinging from one program to the next for the hours-long parade during which we regularly cheer him on.

But it's brutally hot in the confines of the room, too many bodies are packed together generating heat. Hours later, we are sagging and limp and perspiration-stained. These progress meets are easily my least favorite part of ABA. If only Cara lived in proximity she could regularly observe Zack instead of needing these condensed demonstrations I so despise. We're done for the day in our minds, but Cara insists we remain because there's still one pesky program Zack just isn't getting—the "Point" program. The objective is deceptively simple: the therapist puts a desired food or object on the table out of Zack's reach and asks, "What do you want?" to which Zack must respond with a perfectly extended arm and pointing index finger. It's beguilingly simple but developmentally crucial because of what pointing represents. Simply put, he must understand that others cannot read his mind. He must actively engage and direct another person, understanding that his perspective is different from theirs. For typical children this "joint attention" emerges organically, but for our children on the spectrum even this basic gesture must be choreographed in discrete steps. This excruciatingly detailed exercise is prompted tediously until the child makes the connection and finally initiates the gesture on demand.

But Zack's not getting it—even forty-five minutes later. He's exhausted and frantically bored by the drill, sweaty and resting his little head on the table in total exasperation, likely wondering why he's being forced to make such a trivial gesture when he's already demonstrated so much to his fan base. And he doesn't care anymore about the M&Ms or Dorito chip being dangled as behavioral bait. He doesn't want it enough. He's sick and tired and done for the day, and getting more and more frustrated the more objects we place out of reach to change up the reinforcement. He's too irritated and strung out to even look.

By now, even our fearless leader is ready to call it quits and reconvene next month. Her dour expression revealing her disappointment, she murmurs dejectedly, "Zack's been doing so well, I wouldn't have expected this to be so tough for him."

Cara has an annoying habit of talking about Zack in the third person as if he's not right here in the room. She talks about him openly and even critically in his presence. I'll discuss it with her later, too exhausted to take that point up just now, we need to disband. "Can we just please let this go? Absolutely nothing is desirable to him right now, he's uninspired, unmotivated and—"

Suddenly I'm seized by an idea and run sprinting upstairs. I hear Cara calling after me annoyed by the fleeting departure as we're finally winding up, but I'm off and running, and then return with the only foolproof object of desire in the world. If this doesn't work, nothing will.

Re-energized and smiling at Zack while bypassing everyone's irritated and bewildered stares, I ask that everyone inch back a few feet. Zack needs space to concentrate. With a single arm swoop I brush all the chips and candy off the therapy table onto the carpet, then implore Zack to please sit. "Please just one more time, for Mommy." Graciously, with curiosity piqued, he does.

"Okay Zack, what do you want?" I ask, my voice rising in delight as I magically unveil a pint of pristine, unopened Haagen-Dazs vanilla bean ice cream on the far edge of the table! Barely a beat elapses before Zack's arm is darted and outstretched, his index finger perfectly extended in urgency with other fingers properly tucked, nailing the gesture like an Olympic gymnast who just stuck his landing from the vault.

"YES!" we all erupt in loud cheers spontaneously, "YES! Zack you pointed!"

We are giddy with relief after being held hostage. Zack just set us free! Wasting no time, Zack darts quickly with the large spoon in one hand, grabs the frozen pint in the other and tears off out of the room to his private sanctuary in the bouncy castle to enjoy his booty! Ripping off the lid and seal, he thrusts the spoon into the creamy surface with gusto and eagerly lifts huge spoonfuls to his mouth, now flawlessly executing his fine motor grip. Seems Zack can be quite manually dexterous, with proper incentive.

"Well done, Whitney, well done," Cara laughs approvingly and collapses back into her stiff chair. "That was great! And well done to you, Zack!" she hollers out to him remotely as I smile, thinking that right now he couldn't care less about her approbation, only about inhaling the vanilla with no intent to share.

As I walk every last therapist to the door, still giggling and heady, I thank them for what feels like the hundredth time for their earnest dedication over these outsized hours. As I close the door firmly behind them, I reflect on the fact that their heroism lies not just in their willingness to patiently repeat themselves for hours each day, but in their steadfast loyalty to Zack, especially during those excruciating slow-motion stretches when it's seems certain he's not going to catch on.

It's been famously said that "95 percent of life is showing up." I agree, though I'd adjust the expression that 95 percent of life is actually persistence—sheer, dogged persistence in the face of discouraging setbacks and defeat. Nobility lies in scraping oneself off the floor, hoisting oneself up and trying yet again after you've been knocked down so hard you're tempted to surrender all hope that there's any point in rising. But persistence itself is not enough. Success isn't made by ramming one's ahead against the same immovable brick wall, but in realizing that when the wall is immutable, one must find a way to scale it to get to the other side. Informed persistence, realistic and flexible, includes a willingness to abandon strategies that aren't moving you forward, and to replace them with newly devised strategies to find an alternate route to your destination. Shifting course is still persevering, and may even be the most profound form of it because it forces you to get creative and explore alternatives not previously considered. So to my mind, persistence plus raw material equals success. Zack has the raw material; it's my job to persist in stretching, kneading and molding the teachings by whatever creative means necessary to prevail in our mission.

Of course when all else fails, a little ice cream never hurts either.

DON'T FRET

My nerves are bad to-night. Yes, bad. Stay with me.
'Speak to me. Why do you never speak? Speak.
'What are you thinking of? What thinking? What?
'I never know what you are thinking. Think.

—"*THE WASTELAND*," T.S. ELIOT

ZACK IS ON the verge of turning four, and we are yet again tightly gathered for another tiresome monthly progress meet with Cara. Zack had a great stretch for a while, but he's not making steady progress now. He's stuck on the more advanced, higher-level ABA programs. It feels like he's plateaued, and nothing could be scarier than what I'm now seeing. He did grab onto a few more facile words—*yes, no, wait, dog*—along with the universally prescribed ABA phrase, "*I want.*" These words are foundational because they comprise the simplest and most direct means of allowing an autistic child to express intent in sentence form. But for countless months Zack's language has not moved beyond this rote two-word phrase. He uses it for everything and anything, which is becoming every bit as dysfunctional as if he had never learned it.

So expertly did we drill this phrase into his brain that it is now diluted of meaning from overuse. It's not functional so much as robotically scripted, cemented, and now inflexible. We so consistently deprived him of anything he wanted unless he uttered the predicate that now it cannot yield to other iterations such as *Can I have?* or *May I?* With no other new language coming in, this intractable phrase is being rabidly uttered to express every emotion, injury, need and frustration: *I want chip!* . . . *I want sad!* . . . *I want ear ear hurt—I want no ear hurt!* So now we are effectively forced to "unteach" it by demanding other phrases in order to restore his flexibility and discern what Zack means to say. No wonder he's confused by what now feels like unwiring.

Zack's scant other words are in no way generalizing, in part because he has no regular opportunities to practice them outside the room. Words appear on one-dimensional flash cards, in flat books, then regurgitated back to therapists in exchange for food. But in the real world I'm observing that when Zack personally encounters the live version of the saturated labels, they don't register. His failure to connect academics with real life is occurring with frightening regularity—that furry, barking creature is an actual *dog;* that screaming siren you've identified so many times in books is on the *real fire truck* that just passed; the police are real people, not just fictional characters on flat pages. Nowhere, not in TV shows, the park, the community, is Zack identifying what he's supposedly mastered, not anywhere but in that contrived room, one-to-one, heavily prompted, in exchange for bits of food. And now I'm realizing that for children like Zack, literal thinkers, words that are confined to discrete drills and offered in exchange for concrete rewards are no more understood than those mimicked by a well-trained parrot. Not to mention, Zack is totally sick of the drills and chips and sickly sweet candy. More often he swats away the reinforcers angrily, because increasingly, the only thing he really wants is to get the hell out of that claustrophobic room. Now that I'm seeing so little real-world application, I want the same thing.

Zack is technically now *verbal*—he speaks words and truncated sentences—but with crucial qualifiers. He is *verbal* in the room, at the table, in response to specific demands, in joyless and tedious compliance, only because he knows nothing else. But the second he emerges from that room he immediately reverts back to a wordless, uncommunicative and now glazed-over child. It's my job to build upon his therapy gains by constantly probing him to keep speaking outside the room, but I'm also sick and dejected at the mind-numbing protocol. Our efforts are turning against us because Zack has rationally concluded he'd rather forego a drink altogether, if the only way to get it is through constant pecking questions and verbal acrobatics. The prize isn't worth the effort; nothing has been rewarding to him for quite some time because there's only so much change-up possible in his isolated cave.

The ABA rolodex keeps spinning as the therapists mark consecutive words as "mastered" and keep scaling down the target list. But what I'm seeing beneath the spin is that as soon as Zack has conquered one word, he's ushered to the next and the next. So at the end of the week, when the therapist probes words *already taught and mastered* last month, they are no longer retained. No permanence, nor motivation to retain them.

Zack is twirling unproductively in circles. He can only absorb so much without real-world application and direct experience. We are steadily sapping him not just of genuine comprehension but any joy in learning. Given the rote tedium of his days and nights, from Zack's perspective it must indeed feel that there's no light at the end of the tunnel—a devastating concept I understand only too well.

I used to weep when Zack was dragged, screaming, to

perform mandatory drills, but now something more sinister is inhabiting his eyes. A flatness, a dead stare, stoic obedience has replaced fierce resistance: we have beaten him down and drained his fight, and that is sickening me. What's the point of using a phrase like *I want* if he can't use it to get what he really wants, which is to stop all of this? Unbelievably, years after his initial terrifying diagnosis, we've now managed to restore that blank, emotionless mask of autism that we had briefly lifted.

Frightened, I pull Cara aside with an urgent plea. This isn't working anymore, we need to radically change things up and get him out of that room. We're robbing him of his childhood, his peers, he looks more lobotomized than ever. May we move the therapy sessions entirely outside and teach in context in the actual playground, pool, an inflatables gym? May we please start play dates to get some social interaction going?

"No, Whitney, that's not how it works," Cara patiently explains. "Zack must first own language and certain interactive skills *before* we do play dates. Zack doesn't have enough language to engage other kids. He needs to succeed in the more advanced programs first. Play dates are what we get to after the child has mastered certain programs, play dates are themselves several levels higher up after the culmination of other skills."

Deep down I believe we are killing his very soul. So I state the unspeakable, because he is my child and I must know the truth.

"Be honest with me, Cara. You see what's happening. Zack is getting bigger, not better. And I don't blame anyone. We've all tried our best, but he just isn't getting it. He's plateaued and he's not getting there. He's not going to be among that fifty percent who recover, is he? I need to hear it. I'll find a way to cope, but watching it unfold this way is unbearable. He has nothing to look forward to, so why torture him with drills that aren't working and making him miserable? Honestly, I can take this anymore—I can't watch him unravel and lose himself more."

I let it hang in the air as she quietly considers my plea. "Cara," I begin calmly, intruding on her contemplation, "I'm asking you to consider Zack himself, apart from the protocol. Is it possible that Zack is the kind of child who doesn't respond to 40 hours? Can we cut back to twenty, mornings only, then let him play freely? I promise I'll follow through in the natural environment, but let's let the waterslides and inflatables be the motivators."

"The research is clear, we've been over this. He needs 40 hours," she states flatly. "Zack is no different than other kids I've treated, so you need to trust me because twenty hours is as good as none. What you're proposing is wasting his time, and yours."

"We're already wasting our time! I agree that the 40 hours worked initially when it was a novelty, but he's done. He started out strong but he's flat-lined, and I just don't see how it's possible for him to ever catch up or ever be mainstreamed, at the rate he's going."

"Wow! Listen to you wanting more!" she laughs heartily out loud, catching me completely off guard. "Remember when he couldn't even speak a word or count to ten? Now he has words, sentences and number sequence! Come on Whitney, you knew this was going to be a long haul. Yes, some kids do make sudden dramatic leaps forward, but that's never been Zack. Zack does slow and steady. He'll start rolling again, he's just a little stalled. I don't mean to laugh, but you're really forgetting how far he's come."

I nod slowly, disoriented by the abrupt shift of tone, but beneath Cara's cheerful inflection lies something unnerving: the suggestion that I'm greedy to want more—without stagnation, without misery. How ungrateful of me to be dissatisfied! He might never have spoken a single word without ABA.

"Give it time, Whitney, we just need to find another way in. Zack's a little stuck but I have plenty of strategies in my toolbox to get him going again." Cara's voice is beguilingly reassuring and undaunted. "You just keep engaging him, we've got this!"

But I'm no fool. I need only glimpse at children everywhere to know that Zack is falling gravely behind. The gulf between Zack and children even years younger is widening daily. Absent meaningful progress and the promise of a real life or any semblance of it, we are hurting him. We are doing worse than nothing, worse than no intervention. We are actively doing harm.

I walk Cara to the door and close it quietly behind her. I call my closest friend Heather for an impromptu play date with her daughter. Heather immediately picks up on the strain in my voice and compassionately jokes that Zack and I have spent way too much time indoors, that we all need to get out!

Windows down, both kids strapped in, Heather silently turns the key in the ignition. No questions or idle chatter; she can tell I'm not doing well, that Zack isn't doing well, that her company is a desperately-needed oasis. As we back out of her driveway I roll down the window and inhale the pungent freshly-mowed grass and feel enveloped by warm sunshine, a fragrant butter on my emotional burns. I close my bleary eyes and quiet my racing mind as Heather backs out of her driveway. A man approaches Heather's door. It's her gardener.

"Mommy, who's that strange man at our door? I don't recognize him. What's he doing at our house?" I whip around stunned to stare at Heather's daughter, amazed by the volume of words, the syntax and sentence structure, use of possessive text. I'm visibly floored as I turn towards Heather; when did she start doing that?

She apologetically explains that little Dallas has been talking up a storm lately, and that she's also surprised by the precocious speech. "Yes, she's unusually talkative, very verbal." I don't reply, just pivot my face abruptly back out the open car window, straining to breathe and face the light, grateful for the opportunity to avert my eyes and conceal my face which is streaming with tears.

Dallas is only three weeks behind Zack in age, but light years ahead of him in every developmental way—as are all the children who will soon surround us at the park. It's inescapable, no matter where I go. Dallas is *very verbal*. Another dagger to the heart.

STiLL LiFE

In a real dark night of the soul it is always three
o'clock in the morning, day after day.

—*THE CRACK-UP*, F. SCOTT FITZGERALD

I WALK UP the stairs at 1:40 AM and am immediately hit by an odious stench.

"Keith," I scream angrily, "he did it again!"

Purposely closing my throat and inhaling only through nostrils, I enter Zack's room. I try hard not to vomit but my esophagus spasms violently from the putrid and suffocating odor. Another late night where Keith and I were misled by quiescence in the house into assuming Zack was sleeping soundly, when, instead, he was assiduously smearing his feces all over himself and his bedroom. I need only make it halfway upstairs to know instantly what's awaiting me.

At age four, Zack is impervious to personal hygiene, more interested in the tactile pleasures of spreading soft and unformed bowel movements into long streaks everywhere his hands can reach—his hair, his body, the walls, his bed. It's unclear to me if this is a premeditated attempt to escape the confines of his room where we lock him in at night to prevent mid-night wandering. But intent doesn't much matter because it works every time—he gets out because he must be cleaned.

We move in frantic shifts, Keith seizing Zack's filthy body and stripping off his diaper, while I run to start the soapy bath. We pass each other briskly as I reach for latex gloves, the box of Clorox wipes, paper towels, and garbage bags, and drop to my knees. Repeating my posture from the DOJ job I fled, where I at least had the dignity of bending down chronically to measure bathroom stalls, I now return to bended knees for a wholly ignominious task.

Zack's been especially creative tonight. The fecal matter is deeply enmeshed in the carpet fibers, so pervasive that even repeated soakings and vigorous scrubs still leave a putrid light brown residue and dank smell. Moving to his bedroom door I see how the ooze has furrowed and hardened into the grain and grooves of the woodwork all along the ridges of the door in intractable ways, and will take hours to thoroughly remove.

In terms of actual labor, Keith has the easier task tonight because even clotted in his hair and smeared over his body, feces are easier to clean from the child than from the infected walls, carpet and wood grain. Keith and I work diligently and wordlessly. The shock robs us of our voices. What is there to say about the state of our lives right now? By 2:30, I know for sure I can't entirely rid his room of the lingering stench. We'll just have to wait for the fumes to slowly lift over the next few days, during which his room genuinely smells like a zoo. I never let house visitors upstairs, couldn't possibly explain the pervasive odor, it's too humiliating to describe what's been happening lately.

Zack's fecal smearing comes in waves and some weeks it's a nightly ritual. Each night after the first smearing, Keith and I listen silently at his door until we're convinced he's truly asleep. When we check on him at 11:00 PM, if he is in fact asleep we make our way downstairs to collapse on the couch and distractedly watch TV for an hour, knowing neither of us is really diverted. It's not until we retire to bed much later and clumsily make our way up the stairs that one of us is walloped into alertness and screams for the other. The drill continues night after night, sometimes starting as late as 3:00 AM. We engage in the disgusting and degrading ritual of scraping and scooping chunks, all the while straining to breathe as violent gags keep rising in our throats that must be forced back down or surrendered to entirely.

By the time Keith leaves for work the next morning, he is ashen and sleep-deprived from our bleary encounter—but at least he gets to leave. I am trapped here, bitterly reminded that I agreed to such a cruel division of labor. Keith's earned income far exceeded mine at my tiny boutique firm, so it made sense that he would primarily finance Zack's elaborate therapy while I, the parent who had forged a deeper understanding of Zack's issues, would be the one to surrender my career for the sake of his rescue. Lately Keith has been ramping up his work responsibilities, and his career is dramatically taking off. But sometimes I can't help but wonder if those extended hours at night are partly deliberate to avoid what awaits him at home. What should be a source of mutual celebration over his career ascension is instead becoming my mental undoing, as I am seething with corrosive envy every morning he leaves and locks the door behind him. While he's being fed real-world affirmation, professional promotion and income, I am literally drowning in waste. I can see Keith stiffen when he walks through the door every evening, afraid of what new complaint I might angrily hurl at him, awash in my own resentment.

Standing here stonily, in the morning's silence, I can see how far I've fallen—far from the independent and self-reliant professional I'd always envisioned, not remotely accomplished in any way. I'm chained to this denigrating, unpaid forced labor with no tangible reward for all my sacrifice. Standing alone in the aftermath of yet another brutal night, my task will now be to awaken Zack for his morning therapy session, which he will resist with screaming fury at being roused from an exhausted sleep and a long night of his own. Despite my pledge not to allow it, my self-worth has succumbed to miserable self-pity as I routinely chastise Keith for getting to escape the sickness that now defines my life. As his income continues to soar, allowing us to finance the endless intervention, my self-esteem continues to plummet—I am the embodiment of neediness and rage, an insecure shrew. So much for the "corporate pact" vision that was to characterize my marriage: Keith and I are anything but equal partners in this mess.

So this is my life. I am a well-educated woman. I am an accomplished civil rights attorney. I am a woman who spends hours every night on her hands and knees scraping feces off walls. And it's not just fecal smearing. Zack has recently taken up some other demoralizing habits like pica, so he craves and even eats non-food items like candles, twigs or wood chips. He's developed a wicked case of insomnia that even his nightly dose of melatonin sometimes cannot touch. Even as an infant, he never fell asleep before 11:00 PM, but now when he overrides his sleep aide his rowdiness can stretch to 2:00 or 3:00 AM. His occasional tantrums have taken on a feral quality, and he now sinks his teeth not just into his own flesh but mine—my back, my shoulder, my stomach—without notice, my blighted days are punctuated by ruthless bites.

I have entered an entirely new phase with my son and it's a kaleidoscope of horrors. Unpredictability is the norm. I'm stumbling blindly through my life with no exact sense of day and time, as one day melds into the next like an indiscernible mass. I have trouble getting out of bed in the morning. Long after I hear the click of Keith's key in the door to alert me that he's left for work, I lie awake and haunted even though my room is flooded by daylight, the white walls as sterile and antiseptic as an operating room, my bed a reservoir of sloth. The bed sheets are sour with sweat and body odor, permanently stained now because I don't act quickly enough to clean them. Why bother? I hardly see anyone besides the rotating therapists, and no one is expecting anything real from me. So my morning routine exists of rising mechanically, winding myself up for the mighty resistance, wrestling Zack from his slumber and dragging him to the dutiful therapist who calmly steers him into the drills for the next two hours. The therapists are still as earnest and dedicated as ever, but I no longer am. I am broken.

So this is my life. Surgically cut off from the rest of the community, I inhabit a living coma where I detect murky clues from the outside world—but I'm not of it. I've taken to wandering the neighborhood streets to keep from going mad. But it's there on the streets that I get a glimpse of real life. Watching as if from under water, I can see children frolicking in playgrounds, bounding happily into karate classes, eating and chatting with animated zeal beside their attentive parents in restaurants. "Normal" assaults me on every street corner, smothering me with flaunting reminders of how truly dislocated I am from the joys of parenting. It's better when therapists give me a concrete task—buy books with a distinct narrative arc, locate therapy supplies, flashcards, oral motor tools. Then I can busy myself perusing the store shelves for hours hunting down the exact right items—it's at least a goal. But it's those spaces in between where I'm not needed that I inhabit a no-man's land, unemployed and stripped of purpose. The only thing worse than wandering the streets is returning home, my tomb above ground where I'm often greeted by indifference, aggression or anger.

I'm not fun to be around anymore. I used to be quite playful. I used to tell my friends stupendously filthy jokes; my build-up was epic. Now I can't even remember the last time I laughed. My sense of humor may be the greatest casualty of this war. I've no interest in frothy, silly comedies and happy endings. I find solace only in the acerbic reality of stand-up comics, gallows humor that parodies the darker side of life. I used to be a gifted storyteller, a non-judgmental listener, a reliable friend. Friends could tell me anything without fear, and nothing was off-limits. But no one jokes with me anymore or shares their cute stories; they're too busy walking on eggshells. Zack isn't the only one prone to unpredictable volatility. I've begun to lash out at friends whose children are normal because of their innocently clueless remarks, despite that they are still my only close friends.

Loyal friends and close family members have rationally begun avoiding me as I crystallize my fate as a professional victim. I watch it happening, fully aware, but with no incentive to stop it. It's a slippery groove into which I've slid, but I have something that no one else in my life does—a grievous and unjust injury. And that entitles me to school them—my way. There is a very real superiority that comes with being unjustly aggrieved, a license to *educate* others about what truly matters in life so they never dare take it for granted, certainly not in my presence. I may be helpless and out of control, but I retain one last vestige of power—the ability to guilt them. They expect to get lacerated at some point in during our conversation, regardless of their good intentions, until they realize there is nothing good to say to me. After all, what can they say? That it's going to get better? It's not. That they understand? They don't. Don't give me perspective on life, or worse, complain about trivial concerns like which preschool is best. And, by the way, it's all trivial. And the rage does help a little, sometimes.

Time marches forward. It's certainly not going to stand still for me just because my life imploded. Did I expect that it would, that in a show of solidarity for my emergency that friends would resign their jobs, renounce their own aspirations, and devote time to helping me hang flyers and recruit therapists for the cause? Maybe I did—a little. Is it fair that I feel betrayed by their willingness to carry on with their own lives when mine has been so cruelly shattered? Are my expectations of their sacrifices for my plight unrealistic and selfish? I honestly don't know. Matters of fairness abandoned me long ago as I am becoming socially barren.

Throughout this whole ABA therapy ordeal, Zack has always given me enough to get by, enough affection, studious effort—his beautiful face, his fierce gripping embrace have been sustenance enough to remind me that my love for him runs far deeper than my pain. But now, for the first time ever, the scales of compensation are tipping dangerously in the wrong direction.

Insomnia; fecal smearing; pica; tantrums; biting.

A dose of denial and blind faith that it will eventually get better is certainly in my best interest. But I'm living it. And given the permanence of his autism, there's no rational reason to conclude it will get better.

In the meantime, all frivolous photos and other adornments to Zack's room have been stripped from the walls because he has ripped and shattered them into bits. No use repainting his walls which are permanently stained from fecal smearing because he'll just defile them again. One structural change for which I'm ridiculously grateful—vinyl laminate flooring. His bedroom had a stench of urine and feces so strong it wouldn't lift, making it so uninhabitable that we tore up the soiled carpet to do an emergency installation of sturdy and easy-to-wipe flooring. At the very least I can now respond to future fecal smearing with greater speed and efficiency, the stench lingers for fewer days. The installation of wipeable flooring is literally life-changing; now the bar for measuring progress is pathetically low. I'm now so degraded I must contemplate what it really means to experience autism at its worst: daily destructive behaviors quickly emerging and set to full throttle. There's no light at the end of this tunnel; this may become the new normal. In these most helpless hours, and particularly just after Zack unleashes his physical venom on me, despite all I'm doing for him, my resentment is unabated. I can't pretend this is anything but punishment. At its very worst, autism feels like a living, walking, breathing nightmare.

MODERN LEPROSY

In all her intercourse with society, however, there was nothing that made her feel as if she belonged to it. Every gesture, every word, and even the silence of those with whom she came in contact, implied, and often expressed, that she was banished, and as much alone as if she inhabited another sphere, or communicated with the common nature by other organs and senses than the rest of human kind.

—THE SCARLET LETTER,
NATHANIEL HAWTHORNE

FINALLY, A BIRTHDAY party invite! Just when I thought we had become colonized lepers and me a social pariah, a kind and compassionate soul has invited Zack to her daughter's bowling party as she turns four, same age as Zack. This mother is a distant but long-time friend who herself studied special education to earn her master's degree in speech therapy. She works with kids like Zack on a daily basis; she gets it.

Keith and I are overjoyed to be included in the party alongside Zack; all the kids' parents are invited. The venue is just a few blocks from our house: a delightful little bowling alley with duckpins and gutter guards to ensure that small children can easily knock down the pins. The birthday gift is wrapped. Zack is dressed and dapper, and seems excited, so we are off. On our way out the door I pause to consider whether in an abundance of caution I should give Zack a chip of tranquilizer, just in case. I obtained a prescription from Zack's doctor when the melatonin stopped working. I had to quiet his rampant insomnia. I've dosed Zack a few times, during the day, and it worked like a charm, instantly turning him calm and drowsy. But Zack seems steady today and indescribably happy. He gets where he's going.

"C'mon, what are you waiting for? Let's go!" Keith calls out impatiently, and it's obvious he's excited for the party, too. Forget the pill, we're good.

Zack's eyes visibly widen as we pull into the parking lot, and he bounds out of car so hurriedly I have to jump out and yank him back from oncoming traffic. He's flapping and bouncing with such excitement it's clear he understands he's part of something special, which is terrific to behold. Turns out the bowling alley is in the basement level so we steer Zack into the elevator. It's just one floor down and we cram in with a pack of raucous kids and parents, all heading to the same place.

But as the doors slowly come together, Zack's affect instantly goes dark. Within a split second he panics, and as I anxiously reach over to stroke his head he whips around and savagely sinks his teeth into my wrist. I yank back with a stifled yelp but dare not cry out because maybe no one caught it, and I'm not about to draw attention to this deviant act. Rubbing the dark red welts from his bite, I start breathing fast and become laced with dread. *We need the doors to open, now.*

"Zack sweetheart, we're just going down one floor. The doors will open in a second," I whisper soothingly, simultaneously sharing a knowing nod with the other parents that implies a shared understanding. *These kids of ours all have their little tics and fears, don't they?* But the elevator is heading downwards at a creakingly sluggish pace and Zack frantically erupts, "NO DOORS! ALL DONE! NO DOORS!" His high-pitched shrieks pierce the snug confines of the crammed space, instantly alarming everyone trapped inside.

"Zack, honey, I know you're scared," I announce, purposely loud and authoritatively to signal to everyone I have this under control. "But we're almost there. The doors will open, just—"

"NOOO! ALL DONE ALL DONE ALL DONE!" he screeches maniacally. He's caught in a ferocious perseverative spiral that turns physical. Having lost all composure or sense of space, he starts furiously beating his head with both fists while screaming in a prolonged streak, impervious to anything or anyone but his own internalized terror. It would be frightening enough if he blew up this way only in seclusion. But he's terrifying everyone; the scale of his rage, the incomprehensibility—what could possibly drive a child so young into such hideous frenzy in a split second? It's in these times that he's truly gone, warped into reactive savagery by his own secluded universe and inner demons. Overstimulated senses, wild imaginings and exaggerated fears are the only things he's tethered to.

In his blind fit of hysteria he turns towards the steel elevator wall and, in uncontrollable frustration, starts slamming his head repeatedly against it with rapid fury, like a battering ram at high speed. Everyone freezes in place, afraid to breathe or utter a sound, and there's nowhere to move. The elevator is trembling now as the tinny walls reverberate nervously in response to the violently crashing head blows. All this within twenty seconds.

"KEITH!" I scream petrified, "STOP HIM! HOLD HIS HEAD!"

"I CAN"T!" he fires back, enraged. "Zack, STOP IT!" He reaches out to intercept by inserting his hand between Zack and the steel wall but it gets instantly smashed by Zack's skull. "Damn it!" he yells angrily as he jerks his hand back, a deep red indentation already beginning to swell. He glares disgustedly at me as if it's my fault. *What the hell do you expect me to do?* I fire back silently.

Deafened by his screams, I nonetheless hear the elevator finally settle and click into secure position on the basement floor as the doors finally begin creaking open. For a moment no one moves, dumbfounded by the trauma, until one father snaps loudly, "Kids get out of here, now! Get away from that kid! Move!" Everyone scrambles to exit at once, squeezing and thrusting past each other. Stricken and silent, they glance back at us from a safe distance in shock, as if truly having seen a ghost for the first time.

Oh God, now what? My mind is racing. Zack is still screaming, too traumatized from the momentary entrapment to even see the doors have opened, and Keith and I are too paralyzed to stop him. Do we try to exit the elevator with some measure of composure or just duck back in and allow the doors to close so we can escape the scene? The three of us stand immobilized in the vacated elevator as the doors mechanically begin squeaking closed again. *NO!* I suddenly realize we can't allow it. Zack will beat himself even harder if the doors close again on the ride up, the perseverating may never stop. I quickly thrust my arm out between the closing doors, causing them to reflexively rebound back open again. We have no choice but to exit the building another way.

No one speaks to us as we make our way across the room. As we walk, our heads bowed low, I can see other parents hastily reposition their kids towards the bowling, quietly urging them to look away: "Don't stare." I hear music in the distance as the festivities begin, the bowling off to a faltering start, but everyone determined to recover as Keith, Zack and I obligingly exit. The background noise of weighted balls striking the floor, crashing pins and striking gutter guards seems the perfect musical score to complement the battle scene we just enacted for all to see.

Zack continues screaming the same phrase, "ALL DONE! ALL DONE!" immune to the fact that he has moved well past the elevator. I don't even try to quiet him; there's no point. He's stuck in the perseverative cul-de-sac where he will remain for several more hours. Long after the danger has passed, he will keep frantically spinning as if reliving the scene in his mind—he's stuck on repeat play. Keith and I walk briskly now, forcibly shoving Zack toward the stairs before he can inflict further damage to anyone or himself. No time to murmur an apology to the hostess. I just hope my stunned visage is sufficient to communicate my deep regret for bringing Zack here in the first place, for overestimating Zack's ability to attend a single birthday party like a normal child. My throat is closed from all the things I cannot say:

I'm sorry we ruined your party.

I'm sorry we frightened the children.

I hope if we leave early enough the kids can shake off the trauma.

I hope they forget about it by the time they belt out the "Happy Birthday" song.

I hope the birthday girl forgives Zack by the time she blows out the candles.

I hope her wishes come true.

I hope she loves her present, I took a while in picking it out.

I hope everyone has a great time.

I hope we haven't ruined your day.

I hope that you will still think to include us next year, to give us another try after another year of therapy, but I will understand if you decide not to. I will certainly understand if your daughter decides that, despite her very best intentions, this is her day, and the only child she should not be forced by her parents to invite ever again is Zack.

I hope you won't forget about us completely, me especially. I hope you'll stay in touch and maybe check in on me from time to time, just to see how I'm coping. Because I am truly doing the best I can with this child, even if the results don't seem to show it. And despite my attempts to put on a brave face, smear on the makeup, brush out my hair and enter the party with my fixed smile in place, I'm secretly more ostracized than you could ever know. Divided from all of you at this and every party. Banished from the kingdom of happy children and completely humiliated by this deviant child. Please don't be fooled by the resilient exterior, because deep down inside I'm falling apart. Deep down inside, this child is slowly killing me.

The three of us are still trembling as we make our way outside and rush clumsily to the car. It's been a mere twenty minutes since the time we arrived. Keith and I don't speak as he aggressively thrusts the key into the ignition to drive back home. We're both seething towards each other, though neither of us is sure how or why.

Resigned, after a few minutes Keith quietly resolves, "We just won't go there again. He can't handle it."

"Right," I answer miserably "just one more thing we can't do." The number of places we cannot go seems to be growing daily. "Have you noticed how much our world is shrinking because of all the places we can't go with him?" Sensing that I'm provoking a fight, Keith doesn't answer, instead gripping the wheel tightly while grimacing to restrain himself from yet another bombastic confrontation.

Zack keeps perseverating furiously. "NO DOOR! NO BOWLING! NO DOOR!" Seconds pass before he starts the refrain again with identical pitch and fervor, reigniting his insatiable need for reassurance, even as we're driving away with no threat in sight. "NO DOOR! NO BOWLING!" Zack keeps reliving it.

"No, no more bowling," I echo absentmindedly, but my insides are caving in. I'm reliving the scene, too.

I will never get used to this, never grow accustomed to his tantrums, each delivering its own distinct laceration. As humans we are programmed to grow desensitized to certain stimuli with repeated exposure, but each and every outburst cleaves my heart again with equal force. There are some experiences in life to which you never acclimate, perhaps aren't meant to, and watching your child conspicuously lose all physical and emotional control is one of them. Especially when it happens before an audience of horrified spectators whose shock and disgusted glares brand you as the selfish parent with the gall to bring the creature out in public.

Even from my insular perspective, I'm still detached enough to know how Zack's tantrums appear to others. Since Zack presents typically on the outside, even handsomely, people just meeting him have no reason to suspect anything is amiss. It's only natural then, that when my child is unexpectedly triggered to splay out screaming and thrashing, maniacally beating his head with both fists, or savagely tearing into his own flesh, that in their stunned bewilderment they wonder if they are witnessing mental illness, maybe even a psychotic break with reality.

History has famously misjudged our autistic children, sometimes maliciously, sometimes in honest error, but always in an attempt to explain the inexplicable. In early days the grotesque and unnatural behaviors that erupted from our children so mysteriously could only be explained by something otherworldly: the child appeared to be tormented by evil spirits.

Sinister, terrorizing, full-body hysterics, screaming and lashing out, they seemed to be possessed, using words so mangled they must certainly have sounded like someone speaking in tongues.

In his very worst moments, Zack does indeed appear to be not of this world, possessed by something hideous. In moments of intense phobia, he appears even to me truly not part of our world. So looking back at history, looking to what just happened minutes ago, the centuries-old hysteria over people possessed by demons actually does make some sense. All those witches burned at the stake, the possessions and exorcisms—maybe, all along, there was actually a rational medical explanation for what was happening.

History repeats itself today. Even now, the medical causes and symptoms of autism are so poorly understood that modern day doctors are still prone to mischaracterize and misidentify it. The epidemic climb in autism diagnoses over the past decade is itself testimony to the medical confusion and chronic reclassification of that unique set of traits that were once previously thought to be purely cognitive deficit, emotionally disturbed, or obsessive-compulsive disorder. Even now, the diagnostic codes keep shifting to include the full spectrum of behaviors, clinicians still dispute whether Asperger's Syndrome or Fragile X belong to the same classification as autism. Heated debates persist about whether mercury or some other environmental toxin is causing a genetic mutation to otherwise healthy genes. Is autism purely genetic in origin or the product of an immune-compromised susceptibility to pollutants in the environment? Why is the autistic infant's head circumference generally larger than that of typical children? Why do the cerebral lobes and limbic system develop without synapse connections? When and where exactly did the disruption take place—during gestation or post birth? Is the age of an older father or mother to blame? Is it a matter of inflammation to the brain or gut? Why do some children exhibit symptoms early on whereas others appear to develop normally for two or three years and then suddenly snap back and regress developmentally and begin losing words and skills? Most critically, is autism truly on a steady rise or are the epidemic numbers the result of better identification?

No matter how we slice it, autism is all around us and likely has always been, a persistent disorder of the human condition. But for ordinary parents like me, who bleed through these public trials and absorb the cruel judgment of bystanders as if we somehow brought this upon ourselves, we might as well be living in a past century. I am his mother: am I truly expected to lock my child away from society like a leper and provide him no opportunities for social intercourse or growth? Is it my fault when I overestimate his abilities to tolerate certain stimuli, or fail to anticipate what mysterious triggers cause him to erupt in rage? I'm as mystified and haunted by my son's volatile unpredictability as anyone, more so. But I am the one responsible for moderating it under all situations for the sake of public discomfort. *When blame and shame become commonplace, we know that true enlightenment has not yet arrived.*

For me there is an even darker pain than the public glare, because to me each of Zack's outbursts feels truly regressive. Each crumbling is a ruthless reminder that even if Zack is performing well in discrete drills in the therapy room, even if he's had consecutive weeks of emotional composure, it takes only a single meltdown like today's to shatter everything I hoped was evolving. One step forward and two huge demerits back to square one. I believe these fits of rage persist precisely because they are not occurring in the controlled therapy room but in the *real* world with *real* triggers. So the terrible irony is that Zack's true behaviors, the ones that isolate and exclude him from peers and his community, have remained solidly intact and untouched by the mountain of corrective therapy intended to rewire his brain and for which we are paying a fortune. Make no mistake, no matter how many drills he performs correctly, no matter how compliant he is at that table, in reality Zack is highly combustible and largely immune to the very intervention that purports to bring him closer to normal.

"NO DOOR! NO BOWLING! NO MORE DOOR!" Zack sharply interrupts my private trance yet again.

"STOP IT!" I shriek. "JUST STOP. We're done! It's over! Just stop talking!"

Keith glares at me disapprovingly as Zack recoils in shock. But only minutes later the broken record starts replaying, and he's still compulsively incapable of stopping its spin. Zack is not seeking actual reassurance so much as spinning by habit, rotating tediously like those old-fashioned vinyl records which used to trip on a scratch in the grooves over and over in maddening fashion.

Keith gestures anxiously towards Zack as we get out of the car, indicating I should intervene somehow to stop the skipping record.

"Just leave him," my voice trails off wearily.

We enter the house and all is quiet, the mood still and tomblike. Keith exhales deeply and attempts to reach a hostile détente with me. "What are you thinking?" he asks timidly.

"Nothing." I respond flatly.

"Whitney, what are you thinking?"

I cannot say it aloud so I don't. *I must be out of my mind to think this child is ever going to recover.*

MARRiAGE, iNTERRUPTED

*You are not fated to get divorced because you
have a child with autism, but there is a prolonged
vulnerability to divorce for these families.*

—SIGAN L. HARTLEY, PHD, *WEBMD*

AS WE ENTER the house I remain silent to escape the inevitable confrontation. Zack drops to his knees and scurries across the floor to play with some spinning objects as I look on with disdain. Wordlessly, I walk down the stairs to our dark, dank basement: I just need time alone to collect my thoughts, but Keith senses my hostility and follows me down the steps.

"Now what?!" he asks, exasperated.

"I'm just sick of this," I bite back. "It feels like I'm not getting anywhere with him. And it's not like I'm not trying. I have literally worked hours on his therapy books and in that room. All these therapists rotating in and out of our house and for what? No real progress where it counts. We can't even attend a damn birthday party! I've never worked so hard for so little."

"This isn't about you," Keith interjects pointedly, "it's about him, what he needs." From his tone I can feel his profound disappointment in me. He's losing respect for me more and more every day.

"No this isn't just about him, it's about me, too!" I strike back. "You don't get it because you don't live it! You work, you get to carry on with your life exactly the same as if he didn't have autism. But I have lost everything! Every single thing I've worked for my entire life. You have a career, outside validation, you're paid, but I have nothing and it's my life that's ruined! I've lost my job. I'm tied to this therapy 'round the clock, and for what? To get on my hands and knees and try to get this kid to respond to flash cards, then watch him go ballistic the second we set foot outside? *And I hate this!* Do you have any idea how much I hate this new job of mine?"

"What the hell do you want from me, an apology!?" he fires back. "You should be happy I make enough money to support this program. The reality is someone needs to pay the bills around here and we both know I earn more so I'm in a better position to do it. So you do your part and I do mine—only I don't complain about it constantly!"

He's yelling now at the top of his lungs:

"You think I'm not sacrificing for this!? I may never get to retire! I'm working my ass off day and night so we can afford to give him the best therapy, and all I ever hear from you is complaints. I have plenty to complain about, too. I have his entire future on my shoulders to finance! Can you even comprehend the pressure I'm under?"

Oh, you're under pressure? I think sarcastically. *You certainly hide it well behind that façade of claiming to friends that "Zack is fine."* I've overheard his cheerful remarks reassuring friends who ask about Zack, and I'm infuriated by his reductive answer. He's not even here half the time, he's not the one raising this kid, much less sacrificing his entire life.

I remind him again of something I've shouted many times before, "YOU ARE NOT HERE! You are away working, socializing, having your expensive client dinners and golf outings—must be fun! And even when you are here you're not! When you're traveling you're gone, and when you're here you're gone—you are not remotely tuned in to what's actually happening here!"

Enraged, he fires back, "I am here and I do see how hard you and Zack are working! But I don't need to come home to YOU, constantly angry and berating me! You don't have to say a word. I can see it the way you look at me the minute I walk through the door, like this is my fault!" He is searing me now, just as I've seared him. "I mean, coming home to this—to you! You think you're a joy to come home to at the end of a long day? I *dread* it because I know you're just going to unload all this crap on me because of something he did which is not in my control. Do you think I like seeing you so unhappy, seeing what this has turned you into?"

"What?" I counter angrily.

"A misery! YOU ARE A MISERY! It's not him I dread coming home to, it's you!"

I can see in his eyes that I am no longer the woman he married, not the wife or mother he'd imagined. I have changed for the worse, transmogrified into a bitter shrew, the type of wife I'd always sworn I would never become. And in this moment I realize that, in Keith's eyes, the disgrace is not Zack, but my handling of Zack. The disgrace is me.

"Okay then, let's trade places!" I spar. "Gladly. I'd much rather be out there in the world, earning money and self-respect, than trapped in here! But then you get to do this, you get to run this forty-hour program and jump in every time the therapist doesn't show. You wake him up from his nap and drag him kicking and screaming into that room. I give you a week, tops!

Zack would be in a black hole if this was left to you."

Through tightly clenched teeth Keith grinds out the incomprehensible: "You should do this job and *love it*." He speaks distinctly and slowly, clamping down like someone about to blow, "If I had to do it, I'd do it and not complain. I'd do it out of love for my son, and I'd find a way to be happy."

"Oh, right!" I bite back savagely. "Go out there and ask the other autism moms if they're happy, if this fulfills them or gives them some divine sense of purpose!"

I am panting desperately because we are now in true crisis. My son is seriously disabled, now so is my marriage.

"Can't you just—" he states warily, "can't you just take pride in knowing that you are working to save our son?"

"He isn't getting better, goddamnit!" I roar. "He isn't! Not enough to catch up to other kids, or can you not see that? Are you so deep in denial, is your head so deep in the sand that you can't see what's happening here? He's still on the level of a one-year-old, if that, and now we can't even take him out of the house!"

"He's fine." Keith states declaratively, visibly wounded by my assessment of Zack's lack of progress. He abruptly turns and starts striding away fast.

"No, he isn't fine!" I move to get fully in his face, blocking off his exits and denials. "It's not *fine* that our son has brain damage! It's not *fine* that he can't go to a birthday party. None of this is *fine*, but you don't feel it because you can't face it!" My voice turns dangerously vengeful, "So, you can put on that stupid smile for your work friends and keep telling them 'Zack's doing great.' But it's crap, and we both know it. You can shut down and prop up that phony line for your friends, but don't you dare try it with me because I'm the one living it, and don't you dare tell me one more time that I should enjoy this!"

I pause to draw breath and exhale loudly, dogging him even though I know he wants to be left alone. Destroying my husband is not my intent. I just need acknowledgement of my sincere and desperate efforts, of my losses. My tone turns calm. "Look, I love you and this is no one's fault. I know you're working hard and doing the best you can and I'm so sorry if I sound ungrateful. It's just that this is so painful and lonely. It would just help me so much if you just . . . can you just grieve with me about our loss, so I'm not all alone in this?" I implore him beseechingly, achingly, to do the one thing I desperately need. "*Please,* you are the only person in this with me, the only person I can tell the whole truth to. So just between us, can you just admit that you're in as much pain as I am, that deep down you're grieving too?"

"NO!" he roars unexpectedly and I'm taken aback in fear. His face is contorted with fury unlike anything I've ever witnessed in him, or provoked.

"NO! I'm not going to grieve because there's nothing to grieve about! He isn't sick, he isn't in pain, he's a happy, healthy, beautiful little boy and that is all that matters! If you can't see that, then it's your problem—not mine! This isn't about you, it's about him, and he will be fine no matter what. So stop trying to make me feel something I don't!"

"Fine," I whisper, defeated and alone. I turn away slowly, realizing we are not allies but rivals on opposite sides, and the ache is too strong to sit still with it. I must move. Confused, I maunder up the stairs in a trance. Shell-shocked, I walk over to my closet and begin rapidly sorting out items, mechanically sorting and identifying business suits, work wear, tossing them absentmindedly on the floor. Grey, pin-striped dress with matching blazer, navy pants, crisp-collared oxford, business heels, the sartorial uniform of a litigator preparing for courtroom battle, a growing clothes pile at my feet. Finished, I look down at the garments which comprised my former life, now a tangle of suit legs, dresses and blazers breaking over one another in the thick, lifeless heap.

"What are you doing?" Keith asks hesitantly, startling me. I hadn't even heard him come up behind me.

"Cleaning," I answer succinctly. "There are charities which take business wear as donations for women who are starting over in their lives and heading into the workplace. Women recovering from domestic abuse, paroled, starting over. It's a great initiative." My voice trails off.

"But—aren't you going to need these when you head back to work, eventually?" he asks haltingly.

"No." My tone is flat and decisive. "Someone else might as well use them. They're just sitting here gathering dust. These are clothes for a professional. I'm obviously not going back to work any time soon, maybe not ever."

THE FUTILITY OF A FLAT PAGE

Tell me and I forget. Teach me and I remember.
Involve me and I learn.

—BENJAMIN FRANKLIN

HOW DO I use the ABA tool of "social stories" to manage Zack's anger when it ramps from zero to sixty range in seconds? Social stories are crucial to teaching children on the spectrum how to conduct themselves appropriately. The story topic can address any behaviors we seek to encourage, *i.e.* sharing toys, or stifle behaviors that are maladaptive, *i.e.* biting others. The stories are individualized to the child, meaning the therapists write a narrative that illustrates the virtues of preferred behaviors as a way of offering recommendations on how to act; or, in the case of bad behaviors, how not to act. The therapist writes the story, adding any relevant photos, then binds the pages together to create a portable manual which can be referenced by the child and parents alike, specifically at times when the child is engaging in the behaviors at issue. The story is intended to provide object lessons, carefully crafted using language that the child can understand about how to behave in the moment.

Zack's story is intended to reverse his angry behaviors, like screaming and biting, by offering up alternatives like using his words to express his anger. Zack's bites have become dangerous, his jaws so strong that when he locks down, the marks penetrate deep. If his jaws remain locked and not forcibly unclenched, skin breaks and the wound is serious. So Zack's story reads in his voice: "When I get angry I want to bite. But biting hurts people and makes them sad. So I must use my words instead."

Social stories work best when they are read aloud to the child repeatedly, both inside and outside the therapy room, until he truly absorbs and internalizes the lessons about how to behave. The child must then generalize, or apply, those lessons to real-world situations, especially in the live moment when the child's reactive decisions are often made. Zack's anger-management story, "When I Get Angry," has been read aloud to him at least three times daily for weeks. He is so familiar with it he can even recite it by heart, by rote, which is precisely the problem.

Zack's familiarity is the problem because if I'm driving away from the house with him strapped into his seat in the back, and I suddenly turn back the car momentarily to retrieve a forgotten item, Zack becomes instantly enraged. He misinterprets the car's reversal as implying that we're changing the plan, not going out as he was looking forward to. Even when his anger-management story is seated right beside me within arm's reach, before I can even get the story in my grasp, he's already unlocked the safety belt and has pounced forward to savagely bite my shoulder. Forget the story, danger is already here. As I'm frantically prying his jaws off me, I am assaulted relentlessly, all while trying to steer the car to avoid catastrophe. Only after I park the car in the driveway and manually unlock his jaws can I back away from him long enough to explain that we are just picking something up and will head back out. But by then I'm already injured.

It's the same if we park at our downtown destination in the metered lot and begin walking from the car before I realize I forgot to feed the meter. Within seconds of turning back with coins in hand, as I'm explaining to Zack, he assumes we're abandoning our outing. I desperately try to block his teeth and explain, "This will just take a second, honey! We're staying! Mommy just needs to feed—" Too late. His reaction is as swift as it is breathtaking, and publicly humiliating. The day I'd planned, which began with such excited promise, flips instantly into a monstrous public showdown where he's attacking me for the presumed betrayal, and I'm pleading and cursing and physically dragging my screaming son angrily across the concrete. And all this detonation from my uncomprehending child is because I need to fill the meter, which takes thirty seconds. Bystanders recoil abruptly at the sight as this seemingly abusive mom drags and brutalizes her young son; no one realizes I'm the one being scratched and bitten because of a precarious misunderstanding on his part. Sometimes I surrender to the bites and absorb the blows just to keep the peace, for my own self-preservation. No one can comprehend how deeply I'm held hostage to my son's rage.

None of the strategic words of Zack's carefully crafted social story—no matter how persuasive or rehearsed—can anticipate or reverse Zack's trajectory. Explosion eviscerates reason. What the concept of social stories often fails to account for is that in the live moments of an autistic outburst, many children are inaccessible to reason. And in a fit of rage, they are incapable of referencing, much less applying, the wisdom on the flat pages no many how many times the story has been recited aloud. *Words on a flat page don't rise up and translate in the heated moment, because they are not of the moment.*

For a literal thinker like Zack, words and pictures on a flat page remain inert. Zack doesn't think in narrative sequence or coercive "if-then" consequence statements. He reacts in the *now*, violently, with no time lapse between feeling and action. They erupt spontaneously, like a lightning strike. So when and where I need them most in real-world situations that trigger Zack's rage, social stories are worthless.

So tonight we try reading a different book, something whimsical and purely for pleasure, like normal moms do. Lo and behold, Zack is riveted to the Dr. Seuss story about *Yertle the Turtle* and his hegemony as described in captivatingly rhyming verse. My joy rising, I adopt various animated inflections for the different characters as we rhyme down the literary road on the way to that famous *burp*! But midway through a verse something flips inside Zack, a flash of pain. He furiously clamps his teeth into his own wrist several times, drawing blood. I stare at him dumbfounded, and suddenly Zack seizes the slender book from my hands and tears it straight up the spine and slams it to the floor. Bits of lint from the violently ripped pages float and flurry in circles, spiraling downwards as I stumble to understand what just happened—except, I don't care. Now it's my turn to fly into a rage.

"What's the matter with you?!" I scream in exasperation. "IT'S BROKEN! Why would you rip the book? What are you thinking? It's broken now, we can't read it anymore because you broke the book. IT'S BROKEN!" I'm shrieking in fever pitch dangerously close to his face, unhinged myself.

"It's *bro-ken*," he whispers softly staring down at the severed pieces. "It's *bro-ken* . . . it's *bro-ken* . . . " he repeats staccato. His tone tilts upwards into a lilting, sing-song tone as he deliberately turns the words over and over in his mind in concentration over the tethered remains. "It's *broken*," he states decisively, then shifts his gaze to capture mine for confirmation that he has correctly identified the problem.

"Yes," I confirm calmly, "the book is broken and now we can't read it."

"It's broken," he states declaratively, "It's broken. All done reading. No more reading. Book is broken."

It quickly dawns on me: *this is what's penetrating.* Seizing the moment, encouraged, I grab him and excitedly whisk his little body downstairs, planting him firmly as I fling open the refrigerator door and sling a raw egg onto the floor. Zack gazes at the drippy remains of yolk and shattered shell, then looks up at me and declares,

"It's broken! Egg is broken. All done egg, it's broken."

Good boy! I pivot towards an idle glass cup on the kitchen table, pick it up and hurl it forcefully against the wall, shards of glass flying in all directions. I look at him inquisitively.

"It's broken!" he belts out proudly, having caught on fully to the cool experiment. Now a light bulb crashes to the floor, now a pencil is snapped in two, now an old dysfunctional TV remote. *Wow, Mommy's breaking all sorts of stuff, this is fun!* I imagine him thinking. The concept sinks in deeper with each destruction, only now we are finally building something. Genuine comprehension.

Thirty minutes later, exhausted from my physical rant, I laughingly lean back into the living room wall and slink into a heap on the floor with Zack giggling hysterically in my arms. We stay for several minutes, basking in the glow of achievement, and damn does it feels good! *So it's these words, uttered spontaneously in the moment of live action, that broke through the autistic force field.*

As we return to his bedroom and I tenderly lay him down to sleep, I'm reminded again how badly my adoring son wants to please me. He bolts upright and points triumphantly towards the tethered book and announces gleefully, "Book is broken! No more reading! Book is all done!" Zack now not only identifies the object as broken, but appreciates the practical consequences that destroying an object makes it unavailable for future use. *Good.*

Yes Zack, it's very broken, I smile appreciatively into his eager eyes, *but now that you've got the idea let's not make a habit of smashing things all around the house!*

After he drifts off contently to sleep I wander around the house and decide to leave the wreckage intact, conducting an extended drill of my own. Over the next few days I test him, intermittently gesturing towards the various shattered remains around the house, and I'm consistently met with a resounding reply of "It's broken!" In the days that follow Zack looks out the car window and observes a car that seemingly crashed into an interstate barrier and is now sitting perfectly still but severely dented. "Car is broken!" So is the cracked window in that building, so are the tree branches severed from their trunk by a storm which now lay motionless on the ground. We take in an action movie at home and Zack beamingly belts out as vehicles explode in fiery spectacles that the helicopter, police car, building, bridge . . . Entirely unscripted, wholly owned and accurately applied, the new phrase has now entered Zack's lexicon for good—no flashcards, no books, no contrivances.

And interestingly, it only took a single live drill to get him here.

iNDULGENCE

A person who has been punished is not thereby simply less inclined to behave in a given way; at best, he learns how to avoid punishment.

—BEYOND FREEDOM AND DIGNITY,
B.F. SKINNER

"DO NOT LET him stare at lights," Cara admonishes. "Cover his eyes with your hands, clap loudly in his face if you have to: just don't let him fixate!"

Four therapists and I are gathered for our monthly progress meeting.

"Never? I can never let him watch them, not even for a few minutes to reward him after he's worked really hard in the room?"

Turning the corner to age five, Zack has developed a new self-stimulating behavior of staring at lights, whether it's bulbs shielded by lampshades, set in ceilings, or brightening public spaces. He was once so transfixed by the glowing ornamentation on the upper level of the local mall that he tripped over his own feet and hit the floor because he was staring up rather than forward.

"No." Cara commands. "It's a distracting self-stim; we can't allow that. The problem with these kind of perseverative behaviors is our kids get trapped in them to the point that they'd rather stare at lights, flap, line things up, to the exclusion of all else."

Ironically, as she lectures Cara is herself maniacally twisting the ends of her hair through her moving fingers in the identical pattern repeatedly, as she does several times during every stressful progress meeting.

"Wait, it's distracting to whom?" I ask with a distinct edge to my voice. "Not for Zack. He always stops staring to come to the table, and he's still getting all the drills right, so it's not actually interfering."

"That's not the point," Cara brusquely interrupts, but I'm not letting her point go unchecked so quickly. It's been over two years of intensive therapy so I'm not new to this anymore. I've developed some opinions about how Zack learns.

Thinking back to our initial training session, I recall how Cara demonstrated how drills must be executed and how Zack must respond. If there are three different colored cards on the table and Zack is prompted to "touch red," even if he does so correctly, his answer is nevertheless recorded as *incorrect* if his hand flaps on the way down. The only correct response is a straight hit.

Rewiring his brain requires not just epistemic accuracy, but the behavioral appearance of normalcy. This precept made sense to me back in the days when I so desperately wanted Zack to expunge any trace of autism, but over two years later, with a great deal more respect for who he is, I feel like ABA is dedicated to drumming out every last bit of natural impulse and self-expression. It's a systematic annihilation of all that is intimate and personalized to the child in pursuit of the end game of assimilation. Even now, when it's abundantly clear to all involved that Zack will never look or function precisely like his typically developing peers, the drumbeat of normal persists, even at the expense of actual acquisition of skills. So I must ask, "If a stimming behavior isn't wholly absorbing or interfering with Zack's ability to learn, if he still answers the questions correctly, why do we have to suffocate them? It feels unnecessary and unproductive at this point. It's asking too much of him to surrender all his impulses and tics. Why should we, if he's actually getting drills right? Maybe the stims are actually helping him decode the world, allowing him to concentrate on drills. I see typical kids all the time who chew their pencils to help them focus, and we don't force them to stop. So why does Zack have to give up his coping mechanisms?"

"It doesn't look normal," Cara huffs. "Why should I have to explain that to you this far along in the process? After everything we've done and been through, why are you arguing about the most fundamental concepts?"

"Because I don't give a damn how it looks." Something is rising inside me, a feeling of profound injustice toward my son by forcing him to abnegate every ritual that uniquely defines or comforts him, even when the behavior is not harmful or distracting. Far from a hindrance, his various stims might be the only rituals that calm him in an uncertain world, thereby making him more receptive to learning.

"Zack does a million things every day that don't look normal, and we all know that. That's who he is, but he still complies, still does drills, still learns as best he can, so what difference does it make it he flaps or stares from time to time? This whole obedience to the norm is unproductive and wasting time. We all have our stims, our crutches. I bite my nails to the nub and you're always twirling your hair, so why do we get our stims and Zack doesn't?"

My jaw is clenched in agitation. The therapists all shift uncomfortably in their seats at this unexpected confrontation. I'd almost forgotten they were there and I feel badly at their obvious unease. I hate subjecting them to this, but their education is being shaped by the protocol, too, so it's best we all understand the epistemic rationale behind the seemingly fatuous double standard.

"That's a false equivalency, Whitney," Cara responds coolly but with unmistakable asperity. "If you ask me to stop twirling my hair at any time, I can do that." *All evidence is to the contrary: she's yanking her ends so hard right now her hair might just decide give up and fall out on its own,* I think. "And it's not my favorite activity. If someone asks me go to the movies, I'd interrupt immediately and go. But our kids don't abandon their stims unless they're forced to, because they get caught in perseveration to the point they can't let it go and prefer stimming over regular activities. If you leave Zack to his own preferences it will just intensify and get more deeply ingrained."

"*Or,*" I proffer archly, "maybe if we let him indulge in his affinity for lights *from time to time*, they will lose their fascination and hold on him. I've seen him move through several different stims over the years and he seems to abandon and shift constantly over the months. So maybe if we allow it, he'll get satiated and lose interest. I'm just asking, isn't it possible?"

"No, it doesn't work that way." Cara is declaratively incensed. "The research on autism and stims is clear; we need to end it, not encourage it."

Ah, yes, of course, *the research*, that incontrovertible shield against the heretical notion that a parent's expertise and intuition about her own child might ever be more accurate than the one-size-fits-all ABA approach. I respect the scientific research dedicated to our children, but I also resist the notion that in grappling with a disability this complex, a group of detached scientists wholly unacquainted with my particular child knows, with scientific certainty, how he will respond to stimuli simply because he belongs to a diagnostic category called autism. History has proven that the medical community has misunderstood this disability many times, yet still I'm confronted with rigid protocol predicated on the belief that scientists are the sole arbiters of what an autistic child should or should not be allowed to do, the erudite decision-makers about which behaviors we allow and which we stifle. This, despite the scientific acknowledgement that the disability exists on a spectrum, and each child is different.

A flat prohibition against certain behaviors wipes out a panoply of ritualistic comforts for an entire population, some of whom may very well depend on them to function at all. And if we suffocate those adaptive behaviors, even when the child is learning, are we not teaching the child to be ashamed of his own natural impulses, telling him his are disfavored or deviant? And would we do the same to typically developing children, or to ourselves as adults?

Cara has moved on and now speaks authoritatively. "I'll develop a protocol to put the light-staring on extinction," she announces, purposely avoiding eye contact with me and addressing only the therapists. "I'll write up a program with specific steps. The goal is to interrupt Zack every single time he looks up at lights. We can use verbal prompts like 'no looking,' put your hand over his eyes, or even do something aversive like clapping loudly in his face." Sensing my recalcitrance, she states pointedly, "The key in getting him to stop stimming is consistency, which means *everyone* has to be diligent about enforcing the program. The therapists must execute it as often as needed during his sessions, and Mom, you must do it during leisure time. If everyone follows through it shouldn't take more than a month to extinguish the stim."

Extinguish the behavior. Maybe I'm entirely wrong about this, powered only by instinct. After all Cara has expertise, she has Zack's best interests at heart, and I fought hard just to become one of her clients because her reputation is so stellar. A disciple of Lovaas himself, she's undeniably brilliant with mountains of experience. I should defer to her. So I try.

Every evening when Zack emerges from his therapy room the first thing he craves is lights, heading excitedly towards a tall floor lamp to just sit under it and bask in its glow.

"NO!" I bark sharply. It works. He's so startled by my sharp disapproval he immediately recoils in what he perceives as bad behavior. Despite the sickening knot in my stomach I persist throughout the evening, finding varied physical and verbal ways to stop him. It's exhausting. I can't bring myself to clap in his face, so I opt instead for the eye shield, but even this feels cruel. Zack is visually smitten by lights, and now deprived he sneaks furtive darting glances when he thinks I'm not looking, like a criminal. In the ensuing days I overhear the therapists faring better than me in their sessions, routinely clapping and scolding him at every turn. And I can hear Zack yelp helplessly at the repeated strikes.

This feels wrong in more ways than one. For starters, it's not working as scripted because smothering Zack's visual impulses simply gives oxygen to other behaviors like slapping himself. If we upbraid him for looking, he shuts his eyes tightly while his jaws clamp down ferociously on his wrist in anguish. And now, ironically, we have managed to transform what was a self-stimulating behavior into a full-blown obsession and desperate preoccupation to glimpse what's being inexplicably deprived. So now we've managed to create a genuine distraction from Zack's ability to focus and learn, where formerly he was compliant.

But something even more sinister is going on here: we are undermining Zack's autonomy and sense of self-worth. ABA protocol is literally robbing Zack of independence and bodily choices, because we are making them for him. If he felt so empowered, if we hadn't totally hobbled his ability to stand up for himself, I imagine Zack would angrily swat back our hands from his eyes. Which is his right.

After days of rigorous discipline, today I've decided I will not only allow Zack to stare at lights, I will actively encourage it. I will not only permit access, I will hold him up closer to the light so he can get a better look. As soon as the last therapist leaves for the day I lay out a plush blanket at the base of the tall floor lamp for us to lie down together.

"Zack, today we are both going to look at lights for as long as we want." Distrustful at first, he automatically raises his own hand to shield his eyes as he's become accustomed, and with an aching heart I tenderly remove it and explain "not this time." As he begins staring in earnest, his visual lock is not merely inquisitive but reverential. Perhaps he doesn't see a bulb at all but is looking directly inside the mechanical glow—the intricate anatomy, the reverberating filaments, the electron leaps. Zack may actually be perceiving the light differently, and grasp features I can't because his brain is wired differently.

Typically, when a person observes an object the image is inverted on our retina, then our brain reinverts. But Zack's circuitry is different, so his visual interpretation of a common object might literally be different. As I trace his serious glare I realize that he's not just staring, but *studying*—counting, measuring, calculating. Maybe those electrons are speaking to him in a language I can't reach, begging to be understood by a gentle genius with a reverential scrutiny of the mechanical workings. Maybe we vastly underestimated Zack's stimming behavior; maybe there's a dignity to it that we have misunderstood all along. Or maybe he's just a kid who likes staring at lights.

It doesn't matter because, fundamentally, it's an issue of respect. I may never understand it, but that does not mean I can't respect the urge. I don't care whether it's typical; for Zack this is normal. And, provided it doesn't injure anyone or eclipse his ability to keep gaining new information, then Zack should be allowed to retain those distinctive characteristics that make him Zack. Because, instinctively, I understand something that Cara, for all her accumulated expertise, does not: *if I expect Zack to inhabit my world, I must allow him to spend time in his own, too.*

One day, the lights inexplicably cease to hold his attention.

"No more lights!" he announces matter-of-factly when I summon him to lie down. "No more lights, all done lights."

I'll likely never know why the lights lost their magnetism. I only know that for a period of months Zack was transfixed, then indulged, then passed through the stim and then left it permanently behind. Currently in vogue is a new gig of vigorously rubbing two fingers together closely held to his ear so he can listen to the abrasive sound of flesh brushing up against flesh. When I offer up lights, I'm met with an aloof sneer of indifference. I'll need to keep up to stay hip to the evolving trends and stop insulting him with last month's fixation.

Swiftly, on the heels of Zack's unexpected pivot, is yet another progress meeting with Cara fresh off her flight and busily scanning Zack's therapy data. This is good news, she reports. Zack has stopped staring at lights—behavior extinguished. I never told her my tactics. Cara looks up and smiles knowingly at me, as her confidence in ABA protocol is both vindicated and duly reinforced. "Well done, team." She lavishes praise and takes a moment to call me out in front of the team to congratulate me for not giving in to my protective instincts towards Zack and for strictly toeing the protocol line.

"I'm glad you came around to the extinction program, Whitney! See how quickly we got rid of that stim?"

"*Yes,*" I answer obediently as I quickly turn away to conceal a conspicuous eye roll and grin as I lock eyes with Zack who smiles back. I say nothing further. The behavior is now extinct, so no defense is required. And after all, she's the expert here, not me.

iNCONCEiVABLE

Parents who have a child with Autism Spectrum Disorder have a 2% -18% chance of having a second child who is also affected.

—CDC, DATA AND STATISTICS, AUTISM SPECTRUM DISORDER

I MUST KNOW the experience of a typical child. Now that Zack has nascent speech and I've fully metabolized his disability, I can envision living with one foot in each world— special needs and normal. Regardless of my reproductive fate, I'd always hoped to have two children and I finally feel ready to move forward. As with most major life choices, Keith was ready yesterday and is impatient to start trying.

Keith and I had originally planned the children to be spaced closely, and be allies. But now they will be many years apart. But I want desperately to give Zack a sibling and if I'm being brutally honest, I need a moderating influence. I can't have autism be my epitaph of parenting. Irrespective of autism, something within me feels incomplete if I don't at least strive for one more child, come what may.

Our approach to conception is different now: more somber, a reflection of the changed person I have become. There's a reproductive urgency that wasn't there before, too: now that I have made the bold decision to finally move forward, I want to be pregnant right now. My unspoken hurriedness infects our coupling, rendering it more perfunctory than pleasurable, underlain by a desperate need to bridge the temporal lapse between children. Given how deeply I've been shaken by the unexpected, how fearful we are about a repeat performance of disability, we've enlisted a geneticist to inform us of the statistical odds of having another child with autism.

But deep down, I know it's fool's question. No one can predict with scientific accuracy what our odds are of a repeat, because there was nothing whatsoever in our genetic backgrounds to suggest that autism was possible in the first place. Neither Keith nor I have any relatives with autism, or anything resembling a cognitive impairment, in our entire family trees. Moreover, I know only too well that the autism diagnosis is based on a constellation of behavioral symptoms—social difficulties, fixated interests, obsessive or repetitive actions—precisely because no reliable bio-markers exist.

But we came for the reassurance of hearing a doctor tell us we are safe, no matter how far that differs from reality. Our blood was drawn and vigorously tested before this appointment, though I'm unclear what exactly they are looking for. It turns out that only chromosomal abnormalities related to autism, such as a genetic disorder known as "Fragile X," is significant and perceptible, whereas the science pertaining to recurrence is actually derived incidentally from sibling statistics.

We're told that statistic show the odds have indeed risen due to our having already had one child: the scientific community has converged on this point based on nationwide data. Though the increased probability of a repeat of autism in our next child is slight, likely only 3 percent, no truly accurate prediction is possible—for a fascinatingly obvious reason. As the geneticist points out, statistical probabilities about recurrence in siblings depend on the number of siblings born to families already impacted by autism. But given the devastating impact of one child with it, any estimate of recurrence is unduly low because *scientists can't measure the outcome of risks not taken.* Autism truncates families and cuts short reproductive ambitions. Parents who might have intended to have larger broods, once they are hit by autism, surrender their dream and choose to have fewer children to avoid the risk that another might be impacted. Scientifically, these widespread decisions skew the overall incidence rates.

Still, the geneticist reassures us confidently that the odds are overwhelmingly in favor of us having a typically developing child, though my faith in hearty assurances eroded long ago. Absent any genetically certain data, or prenatal diagnostic tests for autism, the choice comes down to a willingness to roll the dice. I won't pretend to be sanguine about where the dice lands. In my heart I know that repeating this experience with a second child will ruin me. I genuinely can't fathom how I will survive it. But nonetheless, I'm prepared to close my eyes tight and gamble once more.

Our lovemaking is neither happy nor healthy because a frantic stopwatch against which we procreate is ever-present for me. Over the years my body has become a lightning rod for tension, perennially stiff and alert with apprehension for what Zack might do next. Even as I'm working arduously to conceive another child, I'm still caring night and day for my son, and the physical consequences on my body are real. I'm angrily impatient to move forward, aware that my urgency is driven less by maternal instincts than a propulsive obsession to break the current pattern and start anew. It's selfish, I know, but undeniable. So while I may fool others about my ambition to become a parent again, I can't trick my own body into relaxing, which I can feel is anything but fertile ground for the delicate business of conception. The first time around was amazingly fluid, conception lubricated by playfulness without any expectation. This feels like an emergency and my body has shut down accordingly.

It's been nine months of trying, nine months of bitter disappointment, me cursing the wheels of justice for grinding so slowly as to cruelly stymie a woman this desperate to move on. Surely, after all I've been through, I deserve this one thing to come easily, but of course nature doesn't work that way. I don't need to consult a fertility specialist to know the destructive impact my mind is wreaking on my body. The enormous pressure I've put on my body to conceive has chased away any chance that it will cooperate. *Damn it! Even if I conceive this very second we are already far behind, the children will already be five whole years apart!* It's no wonder I'm a reproductive brick wall, but I'm incapable of going with the flow.

Enough of this! Time to take matters into my own hands and do the only thing that might work. Given Zack's influence, the mix of resentment and stress, the perpetually rotating therapists and progress meetings, I know deep down that I will not be able to conceive a child in this house. I must distance myself from the therapy, the daily tension, from Zack himself, if I am to truly clear my mind and body. Keith and I must go away somewhere totally transporting, unsuitable for children but ripe for salacious conception. We need a red-light district of my choosing, in one of the most enchantingly bewitching cities on earth. I ask Keith to trust me, and I book the dates strategically.

A month later, Keith and I are away for a single ovulating weekend amidst a backdrop so *Big Easy*, so swinging and jazzy, infused with such a rich ghostly history, that this is the place. One of the trusted therapists in whom I confided about our mission generously agreed to stay at our house with Zack so we could escape and run to the only place guaranteed to break the consuming stress that has hijacked my ovaries. I need to eat beignets, listen to the blues, stare at the intricate, filigree architecture of wrapping balconies, walk the haunted ghost tours where rich spirits surround us. Keith is, as always, far calmer than I am, so it's really just me who needs loosening. So we are unapologetically heading to the red-light district now, for me.

Another month later I have an eerily familiar and unmistakable clogging of my intestines, an unnatural rate of absorption of food, sluggish bowels and distended abdomen. I reach for the clinical stick and am exalted to watch as it obligingly glows a ripe, bright fuchsia. Already I feel different with this conception. The sickness will be more wretched and unabated, the heartburn unbearable, but my intuition speaks that this will result in an entirely different outcome.

A couple of months later and not enthusiastic about being "surprised," we opt to learn gender and discover that we are having a precious baby girl. Suddenly, the chasm between our children in years and gender feels gloriously correct. My joy is also rooted in scientific fact—autism has a gender preference, occurring four times more often in boys than in girls. My daughter's name will be Cassandra, though I will call her Cassie, a feminine and sassy moniker that caught my attention years ago for no reason other than I loved the sound. The lengthier formal name is strictly business, just in case she becomes a brain surgeon and no one wants emergency surgery performed by a boppy "Cassie." Her middle name was already written long ago—she will carry the legacy and memory of Keith's beloved brother whose life was cut short far too early.

All of which makes sense. *Although*, if we approached her name purely as a matter of historical accuracy, from the locus of her *actual* conception, and as a loving tribute to the faithful

city which broke the vicious cycle of infertility as only it could
... her name would be most fittingly, most gratefully—*Cassandra
'N'Orleans' Louisiana,* which does have a cool Dr. Seussian ring
to it that even Zack might like.

THE SCARLET "A"

Speak a little truth and people lose their damn minds.

**—ICE CUBE, "*STRAIGHT OUTTA COMPTON*"
MOVIE QUOTE (2015)**

"TELL NO ONE," Cara admonishes me about revealing Zack's diagnosis, now that I've finally secured a private preschool space where he'll be fully included with mainstream peers, though he is slightly older than they are. Cara's instruction is pointed. My job is to tell his teachers the truth but otherwise pass him off to fellow parents and classmates as merely language-delayed. Cara wants Zack to have abundant play dates and presumes he will have none if other parents know the truth. So *speech-delayed* is the reason I'm sending Zack with a dedicated private therapist to "shadow" him all day in the classroom? Delayed speech is now supposed to account for Zack's habit of ingesting nonfood items like dirt and grass; his likely tendency to trip on the limbs of peers who he's yet to realize are live humans; his obvious auditory processing deficit; and his lack of social skills or genuine play. In truth, the only harm Zack poses to peers is total indifference, so he's more likely to shun than engage them, still unaware of them as potential sources of fun and companionship.

Once again, I'm confronted with the chasm between ABA's expectations and those of the real world where children don't behave remotely like Zack, nor he like them. But this is the scenic backdrop I'm expected to prop behind him no matter how transparent the veneer, nor how weary my arms are from chronically holding it steady. I predict that even these very young, inexperienced children are unlikely to fall for the ruse, especially when they realize that unlike all of them, at age four Zack is not yet toilet trained. *Perhaps I can have a scarlet "A" embroidered on his pull-ups.*

Entering my final months of this second pregnancy I'm far more cumbersome than I was with Zack, slower on my feet, less deft in my movements. At times, this pregnancy felt precarious due to the baby's awkward positioning so far down in my uterus, the pressure on my cervix so acute as to send me sprinting to the doctor, fearful of a sudden abruption. And despite my overall confidence, lurking in the dark reaches of my mind is the distinct possibility that I will be re-enacting this façade once again if my second child is born disabled. I resent more than ever the pressure to conform, to contort who Zack truly is into a more suitable box. As I gingerly broach the topic of daring to reveal Zack's truth to other parents I'm met with swift opposition. It would be a betrayal of Zack's progress to reveal it, now that we've come so far.

"Don't do it, Whitney," Cara states gently. "Remember what I told you about sealing Zack's records down the road to conceal his diagnosis so no public schools will know. We need to preserve that option for your and Zack's sake. I told you, there are ways of keeping his diagnosis private by court-ordered sealing of his records." I do feel obliged to take her advice, reminded once again that while Zack's progress thus far may not be as swift as I'd hoped, Cara is doing her best. And I know she truly has Zack's current and future best interests in mind looking far down the road.

"So, we'll need to manufacture a plausible excuse if Zack does something really strange like—"

"Can we not do that, please?" I interject suddenly.

"Not do what?" Cara asks surprised.

"Can we please not talk about him as if he's not in the room when he's sitting right here, and maybe absorbing every word?"

From the very beginning, Cara has engaged in the unnerving habit of talking about Zack in the third person, even when he's clearly within listening radius. She doesn't mean any harm or insult, it's simply a matter of habit. But it strikes me as disrespectful to him, and ironic that the person who's leading Zack's intensive intervention and thumping for his impending recovery is the same person who inadvertently treats him as though he's entirely oblivious. If we assume Zack *isn't* cueing in and paying attention to our words, doesn't that belie the mission itself, or at least undercut its basic premise? I have no idea exactly how much Zack interprets or discards from the conversations he overhears, but I choose at least to behave *in his presence* as if he comprehends everything; he certainly deserves the benefit of that doubt.

Listening to Cara's authentic concerns, my mind wanders into the woods of a phrase I once heard, "the soft bigotry of low expectations," which means that people reflexively underestimate what others can tolerate or achieve. In Zack's case, the soft bigotry cuts both ways: one is when people dismiss Zack's potential to comprehend or perform, in ways they've already determined, by virtue of his categorical disability. The other cuts just as insidiously in the opposite direction, presuming that parents of typical children can't comprehend or are unwilling to assist in the struggle because they are not personally affected by it. It assumes they are too oblique or unenlightened to extend common sense and compassion to a situation if they have not lived it. Low expectations effectively pit parents of disabled children against those without—to the detriment of all involved.

I pause to remember Cara's experience and dedication to keeping Zack's best interest foremost. Zack's own preference, were he able to articulate it, might indeed favor concealment so that he might start with a clean slate. It might betray him to err on the side of disclosure before he's had a chance to prove himself, without being openly identified as disabled. So, I relent and will introduce him accordingly as *language-delayed*.

The brave front doesn't last long as I march Zack to and from class every day, his private aide also chronically by his side to shadow and assist his every move in class. And when he inevitably behaves as I'd feared, vigorously mouthing puzzle pieces, tripping over conspicuous limbs and ignoring invitations to play, the erected façade is quickly fraying—so much so that the aide reports back that a couple of volunteering mothers expressed innocent alarm over some of his actions.

Truth is not an option, so I'm trapped into continuing to misrepresent it. But increasingly, Zack's peers are starting to shun him, bewildered by why this handsome child is so cold and unfriendly and seems unfeeling, even when he accidentally steps hard on their fingers and they cry out in pain and he just keeps walking. Minor injuries are tolerated by teachers because they know Zack is innocent and not premeditated. Zack benefits from the fact that, at his age, his peers often move and dart at recess so erratically and unpredictably that they, too, are prone to occasionally tripping each other or crashing heads. The difference of course is that when those accidental injuries occur, these kids apologize.

The mystery about Zack's identity extends to me as well. Sometimes I catch glimpses of the parents musing whether I am ignorant that my son is obviously struggling with serious developmental deficits, or that I am acutely aware that he has major issues which I'm deliberately hiding. All this intrigue and deception feels particularly absurd given the low epistemic stakes; this is preschool, not medical school. Children are playing in sandboxes, not dissecting cadavers for life-altering surgery. While Zack sits contentedly at recess watching sand granules slip through his fingers, his peers are eagerly lancing each other in the eyes with sharpened tree sticks, which is considered more normal.

My ache springs from a place that experts don't get: that the chronic pain and shame for a mother like me who can't possibly pass off her child as normal, or minimally delayed, lies in *not* telling the truth. In the real, detailed quotidian life, even children can sense when another child deviates from the norm. So they retreat in confusion, and their parents retreat in distrust.

No one is fooled into believing that a child with Zack's impairments is merely struggling with speech when his limitations are easily judged to be profound within five minutes of meeting him, especially when he refuses to make eye contact or say "hi" during the meet. I'm tired of loud whispers and feeling ashamed of who Zack is, sick of the bogus insistence that I cannot simply tell the truth. He's a kind and decent child with autism who deserves to be accepted and included on that basis alone, irrespective of skills or deficits. He deserves a chance, just like any and every other child. It would frankly benefit the other children to know the truth from an early age, as educational studies consistently state that typical children crystallize their own academic comprehension of math and writing by teaching others whose comprehension is weaker. Once again, all children benefit from the truth.

Tonight I'm surprised I even made it here, barely awake enough to steer the car to the preschool's "Parents' Night," where we are enthusiastically lectured on the vaunted curriculum. I'm just trying to get through this so I can get back to my comfy bed. But in quaint tradition, we parents have been squeezed into pint-sized desks and chairs usually inhabited by our children. It would have looked more suspicious for me to skip this in light of wisps of rumors about Zack. Everything is throbbing as I sit squeezed into this desk, my feet swollen. Fortunately, Zack has already captured the curriculum essentials, which were drummed into him in preparation, so he'll just need the aide to keep prompting him to answer out loud—and not to keep stepping on the other children, and not to eat the crayons . . .

Looking around me I feel starkly naked and exposed, as if everyone in the room knows I'm the one whose child doesn't belong, whose child likely needed a more appropriate special education apart from their kids. My pretext suddenly feels invisible, not because any of the parents are looking at me, but because they seem purposely not to be looking at me. No idle chatter, no knowing smiles, no eye contact whatsoever, as if sparing me the indignity of knowing that the finite concepts being outlined likely don't apply to me or my child.

Even as the teachers go through the roster of parents who proudly identify their children, I feel a momentum building about the fact that I will not be accurately naming my child, not completely. I've pulled the wool over everyone's eyes in the hopes they would glance away and not notice that which cannot help but be seen, that my child is distinctly different from each and every other in the class. The teachers are getting around to calling on me.

"Excuse me," I mutter quickly but, wobbly and unsteady, I slowly rise to my feet. One of the teachers looks startled by my apparent need to make an announcement without first running it by her.

I project my voice loudly: "I'm sorry," I begin, taking in all the stoic glares, eyes tilted upwards in silent unison on me. "I have not been completely honest with you, or your children. I was told by an expert working with my son to leave this information out, but I need to be upfront. My son is Zack and he doesn't just have a language delay, he has autism, which is a serious cognitive and social disability. I'll leave it to your judgment to decide whether and how to explain this to your kids at this young age but—" I stop and draw a breath. "But all the things your children come by naturally, like pointing and talking and socializing—these have to be specifically taught to Zack in therapy over and over. So, every day he has intensive therapy, one-to-one with an aide. That's why he has a shadow in class and now—" I take another deep breath. "Now we need him to have play dates with peers so he can learn to imitate typical behavior, and learn to play." I pause to take in the attitude in the room. I've already said much more than I intended, but the silence is pervasive. Everyone is just so rigidly quiet they themselves resemble fearful preschool children. The vibe I'm getting is not judgmental, just rapt with attention, riveted by the extraordinary circumstances I'm detailing, which they seem to have never encountered before. What this mother is describing is utterly foreign and completely fascinating. *Forge on.*

"So, what I'm asking of you is to help us, Zack and me, please. What Zack needs most is play dates with your children. If you're willing, let them come over during his therapy sessions. The play dates will be supervised by therapists, and I promise your children will have fun. I know . . . I know that Zack may not be their first choice to play with, but he really does care about your children. They matter a great deal to him, he just can't show it yet." I halt embarrassingly. The group is still so deadly silent and watchful, and I feel the need to supply a stronger incentive. "For what it's worth, Zack has been in intensive therapy so many years that there's not a toy roaming the planet that we don't have!" That draws a warm ripple of generous laughter, finally a break in the stoic wave, as I retake my tiny plastic seat.

The teacher-led conversation turns back towards the curriculum and she drones on. When the teachers finally finish, I'm still dazed from my impromptu lecture and lean into the tiny desk to hoist myself to my swollen feet. Unexpectedly, a gracious father quickly extends an outstretched hand to balance me as he applies the other to my lower back to help me stand fully upright. As I gather up the errant school papers to jam into my purse, I look up and am startled to see a sort of formal receiving line extending from one end of the room directly up to me. It's a line of parents waiting their turn to speak with me, applaud me for my efforts, and provide me the contact information to arrange play dates with their children. I am visibly overwhelmed with gratitude at their kindness, pausing occasionally to furtively wipe away a stray tear. I struggle to jot down everyone's information quicker than my pen can scrawl on the random papers. So many names, so many numbers and emails, a fulsome mix of little girls and boys, and their parents.

Overjoyed and exhausted, I report back to Cara the following day about my adventure, including my unexpected disclosure.

"I hope you only told a few of the parents who seemed especially sensitive," she begins apprehensively.

"I told everyone. I couldn't keep it a secret anymore. It's a little hard to sell 'language delayed' when your kid is eating grass, so I just stood up and made an open announcement to the entire room."

"I really wish you hadn't done that, Whitney," Cara sighs, saddened at how quickly I unraveled and blew Zack's cover, so soon after school just started. "Parents are quick to make assumptions."

"No one seemed to mind that Zack has autism once I came clean about who he was and what he needed."

"Yes, but now everyone will know, even if he recovers it will follow him in ways you can't take back. That's why I told you to keep it a secret. Most importantly because he's going to need social interactions, starting now and well into the future and now you've compromised whatever doubt—"

"Zack has twenty-two play dates," I interrupt gleefully. "That's every single child in his class whose parents are perfectly happy to have their typical kids play with Zack. They were literally lined up to hand me their information once I exposed the truth. They seemed to want to help. So let's line up the interactive drills because Zack's social calendar is about to get weighty. I want to get started right away. I'm not taking their generosity for granted, and I don't want Zack to miss a moment of this."

MOMENTS OF CLARITY

I don't want no one to squeeze me, they might take away my life
I don't want no one to squeeze me, they might take away my life
I just want someone to hold me, oh and rock me through the night

—*"GIVE ME ONE REASON"* SONG LYRICS
BY TRACY CHAPMAN

ZACK IS FIVE years old and, after so much time being the sole prince of our house, he must make room for a princess. It's deep into December and I'm about to give birth to my second child, a girl.

For months it's been unclear what Zack has thought was happening inside my expanding belly. I told him, but he could not tell me his feelings, so I don't know exactly what was grasped or lost from my early explanations. I spent a good deal of time during my pregnancy fearing his reaction to the newcomer.

Would he be enraged by the invader of his space? Or is he so completely ensconced in his own world that he won't even notice her? I am more afraid of the latter, the implications being far more somber developmentally regarding his ability to grasp the concept of a sibling. I moved his old rocking chair to make space for a larger denim one in which he'll rock full-body. I remove the stained old chair and drag it into the new baby's room.

Days later I give birth to our daughter, Cassie, who is already looking me squarely in the eyes, even at four days old, which feels miraculous. I whisper serenely into my husband's ear at the hospital, "She doesn't have it." I have become an expert in those minute idiosyncrasies that personify autism—the hasty fleeing of the eyes, the aloof turn of the head, the seeming pained response to voices from overstimulated senses, and even at four days old this child already has differences I can sense. I am being studied attentively by eager new eyes. I am being courted for attention, and it is remarkable that such a thing could occur so early in a life. And suddenly, I am dreading coming home to Zack.

Much is made of the classic maternal conflict in which new mothers worry about whether they can truly love the second child as much as the first. But this new child is locking eyes with mine and there is nothing classic about the way I am feeling, just the sheer desperation of having discovered something that has been missing for so long, something I had learned to live without. And loving my son suddenly feels like a cruel and unnatural exercise, like forcing my stomach to regurgitate something it has already devoured. At this moment, loving my son means forcing my heart to settle for less than what I know I have fallen in love with, and I honestly don't know if I can do it.

As soon as I enter the house I learn that Zack has been restless, agitated, seemingly aware that something momentous has happened. But I don't believe it; he cannot possibly know what's happening yet. I find Zack curled up and sleeping in my bed and I wake him gently, ready to reunite in cuddles. But he wakes up with large haunted eyes and grabs me tightly. He is trembling badly, dark circles underlie both eyes and he's desperate not to let go of me, as if unclenching me even for a second means Mommy may disappear again for days and come back a different person, which I can tell he now thinks I am. He stares down at my deflated stomach and seems crushed by the absence of the buoyant roundness that is gone, and against which he had enjoyed burying his face. He's scaring me a little by being so detached, almost judgmental, so I nervously reach over to the TV remote to restore some familiarity. But Zack startles me by suddenly screaming loudly "NO! NO TV! NO!" For the next thirty minutes I am not permitted to move from that spot where Zack clutches me tightly, not in joy but in sheer distress.

I am at a loss for what to do next, so I steer him over to Cassie's car seat where she's snuggled in, sleeping, so I can gently introduce him. He looks fleetingly down at her but won't touch her or come close.

"Say 'Hi, Cassie!'" I prompt him tentatively. "Go ahead, you can touch the baby. This is Cassie and she's your new sister!" He glances in her direction and abruptly walks out of the room. I'm deflated, crushed at his indifference and remind myself that it may take time, several months, before he really notices her and understands her to be another human child like him. But as he enters his own bedroom Zack stops suddenly in the doorway and shrieks with earsplitting volume. He runs to the corner of the room where his old rocking chair had been and begins pounding his hands and feet angrily on the faded floor where it stayed.

"*Chair!*" is his strangled sob, "*CHAIR!*" A minor detail sure to escape his attention I had thought, but he noticed.

"Chair! Zack Chair! Zack! Chair!"

"Zack, my love," I begin soothingly, "Mommy's already ordered you a new big boy chair and it's coming any day now!

It's coming very soon!"

"NOOO!" he screams, and my stomach starts caving in as I realize I'm not allowed even one hour of happiness in my homecoming with my new baby. *He's going to rob me of this, too.* I feel sickeningly trapped in what feels like an abusive relationship. Zack screams and assaults me in an outburst, then predictably shows remorse, then predictably I forgive him . . . until the next time. What choice do I have but to calmly readjust my emotions yet again, at a time when they are truly fragile from fluctuating hormones and massive sleep deprivation?

"NO CHAIR! NO ZACK! NO CHAIR! NO MOMMY!" he is perseverating frantically and I begin to realize this is not about the absent chair, but instead something deeper.

I kneel before him and try to capture his direct gaze.

"Zack, what is it? You know I love you; you can tell me; use your words. C'mon, use your words, remember? Who's the love of my life? Who is Mommy's one and only favorite boy in the whole entire world?" He knows this exchange, we've had it a hundred times before and, exhausted, I wait for him to call out his name.

"Baby," he says with perfect articulation. He looks me squarely in the eyes. I am so unaccustomed to such direct eye contact from him I freeze.

"Baby is Mommy favorite. Baby is love of Mommy life."

I am too stunned to speak. This is his single longest utterance to date. And it is the most lucid, most coherent and cogent moment of his life, fully engaged and engaging me, fully aware of what he means to say. I cannot explain this linguistic feat, other than it must have been driven by a need to be understood so urgent that even the bondage of autism could not suppress it. *Baby is Mommy's favorite.* There it is, that's why he walked away so brusquely. His eyes are overflowing with fast tears and locked longingly on mine. He is searching my eyes; he needs an answer.

"NO, my love, NO. You're wrong. I could never love anyone more than you, I couldn't even if I tried. *You* are my first love, the first love of my life. You will always be my first love and greatest little boy on earth. *Always.*"

My voice is quivering because I cannot be sure if he truly understands my words, and I need him to understand, just as he needs me to understand. We have never had a true conversation, and never an exchange about anything as important as this. And I realize at this moment that there are still many crucial truths about Zack that I have yet to uncover. Does he feel love deeply, and does he feels it for me? Is he capable of comprehending complexity and change and maybe even birth? He is capable of experiencing jealousy and loss as much as any other person, maybe even more? These are horrible discoveries for Zack, but they are magnificent for me.

And once again, he has given me more than enough to compensate for his previous anger—he's gone further than ever before in explaining just how much he's suffering and why, and what he needs from me to reassure him. Yes, there's a soul inside this remarkable child that needs nurturing. He feels justifiably threatened. Once again, Zack is magical, performing the astonishing feat of rescuing me from despair by finding the right sequence of words at the right moment to prove his love for me and insist that my faith be restored. No matter what, no matter who else enters our orbit, he belongs with me and I with him—always.

He suddenly breaks eye contact with me and thrusts his quaking little body into mine, sobbing uncontrollably and gripping me hard. "Mommy! Mommy! Mommy!" he sobs. He need not stop. I can't get enough of the record this time.

Still sore from childbirth, I gingerly slink down to the ground and slowly wrap my arms and legs around him fully, as I've done so many times before today. Together we rock gently on the floor, creating our own physical rocking chair. No more words are needed; we understand each other perfectly. Our love is deep, mutual and permanent. And in that brief communication of his, those rare and astonishing moments of clarity, I know that he knows it, too.

THE ECLiPSE

I've looked at love from both sides now
From give and take and still somehow
It's love's illusions I recall
I really don't know love at all.

—"*BOTH SIDES NOW*" SONG LYRICS
BY JONI MITCHELL

CHARLES DICKENS FAMOUSLY wrote of the dichotomy between warring political factions: "It was the best of times; it was the worst of times." There is no better way to describe the painful chasm in my house six months after bringing Cassie home. My two children could not be more different. Separated by five years, one child expresses need in raging outbursts which provoke my hostility, while the other is a tranquil and remarkably perceptive infant who seems already to comprehend nuances about life far beyond her months. She seems to have absorbed that her brother functions differently than the rest of us. She observes him with a calm, detached smile, which suggests compassion, while Zack continues to glare and revile her presence. While I deeply love both of my children, I dare not ask myself whose personality I prefer. I can't hide how smitten I am with my daughter, nor my growing antipathy towards my son.

Over the past months I swear Zack has transmogrified into a virtual vampire. He stays up into the wee morning hours, wreaking nocturnal havoc by bounding around loudly in his room to create a distraction from the many times I must visit Cassie throughout the night for her feeds. Zack is so acutely sensitive to my movements, my wakefulness, that almost on cue he awakens to stomp loudly on the floor of his bedroom seemingly in protest to all the attention his sister is now getting. He is erupting daily into feral tantrums and aggression towards me. His outbursts are triggered by slights as simple as Cassie's hungry whine, the sight of her nursing or me changing her diapers. Within seconds of watching her, his angry tirade begins, and due to his burgeoning weight to now at sixty pounds, his physical explosions literally send tremors throughout the house. On the first floor's ceiling, light fixtures and bulbs shatter from his slamming on the floor above. Water comes spurting through ceiling light fixtures because of his vengeful decision to overflow the bathtub upstairs. His fists pound so regularly on his bedroom walls that portions eventually cave as he craters them into large holes and exposed pink rows of cottony insulation, which he now eats in fistfuls only to forcefully vomit up hours later onto the living room or kitchen floor.

Worse than the house damage is what Zack's doing to me. He lashes out at me with piercing bites—simply opening the refrigerator door to grab Cassie's bottle I'm met with a vengeful bite on the wrist. His jaws are so practiced and determined the wounds are now bloody, piercing the flesh and breaking capillaries. Once, just after I nursed Cassie, he actually lurched over her lying in my arms and bit my breast. For Cassie's sake I remain sanguine and absorb the exquisite pain, biting down hard as tears spring to my eyes. I remain silent, not wanting to signal my pain at the savagery Zack is capable of. For as long as Cassie's incapable of understanding the whole truth about Zack, I am determined that she believe Zack is typical, that nothing about his behavior is extraordinary. I try to remind myself as well that to some degree this is normal and even what I'd hoped for, that Zack would exhibit some level of jealousy over the new baby who has distracted my sole attention from him. Sibling rivalry is typical, so it's developmentally important that Zack learn to share me. But I'm exhausted from late-night feedings, and suffering chapped, sore nipples and sleep deprivation, and furious that I have other wounds inflicted by Zack. My patience is at a dangerous tipping point.

Living in Cassie's shadow can't be easy for Zack. She is an absolute gem of an infant. Animated and responsive, she inspires me to engage her in long conversations about everything from politics to lullabies. Not that she comprehends what I'm saying, though she's so keenly attentive I swear she actually might. It's just thrilling to see how absorbed she is by my every word, occasionally crinkling her little nose with a furrowed brow when she disagrees. Her eye contact is prolonged and sustained, solemn when she gathers from my tone that our topic is serious, but sparkling and animated when the story is fanciful, especially when it involves tickling. She emits laughs so deep they quake her body.

Unlike Zack as a baby, Cassie is exceptionally watchful of my every move. To me she seems even more advanced than a typical six-month-old in the way she studies me—my voice, my gait, my gestures—as if precociously trying to absorb what it means to be a woman. Even breastfeeding is coming more easily, and in those precious moments when she and I are alone, my flow is healthy and abundant, likely because I'm much so more relaxed with her. In short, Cassie exhibits everything Zack did not, and more. I feel truly appreciated, indispensable, valued. I'm not just smitten but truly grateful to my daughter for allowing me finally to know true reciprocal joy and interdependence. So this is why so many parents describe newborns as transformative, revolutionary and all-encompassing. Now I get it. Now I can't pretend that I don't.

I should keep my feelings in check so Zack doesn't suspect anything, but I honestly can't help this. From the moment I first accepted that Cassie did not have autism, I was determined to keep one foot happily planted in each world—special needs and typically developing. But my feet, brain and heart have been totally hijacked by this girl. I've spent years on my hands and knees tending to Zack's every need, been swiped and bitten and smeared for so long, so this time alone with Cassie feels *earned*, whether Zack can handle it or not. I just wish Zack's therapists would step up their hours to keep him occupied more of the day so I could spend more uninterrupted time with her.

I confess, I'm scared of my growing resentment towards Zack. I cannot see a way out or how will it ever subside in the face of such obvious, lasting discrepancies between my two children. I've never been one to repress my fantasies, the theme of which are now overwhelmingly versions of "starting over." No matter how bleak the situation was with Zack these past five years, never did I ever want him *gone*. If anything, in my darkest hours *I* wanted to be the one enveloped into the ground to put an end to the pain. But now I indulge in "wish fulfillment" imaginings.

Just for a moment, what if Cassie was our first and only child? What if Keith and I could start over with just her and then have just one more typical child? Now that we know it's reproductively possible, the notion is intoxicating, the vision of Cassie as the older sibling to another adorable healthy baby, rounding out the family to the four I'd originally envisioned, before all hell broke loose.

No one who hasn't walked in my shoes gets to judge me. How could any parent who's just tasted the alternative to being hit, bitten, and defiled not secretly yearn to turn her back on the past? Shameful and treasonous thoughts, perhaps, but also natural in light of what I've lived.

But I must rein it in. The situation is that I have two children equally deserving of my love. And if my affinity for one isn't coming quite as naturally as before, I'll fake it. Lavish him with kisses and hugs, remind myself what a gentle and innocent being he is. Retrain myself to tolerate his behaviors; retrain my mind to behave as if my feelings haven't changed, and pray for the genuine feelings to catch up with the affectionate pretense.

But another hideous reality emerges. It's unsafe to leave Cassie alone with Zack; she could be in genuine danger.

My brief visit to the toilet yesterday was interrupted by a sudden frantic scream that had me tearing and tripping downstairs before I'd even finished. It seemed Zack passed alongside Cassie as she bobbed happily in her bouncy chair where I'd momentarily left her. Zack pushed the chair ruthlessly forward, causing Cassie to smack the wood floor hard, face first. Still strapped in, her face struck the dangling fidget toys affixed to the upper bar of the chair, causing angry red indentations and scratches along her forehead. Another day while Keith was on watch, Zack seemed safely occupied on an indoor treadmill with Cassie playing quietly beside him on the floor. Within seconds, with Keith's back turned, Zack hopped off the moving belt and viciously thrust her body towards it, causing an elongated, bubbling burn to rip across her tiny back as she shrieked in terror and searing pain.

Poor Cassie is confounded at why her brother seems to hate her. She's honestly trying to make sense of why he's ready at a moment's notice to inflict serious, premeditated injury. She's far too young to understand Zack's condition. Many times I've tried patiently explaining to Zack how much Cassie adores him, looks up to him, can't wait to become his very best friend. But it's unpersuasive, not to mention untrue: all she feels about Zack is pure terror. Upon seeing Cassie's bloody back welts I immediately flew into a violent rage, grasping Zack hard by the arm and dragging him to look at her burns, screaming at the top of my lungs, "FOR GOD'S SAKE, ZACK, SHE'S A BABY! She's not remotely a threat to you!" I must bite my tongue hard before I spew something truly hateful. Even if he doesn't fully grasp the words, he definitely absorbs the vitriol. I am the adult here, but I can see how easily my impulses will devour both Zack and me if I don't clamp down very hard.

One day later, upon seeing carnivorous, unmistakable bite marks on Cassie's tiny plump arm, I'm truly aghast that Zack would go this far. "STOP IT! DO NOT TOUCH HER, EVER!" My scream is at fever pitch, so shrill that I now sound every bit as volatile and deafening as he does in his worst tantrums.

I will terrify him into obedience if that's what it takes to keep her safe, knowing that the more protective my reflexes are towards her, the more loudly I scream at him, and the more he will believe I prefer her. With every verbal laceration, I validate his deepest fears—that he's been replaced. And given the vicious "catch-22" into which he's put me, the more I defend Cassie and lash out on her behalf, the more he will grow to hate her.

One early evening, I lapse into a deep sleep the second I lie down. In my semi-conscious state I hear echoes of a steady wail intermingled with my dreams. But when the wail breaks into a sudden blood-curdling screech I jolt awake, foggy and furious. *Damn it, can I have one single moment of peace?* Racing down the staircase, my feet barely touching the steps, I'm stopped cold by an inexplicable mirage—Zack crouched down on both knees, covered in soft brown smears along his face and torso, with Cassie seated beside him similarly smeared.

"Zack!" I gasp in disbelief, "what are you doing?"

But the smell is actually scrumptious; Zack must have gotten hold of the pan of underdone, cooling brownies I just made and absconded with them. The sheer physics are impossible—I placed the pan well out of reach above the kitchen counter in a closed cabinet, precisely so no one would be seduced by the smell. Zack can't climb up a tall chair, much less onto the kitchen counter, or the cabinet above it. It's impossible, but the proof is unfolding before my eyes that Zack somehow made it happen, because no one else is home. As he fitfully jams his face with cake with one fist, he sloppily shovels some into Cassie's mouth with the other as she rebelliously spits and shrieks in rage. *Is he trying to feed her, or maybe just silence her?*

Spying me on the stairs, he suddenly declares with perfect diction, "Cassie wants brownies!" I go from shock to awe as I stifle a raucous laugh. I dare not giggle when poor Cassie is so inflamed, but I can't help but admire my prince. How spontaneous an act of self-preservation! *Very well done, Zack*, I smile approvingly, *you've just mastered the art of manipulation*. For a child with so few words, how cleverly he just arranged them to lay the blame at Cassie's feet, a transparent effort to save his own ass. *Now that's how a typical child subverts his sibling; that's an important developmental and cognitive achievement*. I absolutely love it!

As I approach them on the ground, Zack quickly ducks his head and shuffles back towards the wall in anticipation. *Surely mommy will scream again*, he must think. He knows he's been bad in more ways than one, so punishment is imminent. But he didn't just defy physics and execute a superb theft. *He shared the booty with his sister*.

Smiling wordlessly, I kneel down and tenderly begin wiping Cassie's screaming face, now beet red and contorted by rage. I scoop her up swiftly and carry her into her bedroom, quietly closing the door behind me as I bounce and sway to calm her.

I have no intention of depriving Zack of cake for which he took great risk and displayed great ingenuity against all odds, against the prospect of punishment, against the laws of physics. No, these brownies weren't just seized, they were earned.

It really was a noble gesture by Zack to involve Cassie. Maybe he aligned himself with her because he reasoned that if mommy values her so much, she must be worth valuing. Or maybe I underestimated Zack's wiliness; it was brilliantly cunning to first enlist and then blame the enemy. Whether Zack acted out of a momentary lapse of hostility or for strategic reasons is secondary. The point is, he assessed a problem—both brownies and sister seem unattainable—and plotted to solve it. *Come on, Cassie, stop whining and go to sleep*, I urge her silently, bouncing impatiently. *Zack and I need to talk.*

As I descend the stairs again Zack, deliberately left alone with the pan, begins rapidly guzzling the remains so that the crime will have been worth the punishment. Darting anticipatory looks at me, he quickly scoops up a clump and offers it up, stating "Hi Mommy! Mommy want brownies? Mommy say, 'I want brownies, yes!'"

I appreciate the verbal prompt as I gratefully accept the cake, relax and slink to the floor. "Thank you, my love," I whisper as I look into his rich, beautiful dark eyes. Suddenly, the wick is relit, our love rekindled as I am reminded how desperately he wants to please me. He's showing me right this very moment, tenderly feeding me cake, and scanning my face for signs of distress.

In his watery eyes I see regret mixed with fear. Contrition and apology. He inspects me closely, then relapses into his particular verbal stim of asking repeatedly, "You OK? Mommy, are you OK? You OK?" This is his default phrase when Zack suspects I'm angry or anxious: he perseverates asking me this on a loop until I reassure him. Not just with words, because Zack is no fool. Much like an angry wife who falsely assures her spouse,

"I'm fine!" with a deliberate edge to her voice, Zack cues in to the bitter inflection and knows when I'm not. After years of studying me as much as I do him, Zack knows that when the spoken words are incongruous with the real feelings behind them they are insincere, so he keeps probing for truth. In this instance he even grasps my chin and pivots my face toward his so he can look directly into my eyes, and only then, when I calmly answer that I'm truly fine, is he satisfied. "Yes," I whisper lovingly while stroking his soft, abundant hair, "yes, I am OK, thank you for asking," I whisper hoarsely as tears begin welling up and spilling over.

As I allow him to feed me, all my resentment drains and I feel ashamed for my intolerance. Zack has not been eclipsed by Cassie. I was distracted by her charms, but my love for Zack remains wholly intact, most especially in this moment as he gently feeds me, despite what I have put him through these past months. He wants only to be loved, to feel as important to me as he always has been, to be cherished. Even in my darkest hours, he surprises me and turns me around. I cannot help but worship him—still.

THE COMMODIZATION OF HOPE

"The second day, I really remember, we got into the car and we were driving home—all of the sudden she said, 'I want cookie!.' She'd never said anything spontaneously like that before."

— "AWAKENING ASHLEY, TOMOTIS METHOD," *THE TODAY SHOW,* NBC (MAY 5, 2003)

TOMOTIS LISTENING THERAPY is now being touted as a groundbreaking intervention to improve auditory functioning in kids. The theory behind it posits that since autism is a sensory integration and communication disorder, "positive and lasting changes occur [in the autistic child] by stimulating the auditory system through channeling of certain sounds delivered to the child's brain via headphone listening." Among the palliative effects listed by vendors are:

- Decreased hypersensitivity to sound, or as one mother put it, "He can now hear the vacuum cleaner or the mixer without losing it."

- Fewer temper tantrums and less repetitive behavior. Children will also start paying more attention, and as they become less tactile-defensive, their desire to reach out will increase and they may start to interact with others. This makes them more social, more affectionate.

- For autistic children who do not speak, receptive language is likely to improve. They may try to vocalize more and start to babble, experimenting with their voice.

- For autistic children with more developed language skills, the expressive language may improve. They may use longer sentences, and find more appropriate words to describe things. They may also use personal pronouns, like "I" and "You" more correctly, instead of referring to themselves in the third person. Better mastery of language leads to an increased desire to communicate.

Despite years without fanfare, Tomotis became instantly popularized when the media spotlighted one little nonverbal girl who, after mere weeks of wearing headphones, spontaneously spoke a sentence. It's extraordinarily good fortune for me that this intervention happens to be headquartered just miles from my house. Cara unreservedly recommends that Zack participate, in addition to his ABA, so for $3,000 per treatment of consecutive listening *loops*, I feel compelled to try.

My initial research into Tomotis does not reveal concrete data or statistics, only broad and unsubstantiated claims by anonymous parents who enthusiastically report tangible changes. Still, I join the stampede of parents seeking to reverse the linguistic tides. When we enroll, there is no preliminary intake or evaluation process to determine whether Zack is a suitable candidate, because no such scientific screenings exist. Payment is due upfront and, once ushered through the turnstile, we're blocked in with no turning back and no remuneration if the mightily expensive loops fail.

One month later, as I'd secretly feared and predicted, there is no discernible progress in Zack. Which is not to say that the occupational therapists administering the headphones aren't straining to identify perceptible improvements. *See how he's turning his head to the left a little when you call out his name? See how he's walking a bit straighter and more upright?* Even the most inconsequential details are touted as proof, if one looks closely enough. But if a treatment is producing real quantifiable gains, why are we having to look so hard to see it? Shouldn't it be obvious in the form of more words spoken, objectively identifiable receptive skills, more interactive and reciprocal dialogue, or were the predictions ragingly inaccurate? Perhaps he just needs more loops—another $3,000, please.

I'm squarely immersed in the horde of parents who hemorrhaged massive income for a beguiling promise that originated with a single anecdote about a single child. In response to the therapists' insistence that Zack has made calculable gains, I confront them with questions that should have been asked at the outset: What specific criteria are you using to evaluate whether and which children will respond? Where is the recorded data? How many total children made scientifically identifiable improvement compared to the overall number of children treated? For those children who made measurable progress, how many consecutive listening loops were required? And critically, for those children who made identifiable progress, did these gains outlive the treatment itself or were they exhibited only during listening sessions and later become irretrievable?

The merchants are acutely aware that an attorney is asking

pointed and probing questions about services advertised and marketed claiming to produce specific results. I easily sense their trepidation rising. They have no intake evaluation; their progress claims were not meant to be taken literally for each child; results weren't actually guaranteed. They sincerely apologize if I feel misled.

Their sincerity is so earnest, their confidence in the treatment so durable, that they offer to provide Zack with an additional round of loops at no charge. *Surely I'll see more results if we stick with the protocol another few months.* "No, thank you," I respond.

As I stride toward the office to exit for the last time, I overhear a parent angrily contesting the insult of being charged massive amounts for a treatment which seems to have actually harmed her son. Following loops, he's now viciously pounding his head and is palpably more perseverative than when he first entered. As the therapists flounder to placate her, I feel my stomach caving. On the comparative spectrum of brazen insults, at least the "treatment" didn't provoke regressive behavior in my son. I could at least afford to be swindled, although others cannot.

Autism is its own universe, and as I've come to discover, a mercenary one. The range of medical and behavioral "cures" available to rid our children of what ails them is vast:

- gluten-free, casein-free diet
- chelation
- hyperbaric oxygen chamber
- Tomotis headphone therapy
- speech therapy
- occupational therapy
- music therapy
- horseback riding therapy
- Applied Behavioral Analysis ("ABA")

After years of hemorrhaging money while strapped to the racetrack of recovery, I can now appreciate how easy it is for us parents to get entrapped by the fretful mirage of *"if only."* "If only" I had pursued (insert marketed intervention), maybe my child would be in an entirely different and better place right now. What this guilt trip overlooks is that many of these treatments are subjective—not scientific—and are unproven to work across a broad representation of children.

Parents desperately groping in the dark for that magical elixir will naturally grab onto trends and fads that project hope—anything to rescue their child. Merchants know the lengths to which desperate parents will go. Some exploit that desperation with broad claims of amelioration, though without specific data about how many children in their care made quantifiable gains, compared with those who did not. What merchants frequently don't advertise includes: a way of assessing, prior to parental commitment, whether their unique treatment is likely to work with a particular phenotype within the spectrum; how long the treatment must be sustained; whether the improvements are permanent or only temporary while the treatment is being administered; or what concrete and measurable progress has been proven across a genuinely representative group of children on the spectrum.

To the point, I asked my ABA merchant, "Hey, Cara, I've come to know tons of autistic kids, and I know you personally are treating at least ten in our area, in addition to your caseload in New York. So, if it's true that as many as 50 percent of kids recover and become mainstreamed from ABA, why is it I don't know a single one?"

"Well, of course, parents are not going to broadcast that their mainstreamed kids once had autism! You probably already know kids who are mainstreamed, but you don't realize it."

I've done some due diligence to satisfy my curiosity about

the vaunted Ivar Lovaas and learned that the celebrated results from his original 1950s ABA trials have *never* been duplicated. I also have read that in order to ensure compliance and results from the autistic children in his experimental care, Lovaas physically struck them, and worse, to create "aversions" if they refused to respond to drills.

"Cara, I learned something deeply disturbing: that Lovaas actually hit kids to get them to speak."

Unfazed, Cara replies, "Look, Lovaas was strict, he had to be because he was breaking new ground. Did he occasionally slap them from time to time? Yes, but that wasn't the norm or the reason for their compliance."

If I was a nonverbal child with a profound disability getting smacked hard in the face, I'm pretty sure I'd do anything to stop it. It's unsurprising that such tactics produced results, and that civilized treatment of our children might not yield those same undeserved results. Continuing, Cara explains the stark disparity I'm seeing between promises made and outcomes realized.

"I do see a big difference in outcomes between the kids I'm treating here versus New York, but that has a lot to do with the parents' commitment to the *forty* hours. My parents in New York are relentless in making sure their kids are occupied constantly in therapies, not just ABA forty hours, but on top of that the kids are in speech therapy, occupational therapy . . . Those parents never let up on keeping their kids engaged 'round the clock. So, my New York parents are definitely getting better results."

I see. It's partly my fault that Zack isn't recovering, because I'm still not doing enough.

The history of autism includes a now-infamous Dr. Leo Kanner, known as the father of child psychology. He formulated the "Kanner theory" of autism, which is now derided and debunked as preposterous. Kanner posited that autism developed as a result of mothers who deprived their newborns of overt love and affection, showing only cold indifference to their infants who then went on to develop an affliction known for its aloofness and indifference called autism. The children themselves responded to the affection deprivation by becoming correspondingly detached and indifferent, helpless products of an unloving and unfeeling "refrigerator mom."

How far we've come from that archaic notion! Looking back now it seems absurd that there was a time when the fault of autism was laid at the feet of mothers who even back then were desperately struggling to connect with their children and decipher the inexplicable and misunderstood affliction. I cannot help but consider a bitter irony from my own experience.

No, Dr. Kanner. You seem to have inverted an important temporal point. There was nothing frigid about my parenting when my son was a newborn; the deep freeze set in after he was diagnosed with an incurable brain disorder. After I lost my job, my peace of mind, and a considerable amount of income, only then did I turn a little frosty. So would anyone.

It seems now that we've managed to find an alternate theory for assigning blame, though the bearer of shame remains the same. After all, once all the invoices are paid and all the hours put in, someone must be held accountable for the failure of the child to recover.

As I reflect on Cara's insinuation, my heart aches over the intense pressure for parents to do absolutely everything in their financial and emotional power to rescue their child. We investigate every conceivable option and dive in deep. No matter how unrealistic or unaffordable the treatment, no matter how unproven their efficacy, no matter whether your health insurance covers it or not, parents are expected to intervene early and often. Listening to Cara's passive recrimination, I can't help but conclude that when it comes to blaming parents and holding them accountable for their child's failure to recover, we haven't really come all that far from Leo Kanner after all.

Parents comprise the population of people desperate to do anything to cure our children amidst an industry eager to capitalize on our collective grief. It is a mercenary exchange in which money is traded for false hope. *If only.* This insidious phrase assumes that the millions of parents whose children do get the *super-intervention*, yet still don't recover, must surely be doing *something else* wrong. The assumption is that other remedies are out there and it is incumbent upon the *responsible parent* to find them and buy them.

Take a moment to Google the term *ABA* and you will be bombarded with direct and easy solutions to what ails our kids. So costly yet so simple, so simple it's a wonder that with all these purported *treatments* we aren't we seeing more and more recoveries of kids on the spectrum. It's a wonder that the headlines aren't clammoring about the epidemic of recoveries rather than the persistence of children entering adulthood who increasingly "fall off the cliff" of supports when they become ineligible for school at age twenty-one. Parents are being misled into a hall of mirrors, distracted by reflections of progress that aren't tangible or measurable, and told that even the most imperceptible changes in their child represents real growth.

What we're not told is that maybe, *just maybe,* our child has an incurable and intractable brain disorder that will only respond a finite amount to any intervention, regardless of the intensity and cost that bankrupts some families. Maybe, autism really is that inscrutable and permanent. I wonder.

Since the outset of this journey, I've never lost sight of the fact that Keith and I were able to afford the expensive interventions for Zack that other families couldn't. The tragic irony I'd love to impart to those less financially fortunate is that we might have been better off with less money and fewer choices, because with financial ability comes the corresponding obligation to explore every option you can afford. How can you do anything less when so much is at stake? But affluence cannot save Zack; it just gave us the illusion that we could.

Zack has certainly made concrete gains through his many years of ABA, but might he have made similar gains in a public preschool autism program for no cost? Might he have ended up looking identical to how he looks now at age five, or even better if he had been consistently exposed to other autistic peers in the program with whom he might have made a genuine connection? Everyone has had a stake in Zack's ABA—the consultant has her visits; the therapists get résumé experience; I get the satisfaction of administering the very best behavioral intervention on the market. *Except that providing the best that money can buy is not the same as providing the best intervention.* Because now I know for certain that we have not met all of Zack's needs.

I don't dispute that some interventions ameliorate symptoms and succeed in some children. As always, the progress is individualized. So, for any intervention there will be certain children with autism who will improve dramatically. *The key is that it's a matter of probabilities as to how many are helped against the backdrop of how many total children tried the identical interventions with no tangible improvement.* My dispute is with interventions that claim indiscriminate success and market to the autism population at large, without providing full data disclosure. They lure parents into believing that the more we spend on intervention, the better the odds of improvement.

As we seek to justify our massive expenses and allow merchants to do the same, we risk losing sight of the governing principle—treatment must actually move the child forward in discernible ways that allow him to better function and engage in the world. It's why, knowing what I now know, I have far more respect for the diagnostician who admits that autism is variable and that no one can predict the outcome for any given child.

The media spotlighting the exceedingly rare recovery story isn't helping. The tendency to feature the infinitely sexier story about "the amazing breakthrough" only further peddles the mercenary commodization of false hope. I don't fault the media for covering the breakthrough story, but for failing to put in context that the very reason it's newsworthy is because it's the exception to the rule. I fault those stories which hype the child's breakthrough but fail to inquire of the merchant how many total other children who received the identical treatment failed to make any definable progress. Those stories would require the merchant to explain how and why this particular child responded whereas others did not, or admit that the merchant truly does not know.

To report responsibly and defuse false hope, the media would be wise to ask, for the "breakthrough child," about the length of time the treatment was administered, for what total cost, what portion was covered by health insurance, and what are the financial or other mitigating remedies for parents for whom the identical treatment is tried and failed. Were parents reimbursed or is the game played as a matter of luck? *Pay your money and take your chances, but be advised that the house gets paid whether or not your child responds.*

Hope predicated on the rarest of outcomes is not hope at all but a mirage dangled to induce payment. Hope predicated on the thrilling breakthrough story that fails to account for the legions of children for whom the identical treatment has been tried and failed, is failing to hold merchants accountable to the consumers they purport to serve. Hope that is not predicated on hard, provable data and statistics is simply *false hope*, a lottery ticket for those willing to pay. But if the odds that a particular treatment actually succeeds is as unattainably low as winning the lottery, if consumers are informed of the realistic probabilities of success, parents might think twice before laying out their hard-earned income for an exceedingly rare result. And if they are, unscrupulous merchants who seek to exploit parents' desperate attempts to rescue their children might then go out of business.

In the wise and embittered words regarding racial disparity, famed author Ta-Nehisi Coates said, "Hope is not feel-goodism built on the belief in unicorns . . . Hope is not magical. Hope is earned." And while the parents agonize about whether they've done enough, sacrificed enough of their lives, expended enough energy every waking hour, the wheels of commerce keep spinning. And while the merchants bleed the families dry, the child continues to flap.

REWRITE
THE FAIRYTALE

But somebody's gonna have to answer
The time is coming soon
Amidst all these questions and contradictions
There are some who seek the truth

—"*WHY*" SONG LYRICS BY TRACY CHAPMAN

WIDE AWAKE BESIDE Keith in the middle of the night, I can't sleep because I must finally acknowledge a truth that has been staring me in the face: Zack is at the critical age of five and he is not going to make it.

For at least the past year, Zack has not made any meaningful strides. Three years and hundreds of thousands of dollars after our ABA therapy first began, after observing hundreds of other children who received comparable intervention at an early age, I no longer buy into the ABA statistics of recovery. At best, ABA is helping a very slight percentage of children to attain conceptual mastery sufficient to mainstream. At worst, ABA is churning out legions of autistic children whose main accomplishments are compliance, rote memorization, and attendance to task rather than genuine function.

Whether I'm right or wrong about the overall numbers, I'm right about Zack. In my heart I know. I need only glance at him to know that Zack has not mastered enough functional skills or compensating behaviors to ever pass for normal or become mainstreamed in general education by the time he gets to kindergarten. The pivotal battle is over and we have lost.

It's agony to utter the words aloud. With them, I finally kill the fairytale that Zack would be functionally normal and be fully included in school, have regular play dates with peers, develop typical romantic relationships, go to college, marry, and so much more. Also shattered is the fairytale that hard work pays off, that if you do everything right, work diligently day and night and throw all your energy and resources into a project, your efforts will yield corresponding results. For the first time in my life, all of my dedication and intense work ethic didn't pay off, and my absolute best fell short of success. Slowly I turn my head on the pillow toward a slumbering Keith and gently rouse him from his sleep. *We need to talk, there are things I need to understand.*

"Keith, he's not going to make it," I whisper calmly as he awakens groggily. "I've been struggling with this for so long but, I need to just say it, out loud, to you. Zack isn't going to make it."

Keith stares upwards at the ceiling serene and composed as he responds, "I know."

"You do? You've been watching this happen, too, and you agree he isn't catching up enough and isn't going to make it?"

"Yes," he replies calmly. No trace of disappointment or regret—just calm.

I'm amazed by his equanimity and sit up to face him. "Keith, how are you okay with this? I'm not attacking you. I mean it. I'm ready to listen. I just don't understand how you don't seem at all shattered or even disappointed by this, you've never have felt that way. Have you?"

"Because Zack is fine, he always was," he says. "I know you don't believe me when I say he's fine, but I mean it. Zack will be fine regardless." Answering my bewildered expression he continues. "You think I don't see what's happening with him and all the work you've been doing, but I do. And we have both done our absolute best to help him, the best therapies, best interventions, all the love and support we've given to him. And, if after all the hours and dedication we've put in he still doesn't recover, then he wasn't meant to. Then this is who he is—a healthy, happy and loving little boy . . . with autism."

I am speechless at his candor, his ability to slice through any artifice and get right to the bottom line with such clarity and, as I'm just now realizing, foresight. Because it seems Keith long ago seized upon a truth that, in my frantic attempts to rescue Zack I did not—the possibility that Zack's autism might be so ingrained that it's impervious to even the strictest and earliest attempts to reverse it. What Keith kept to himself was an understanding that Zack might always remain fundamentally the same child he was at birth, and that this outcome was fine. All these years that I thought Keith was passive and deliberately in denial, it was he who foresaw the "worst-case scenario" and accepted it. It was Keith who was both prescient and prepared for Zack to emerge unchanged. He made peace with it and adored Zack unconditionally, regardless of outcome. I'm captivated by Keith's every word.

". . . and, if he never gets better than this current functioning level, if his autism means he ends up living with us for the rest of our lives, then that is fine, too. Because I love him so much. He's such a pure and loving child that I'm happy that he will always be tied to us and dependent. He doesn't have to recover or be independent to make me happy or be happy himself. And that's all that matters. I don't care if he's like everyone else." Keith's voice cuts off suddenly as he swallows hard, still calm but momentarily overwhelmed by his intense love for our special child.

I stare at him in stunned silence, letting his words fully sink in. I had no idea this was how he had processed Zack's disability, but then again I never asked without anger. All these years that Keith kept saying Zack was "fine," this extraordinary man was actually telling the truth.

It feels strange to allow for a different perspective on Zack. I've been so enraged, so tightly bound to the race to cross that vaunted finish line, that I lost sight of any outcome short of recovery as acceptable. Tolerance for competing viewpoints is not a muscle I have exercised in quite some time. Living inside my own mind, feeling abandoned and alone, I never gave alternative perspectives a chance. I never imagined that my husband had metabolized Zack's failure to recover so differently, that he was actually watching Zack every bit as closely as I was, but arrived at a different conclusion which he carried alone because he knew I couldn't bear it.

Forgiveness is both an act and a character trait that has not come easily for me since this all started. Initially, I could not forgive myself for past misdeeds that I believed were in some cosmic way responsible for my fate of being unemployed, chained to the house and tethered to a task I despised. I've been unable to forgive my husband for his supposed denial of the seriousness of Zack's prognosis. I equated Keith's reference to Zack being "fine" as his refusal to acknowledge Zack's situation as a tragedy, and so it was either Keith's deliberate defiance or insipid failure to fully grasp the facts. As Zack's aggressive behaviors began to emerge, I routinely extended a charitable interpretation to his ferocious bites and smacks because I knew they were not maliciously intended, but instead just a byproduct of his intense frustration at not being able to express himself verbally. But I have not extended the same charity to my husband, nor to his legitimate interpretation of Zack's condition because it differed so agonizingly from mine. I've been intolerant of his tolerance.

Then he wasn't meant to recover, so says Zack's father. I must sit with this for a while as Keith, having spoken his piece, drifts soundly back off to sleep. I've been grieving over a child who is alive and happy. A mother bereaved, only my child is able to laugh and run free and maybe even a great deal more if I'm willing to contemplate a different outcome for him. If I abandon my ambition to rewire his brain and surrender my insatiable habit of comparing him unfavorably to typically developing children, I might see clear to a different path and become of far greater use. I've been an animal lunging at a lure dangled endlessly before my eyes, but permanently out of reach. And now it's time to stop. Stop lashing out at friends and, instead, let them help me any way they can. I know now I can't survive this journey alone, and neither can Zack, and neither can my marriage to this extraordinary man I just met. . . again.

An oft-quoted definition of insanity is to continue to do the identical actions and expect different results. Right now, the only thought more terrifying than dismantling Zack's home therapy program is sticking with it, because I know we're not to get Zack where he needs to go by relentlessly dragooning him to the same tried and tested methods which have failed him. I don't take for granted the very real gains that ABA protocol achieved—his nascent language, early reading, enhanced auditory comprehension, and the importance of being able to sit and comply with teaching demands. I don't want to eviscerate the program but only to modify it so that we keep pushing him to read and learn as long as he demonstrates progress.

I should not make therapy decisions impulsively, but I'm actually at my least emotional right now. I am a scientist parsing facts, looking for evidence, and contemplating new theories. It's time to stop chasing "normal" and acquiescing to the forty-hour mandate; it will be replaced by twenty hours to be administered mornings only. I'm not asking permission. I'll notify Cara on her next progress visit after I've evaluated how the new hours are working for Zack. No longer under a fairytale spell, I can lean on my own cultivated expertise about Zack, think outside the ABA box, and craft an alternate ending to his story with an entirely different purpose and new chapters. Let's begin.

CHAPTER 1: IS IT POSSIBLE THAT ZACK CAN LEAD A FULL AND PRODUCTIVE LIFE EVEN IF HE NEVER RECOVERS?

I'll let my mind go to the place I feared most and imagine Zack's dependence on others for the rest of his life, even when I'm gone. I'm aware of a few outstanding day and residential programs in my area for adults with disabilities. The adults each have a one-to-one aide and live in regular apartment buildings around town which they share with another other disabled peer. They assume regular household chores and daily schedules which include recreation and part-time employment. No caretaker can possibly take my place with Zack, but if the aide is attentive, qualified and kind, would Zack ending up in residential care be the worst thing? Or might it lead to a contented, protected and more productive life, given his limitations? Aides, known as *direct support providers,* aren't paid well, not nearly commensurate with their enormous daily responsibilities. The type of person who studies and trains to become an aide to a disabled adult is indisputably extraordinary. Maybe one day I'll advocate for well-deserved higher wages. This future is certainly not what I imagined or dreamed for Zack when he was born, but I can certainly envision far worse scenarios even for typical children who fall upon hard times, become addicted to opioids, or are miserable in their adult lives because their ambitions didn't go as planned. *I might even know an adult whose future and ambition didn't go as planned.* But Zack's life still has the potential to be as happy, fulfilling and productive as those who possess greater natural advantages and skills.

Zack does have unusual skills, obsessive and exacting rituals that could be put to efficient economic use if nurtured and trained up into the right kind of task. Maybe the child who loves to visually scrutinize details of objects could be trained to be a TSA employee at the airport who examines photographic screenings of luggage to identify any banned products. I recently heard of a car wash that exclusively hires adults on the spectrum to perform all the cleaning and drying labor, precisely because of their remarkable and ritualistic attention to detail. The employer, who himself has an adult brother with autism, claims his are the most stellar employees—punctual, honest, industrious employees who work from the moment they arrive until their tasks are completed. This employer boasts that he tapped into an unmet workforce potential that's yielding profit and market benefits he'd never previously known.

Given the ways Zack decodes the world, I can easily understand why people on the spectrum who are properly trained for tasks others might eschew would perform them not merely as well, but better than their non-disabled peers. Our kids are powered by an innate ability to excel at tasks too tediously rote and complicated for others to maintain. Plumbing intricacies, architectural details, software testing, cosmetics application, animal grooming, hospital and hotel room cleaning, detailed home inspections—job opportunities range as far as the imaginative eye can see. I've heard that large software companies are catching on and selectively choosing autistic employees for those unique, discrete tasks for which they are innately qualified. Sounds like a very good wave to ride.

The more I consider it, the more I realize I may have less to fear than I first imagined, and that it is rationally possible for Zack to have a productive place in society regardless of whether he overcomes autism. Maybe the key lies in working with his disability and unique attributes rather than rewiring them, in finding those niches for which he and others like him are already wired. Maybe *normalcy* is not what's precious; certainly it's not a guarantee of those things I desperately want for my son. If I'm to survive intact, my focus must shift towards identifying productive roles that Zack is competently able to perform, to the best of his ability and limitations, with an attentiveness on what he can do instead of on what he cannot.

I consider the adults I know from my own childhood who grew up to become disenchanted, unproductive, and deeply unhappy. Zack is none of these things yet. He is strongly motivated and industrious with genuine passion and intense drive. So, we must channel and shape that energy into employable skills that allow him to contribute as an adult. But if Zack's potential is to be fully realized, I must first get him over his intense phobias that are constricting his ability to access so many places and become a true participant in his community. I'm going to have to make some mental adjustments of my own.

CHAPTER 2: WHO IS THIS CHILD AND WHAT AM I SO ASHAMED OF?

One need only reference the news to learn of the depraved ways with which purportedly typical people treat one another. Gunfire fatalities are triggered by something as trivial as road rage. Esteemed professionals and clergymen entrusted to positions of power commit heinous acts of abuse towards subordinates, even children, in their care. Packs of teens ruthlessly bully a vulnerable peer who then tragically takes her life. Parents understand all too well the cruelty that teens, whose brains have not fully biologically matured, can inflict upon one another as they fail to appreciate the devastating and even criminal consequences. News is rife with incidents of date rape committed by unscrupulous and entitled young men against inebriated and unconscious young women. Revenge porn, hacking, exposing private secrets and photos to the world premeditated to humiliate and undo others, bigotry, racism, harassment, misogyny, assault—isn't that the stuff of shame? I had trouble getting out of bed to assist my disabled son in those early days. Imagine if my son had raped an unconscious girl behind a dumpster. How difficult it would be to rise from my bed to defend him in court?

But that is not my son. When Zack physically lashes out, it's a defensive reaction to something aversive or terrifying. He does not premeditate or intentionally inflict harm on others. He does not derive pleasure from holding down or degrading others for his own gain. He is fundamentally incapable of deceit or subterfuge. He is neither a bigot nor does he consider himself superior to others. All are equal in his unpolluted eyes. Zack is simply an innocent child trying to navigate a world that doesn't speak his language.

What exactly has me fleeing home in disgrace when Zack explodes in public? Against the backdrop of truly demoralizing behavior exhibited by others in our society, why do I bow my head in burning shame and vacate the premises? And when I occasionally lash out verbally at gaping bystanders in bitter defensiveness, what signal am I inadvertently sending to Zack about how I view him? That I am so mortified by his behavior, so angry to have been dealt this hand—this child—that I'm ready to smack down others in rage?

Zack is a child with a profound disability that causes him occasionally to lose control. We all lose control at times. The difference is we don't commonly do it in public. Even as bookstore shelves are stocked to overflowing with self-help books on managing anger, anxiety and panic attacks, I still feel compelled to grovel and seek forgiveness for my disabled child because he struggles with the identical issues and lacks the capacity to be comforted by the same self-help books the rest of us are reading.

CHAPTER 3: DO i HAVE THE COURAGE TO HELP ZACK TRULY JOiN THE WORLD?

Zack has been thoroughly preoccupied with intensive drills in a confined room, but he has not meaningfully inhabited the real world. He has not experienced enough of all the recreational choices the world has to offer to make educated decisions about how he wants to spend his time. But even when exposed to social venues, he has been so hobbled by intense and misguided fears that he still has not truly accessed the facilities. And now I must override those fears by any means necessary. I must teach him through brutal exposure what's really going to happen to him when we resist his instinct to flee, and instead, stay rooted to the spot for as long as it takes for him to understand what truly awaits him, what treasures exist in his community that others enjoy to which he, too, is entitled. My methods will be unorthodox and, to outward appearances, ruthless. Given Zack's furious protest against remaining in places he fears, I will need to physically restrain him—sit on him, hold him down while he is writhing and screaming. And now I must truly withstand the public scorn and backlash that's sure to accompany us everywhere we go, in each and every venue into which I forcibly shove him.

But I've already endured the stares and remarks that come with having a conspicuously unusual child who yelps and flaps and bounces for no apparent reason. Surely I can endure the ridicule once more in pursuit of the noble goal of getting Zack truly integrated into his environment. I have spent enough of his life dragging him kicking and screaming away from venues; this time I will drag him toward them, with a mission. I will not be able to explain to strangers, who look on with horror, why I am adopting such austere methods. They can't know that I've tried every single less invasive alternate in trying to get my son over his fears. Social stories, verbal encouragement, physical prompts and unyielding emotional support are insufficient; we are at the end of the line and there is no other option than battle. My son will not be confined to the house and virtual institutional living as long as I have the personal resources to prevent it.

And really, what do I have to fear at this point from the public condemnation I have already experienced so many times before with Zack? Cruel remarks will be slung at me. *But can anything anyone says begin to compete with the private disgrace and terrifying thoughts I myself have already thought about me and my son?* No. *Is there any injury a stranger can inflict upon me with words that can possibly rival the wound inflicted by Zack's initial diagnosis, and my realization that he is permanently cognitively disabled?* No. There is nothing anyone can take from me that my years of living in shame, pain, and profound disappointment in early intervention have not already fed upon; there's nothing left to ravage. And, on a genuinely positive note, there is nothing anyone can hurl at me that will convince me that my son is anything other than precious and worthy of the extreme measures I intend to take to save him. Right now, my son cannot leave the house and participate in the world; if this remains the case then I have already lost everything. But if I take a momentous and educated risk on my son—and win—the tides may turn forever in our favor. And in contrast to all the money hemorrhaged so far on behavioral interventions, this risk is free. The only tools required are courage, persistence and a willingness to endure public scrutiny. In exchange for Zack's life, that's a risk I'm now willing to take.

Bystanders cannot know, in the violent moments they will witness, that as uncomfortable as they feel watching, I am ten times more uncomfortable. And desperate. *But not ashamed, not any more.*

Zack is not going to recover from autism through ABA or any other means. Suddenly, this conclusion which I've railed against for so long is finally liberating me. Ironically, it's not until all hope of a normal life for Zack has been eliminated that I can contemplate the possibility of a real life for my disabled son. And this is not resignation; if anything, it feels like rebirth. It's time to topple the status quo—of shame and disgrace, of false hope and invisible progress. Time to take a wrecking ball to the traditional expectations to which both Zack and I have ceded for far too long. I don't know how this will end, I just know I'm ready to take a serious risk that for once feels within my control and for which I'm prepared to be held fully accountable. I'm tired of losing our lives and watching our universe contract. I'm willing to go to radical and unknown lengths to prevent that from happening.

I don't know how this will end, but one thing is certain: we're going out and I'm done apologizing for my child.

THiS iS GOiNG TO HURT

There are some things one can only achieve by a deliberate leap in the opposite direction.

—FRANZ KAFKA

"KEITH, I WANT to take him out; I want to take him to all the places he's afraid of," I announce one evening.

"What . . . why? What does Cara think?"

"I'm not telling Cara. I asked her not to come down this month. I just need a little break from the monthly progress meetings, time to try something new."

"Zack's getting out enough. There are still enough places he can manage, so we don't need to force him."

"Zack needs more than just heading back to the same few places he can manage," I respond. "I know you're always saying he's such a happy little boy, but imagine how much happier he'd be if he could go anywhere without fear. Did it ever dawn on you that maybe he's sick and tired of his life, sick of feeling afraid of dark indoor spaces for reasons he himself doesn't fully understand? I've tried everything in our arsenal to get him over his phobias, but nothing is translating from flashcards, books or social stories. I can't reason with him ahead of time or in the moment, so there's only one thing left that might work."

"So what exactly are you thinking of doing?"

"I'm going to drag him into the places he fears and physically restrain him for as long as it takes to show him he has nothing to fear. I'll go in baby steps, inch by inch, and I'll be right there with him whispering in his ear every step of the way. We're not leaving just because he starts screaming. We're going to ride it out until he stops, even if it's just from sheer exhaustion. But we'll never know what he's capable of overcoming if we keep fleeing the scene the minute things get rough."

"So you're going to hold him down against his will after everything he's been through? That's barbaric and completely unfair to him. What about respecting his voice like you're always saying? Obviously, if he's screaming, he's trying to tell you he feels unsafe and needs to leave, and if you override that you are deliberately ignoring his communication, which is what you're always preaching needs to be respected!"

Keith is not wrong. What I'm proposing is wholly inconsistent with my own policy of respecting Zack's voice. But his screaming terror is borne of a misunderstanding about the danger he perceives, and I know for certain there are activities and venues Zack would adore if he understood he had nothing to fear. Even if it requires forcible exposure and suppressing his will in favor of a greater truth he's yet to discover about himself, I believe we must err on the side of giving him accurate information in furtherance of him eventually making informed choices. Nothing short of forcible and repeat exposure will work, so now I'm prepared to take the path of greatest resistance on Zack's behalf. I'm not looking forward to traumatizing my child, nor am I seeking to incite a tantrum. To the contrary, the objective is to push past that initial explosive reaction for the sake of his comprehension. This is not my first choice, but it is now my only choice.

"Keith, this is the only life he gets; it's the only life we get, and it's shrinking fast. He's not making the kind of progress in therapy to overcome his phobias, and every time we give in and let him escape, he's still traumatized anyway and his phobias are getting more deeply ingrained. Soon we'll hit a point where we can't get him out of the house, on a plane, into a hospital, even if it's urgent. All we're doing now is ensuring he stays stuck. I need to break the pattern, now, while he's still young and I'm still physically strong enough to do it. You've always said this is about him, and we owe him this. If he's not going to acquire enough speech or relationships to sustain him, the least we can do is get him as strong and functional as he's capable of being. We owe him a life, and we deserve a life, too."

"But it's physically painful for him." Keith counters. "Look how he reacts whenever we're in a bowling alley or movie theater. He grabs his ears and covers them frantically like he's in real pain. Obviously the crowds and chaos is too much for him. He's over stimulated and painfully sensitive, and now you're talking about deliberately inflicting more pain. That's just wrong!"

I expected Keith's reaction and love him even more because of what it represents—his protective and fervent defense of Zack, his willingness to go extreme lengths to ensure that Zack is never in pain. But what I'm suggesting is that Zack is already in pain and we're not helping him adapt to the world if we're constantly striving to avoid unpleasant encounters with it. At some point, Keith and I will be gone and Zack will have to confront his fears, or else be confined to institutional living. I'm every bit as much on my son's side, and I have studied Zack's intense reactions to dark interior spaces where he lacks visual cues to guide him. And I've come to believe we've drawn the wrong conclusions from the exterior manifestations of Zack's anxiety.

"I've been watching Zack closely and he covers his ears and beats his head when he's terrified and feels out of control, not because the noise is physically painful. Think about it: he manages outdoor sporting events, like games in packed stadiums where he's surrounded by loud cheering, and he doesn't even flinch— because everything he needs to know about his surroundings can be seen. He's thrilled by amusement parks despite all the crowds and chaos. The only time he tantrums is on rides which guide him indoors, which is ironically much calmer and quieter. It's the fear of the visual unknown that terrifies him, so when he's being led into an indoor space he panics because he lacks the visual information and that's what triggers the terror. The frantic clamping down on his ears is just how he expresses his dread. So, we have to reset the record playing inside his mind."

I'm met with a quizzical gaze, but I recall a discussion I had with an autism expert who lectured recently at a conference. He raised an interesting behavioral point, the science of *negative reinforcement*, which posits that people are not just motivated by reward, but by avoidance of negative consequences. Drivers hit the brakes at a red light not because it's inherently satisfying, but to avoid getting pulled over, ticketed or having a collision. He made a fascinating connection. When parents surrender to their autistic child's tantrum and abandon the cause, they inadvertently reinforce the tantrum as an effective means of avoiding aversions.

Put another way, giving in to the tantrum negatively reinforces that escape mechanism, thereby crystallizing in the child's mind that the tantrum is useful in escaping whatever he finds aversive. Unsurprisingly, the child begins to invoke the tantrum habitually in response to those things he wishes to avoid. But in Zack's case, allowing him to escape feared venues via tantrum has the compound effect of reinforcing the phobia itself. Allowing him to flee the scene confirms his exaggerated fears by signaling to him that he was right to escape because there was indeed something to fear.

As Keith silently marinates on the larger scientific backdrop, it's clear to him that I've put in a great deal of time examining this issue.

The role of intense eidetic memory in the mind of an autistic child strikes me as essential in explaining the residual fears that play on long after the perceived danger is avoided. Autistic children experience the world in a repetitive way, often engaging in ritualistic comforts of flapping, and lining up objects in order to impose a measure of personal order on chaos. It's not surprising that when the child is thrust into an unfamiliar situation outside the boundaries of the world to which he's accustomed, he experiences disorientation and internal chaos. The explosive child is not to blame; the outburst is a reflection of true terror, entirely authentic and not premeditated. What hobbles children like Zack is the inability to rationally assess the danger or apply coping mechanisms to manage anxiety triggered by the unpredictable. Simply put, they have no way to de-escalate.

Keith is still deep in thought as I persist. "I know you may not agree, but I feel like this is our best chance. I know you're skeptical, I don't need you to participate in the restraint, but I need you not to interfere no matter how bad it gets, because you're going to want to stop me once he starts screaming. But I can't fight you and him at the same time, so I need you to stand back and let me do this without interfering. The more hysterical he gets, the calmer I need to be, and I can't do that if you're yelling at me."

My husband isn't yelling. He looks down quietly; he has relented; he understands. He looks bewildered, but he trusts me and my expertise about Zack. And maybe he agrees to it because deep down he realizes the danger in letting Zack's world continue to constrict as he grows older until we fade from view. He offers one last protest: "It will hurt him, won't it? Even if he calms down eventually, physically, emotionally, this will really hurt him," he whispers, his face a portrait of sadness.

"Yes, it will," I answer. "It's going to hurt all of us for a while, and I honestly don't know for how long. I don't even know if this is the right thing to do or whether it will backfire and Zack will be even more traumatized than ever. I just know we have to try; nothing is going to change for him if we don't at least try." My voice breaks in anguish. "I just can't keep watching him lose his life anymore, and I don't have any ideas left."

Days later, I happen to catch a TV show featuring a profoundly impacted adult with autism named Sue Rubin. This young woman has no expressive speech and as a child was forced to wear a helmet to protect her skull during episodes in which she rammed her head against walls in frustration. The frustration was because she was not being understood for who she was, that is, a person who understood every single word being said about her in her presence, a girl who overheard musings about whether she was retarded, crazy or incompetent. Then, miraculously, one day she was introduced to a typing mechanism that allowed her to communicate letter by letter. And she had plenty to say about how clearly she comprehended every word and everything in her world, including her own autism. As an adult she writes regularly and has received her PhD for her brilliant prose, a thesis completed by typing one letter at a time in painstaking but dedicated detail.

Sue eloquently describes the experience of being mentally astute even though trapped inside a disobedient body. She tells of fighting to express herself somehow back in those days when everyone around her mistakenly believed she couldn't. She even explains her unusual affinity for holding varied metal spoons in her hands and fondling them at the sink while water drips over her fingers. She herself doesn't understand her tactile need to repeatedly handle the spoons, she just knows she needs them. The mesmerized interviewer asked Sue what she most wants people to understand about individuals with autism. She types slowly but deliberately, systematically pecking at the keys, one letter at a time: *P-r-e-s-u-m-e c-o-m-p-e-t-e-n-c-e*. Presume competence. Indeed.

PULL BACK THE CURTAIN

Success is not the result of spontaneous combustion; you must set yourself on fire.

—ANONYMOUS

AS WE APPROACH the Sesame Street "Live Elmo" show, I'm losing my nerve. Zack's going to viscerally explode; he's going to spit and hurl and writhe and scream and everyone will be watching. It could get gravely serious if he starts bashing his head into the tile floor; he could get a concussion. I may get struck in the face. I may get bitten to the point of bleeding, all this uncertainty atop the ultimate question of whether this will even work. Bones could splinter, he might not calm down for several days. He could spiral into a depressive tailspin, all alone in his room replaying the physical trauma and unable to sleep or eat.

Oh God, this is wrong, bad for Zack, bad for me.

Stop it, you know exactly what's coming from all sides, you've been down this road a hundred times before and this is qualitatively different.

This isn't about a public spectacle but a serious undertaking to give Zack his life. I've done nothing wrong and neither has he. *So turn it down, turn it off. Yes, he will shriek and flail and humiliate me, so what? I've been here before and I'm still standing.* This is for a child who does not have a cruel bone in his body who would never intentionally harm or frighten another person. He will not aim his fire at anyone, nor point a lethal weapon in their direction.

We've arrived, all three of us sitting very still in the parking lot as I mentally prepare for battle. Keith slowly withdraws the key from the ignition, opens the car doors and leads a bounding and unsuspecting Zack into the sun drenched parking lot outside the massive concert auditorium. I remain seated for a few beats longer and draw a deep deliberate breath and exhale slowly. *He's not a criminal nor liar nor hypocrite nor bully . . . he is not . . . he is not . . . he is not . . .* Fuck it! I'm going in.

In the auditorium, no sooner than the steely auditorium door swing closed behind us does Zack immediately reel back and plunge towards the door to frantically grasp at his escape. At 65 pounds now, his furious strength is a troubling match for mine. In abject anger his jaw and limb strength is staggering, he's a thoroughbred of resistance.

My buoyant child turned savage in seconds, the internal flip switched. He's inside desperately slamming his fists and grasping at the metal door bar to claw his way out. I quickly seize him by the shoulders and diligently pry his gripping fingers from the bar as he jerks his head back in a quick and sudden motion, like an animal trying to break free of a trap, and he smashes his skull into my chin in fierce rebellion. I roll my tongue to release the pain and taste the metallic taint of blood. I give up on the grappling fingers, wrap both arms tightly around his torso and yank him back fiercely as we both tumble angrily to the floor. Zack momentarily escapes my grip and scrambles urgently back towards the door, but I leap on top of him in full force, pinning his entire body flat to the ground.

Damn it, this was a mistake, too ambitious, detonation happened immediately before I was ready, give it up.

I thought we'd at least make it a few steps inside before the realization struck him, at least partway to the show entrance where the huge red velvet drape hangs in fat, lazy, protruding folds several feet away. I should have stopped him just outside the door and gotten a firmer grip on his body, but now we're turning wildly over and over each other in flagrant display along the filthy floor.

Keith rushes to a remote corner in disgrace. I lose sight of him in the chaos, my focus unhinged but remaining solely on the enraged child writhing in my grip, mouth gaping as he now attempts to bite his way out of lockdown. I can't spare seconds even to glance at the horrified throngs of people gathered suddenly, watching the grotesque display, unsure whether to intrude physically or duck back and shield their children's eyes in protection.

Breathlessly, I pivot myself to secure Zack's entire body between my thighs as I clamp down tightly and interlock my feet to prevent rupturing the barrier. I lock together both arms to restrain his flailing torso, but I miss a beat. His head slams hard down to the floor, one strike against the hard surface, before I instantly untangle my right leg and extend it to shield his battering skull from repeated rhythmic blows.

My leg begins quaking as muscles alternately flex and slacken to absorb the furious strikes, and I can feel parts already beginning to swell up in anger. I pivot back, grabbing his skull in my right curled arm grip, and begin dragging him towards that plush curtain, dragging and scraping across the sludge of soda, popcorn and stickiness that coats the floor and now both of us. Zack is hobbled and shrieking at an alarmingly high pitch, but I keep heaving and dragging us both, inch by dreadful inch, in heavy guttural grunts as remarks spontaneously erupt all around us,

"Hey, lady," comes the shouting sneer. "Your kid obviously doesn't want to go to the show! What the hell kind of mother forces a kid against his will?" The collective herd roils and moans in agreement.

"Let him go, you asshole! What the hell is the matter with you? He's just a little kid, for God's sake!"

"Hey, lady! Maybe you're the moron if you can't figure out your kid is freaking and wants to leave! Why don't you stop causing a scene and leave him the hell alone?"

I'm too beaten down to utter a syllable, much less a defense, though I desperately long to scream it out, just like those wretched silent screams in nightmares where you strain to speak but discover you have no voice. Grunting and dragging at a dizzyingly slow pace, my vision is suddenly blurred by tiny capillaries bursting inside my eyelids in response to the fierce and prolonged physical restraint. As my heart gallops, full-body chills and tremors through me spread as my strength begins breaking and yielding to Zack's. Maybe permanent damage, my fault. . . . I am actively harming my child, the reverberations of which are an entirely separate matter yet to be determined. And that's just the immediate trauma. Imagine how long Zack will perseverate and "spin" the terrorizing record; the ripple effects could last for days. I can't hold on much longer. *We're not going to make this . . .*

An icy shock sprints down my back as I reflexively arch and stare wildly in confusion. Someone just threw their soda at me.

"Bitch!" he spits and spats a viscous wad which lands on my right arm. Momentarily stunned by the cold shock but unable to release my grip, I quickly shake my head to disperse the soda as it streaks pale brown ooze across the floor. I'm definitely not giving up now. We are at war, Zack and me, thoroughly turned inside out, everything that was once private now publicly exposed as we wrestle along the dingy, dank floor. Hastily, I look around for a moment and steal a glance at Keith who is shrunken down in pain, angrily shaking his head at me in profound disapproval and disappointment. I longed to see a shred of admiration in his eyes, but Keith has concluded this is wrong. *It's over, we need to leave, this isn't working,* he silently pleads. Zack is unraveling just as Keith predicted, and the crowd's reaction to it even more horrible than I had imagined. In his disgusted visage I can read the outrage, *Enough! Haven't you tortured Zack enough? How badly do you need to win at his expense? It's over, this totally failed and now you're just exposing him to more scorn and pain! Surrender, for God's sake, he can't do it and it's cruel to keep pushing him!*

No, I'm not giving up, I think, turning my back on Keith. He's not with me in this, he's in agony over Zack's pain, but it's enough that Keith has stayed true to our pact without interfering.

Suddenly, from somewhere up above an invisible cloak descends and slowly envelops me. These are the very moments I've been dreading, but also building towards, so I don my invisible armor, now impervious to the spectator ridicule because I truly don't care what they think. I can't afford to care, can't afford to be humiliated into retreating, can't assuage their discontent and still get Zack where he needs to go.

Autism is angry. The infuriated beast of defiance is rearing its head, snarling, writhing, biting, only I'm not trying to defeat the beast or even subdue it. I need its passion and power. It's this very passion that fuels the resistance with which I must align myself, harnessing and channeling that live energy and redirecting it towards something Zack craves but wrongly fears. Like live theater.

OK, get in his head now, talk back to his thoughts. Keep it simple.

"Zack, you are doing it! I know you're afraid, but all you have to do is stay here, you're already doing it, you've already won. Just stay and watch, sit and watch, that's it. You did it. You're doing it. You did it!" A simple and repetitive mantra to penetrate the panic and break through the force field. "You are doing it, Zack! That's it, you are doing it! Almost done, no more, just sit, you did it." We keep crawling closer to that red curtain.

In a now recovered and controlled voice I loudly announce to all in proximity, "My son has autism and he's terrified. I'm working with him to get his fears under control." That's it, that's all I can muster and all I owe you, my terse but fulsome explanation. My tone is controlled because I'm not actually angry at the public smackdown. I expected it and respect the sincere protective impulse to intervene on my child's behalf. They are shaming me in support of Zack and are owed an explanation. My resolve holds.

I am Teflon in defense of my son, emboldened to go to extremes to rescue him from a life imprisoned by fear, as real as any institutional confinement. I used to feel the shards of glass from his explosions lacerate me straight through the heart, the public disgust leaching into my pores, but now the daggers bounce off like me like toy darts. I'm convinced of the rightness of my mission and my son's life is not your hands, it's in mine. So I am not letting up until we get to the Promised Land. Feel free to stare and judge out loud, but please do not interfere because, however hideous it looks, I'm working with my son and I'm getting him to that damned plush red curtain.

Years of observation have made me an expert on the precise idiosyncrasies and mannerisms, the sudden jerks and pops of the head, the involuntary smacks and starts, even his gaping mouth seconds before it lunges to bite my right forearm. I've been here too many times, planted myself too deeply inside Zack's mind, not to anticipate his every move. Like a well-choreographed wrestling match I follow both from behind and a second ahead—dart, pivot, block, duck—each consecutive reflex part of the interactive dance as I move in synchronicity with him to prevent us both from injury, even as I continue to drag him by the body, inch by agonizing inch.

The public avenger comes striding towards us, not a member of the gaping general public, but a manager summoned to the scene.

"Miss, I'm afraid this is too disruptive to the other patrons to let this continue. I'm afraid you'll have to leave." No response. Repeat with emphasis. "Miss, you are creating a public disturbance and I need to escort you and your child out of the auditorium right now."

"No," I respond calmly without looking up. "I'm not going anywhere." As I take a second to scan his face, what I catch in his visual exchange with the security guards is enough to make me actually laugh. His look reads, *Crap, we've got a live one here. She's saying she won't leave. What the hell do I do now?*

"Ma'am, I appreciate that you're trying to handle this situation as best you can, but you can't be doing this in here. You're going to have to take this outside. You're disturbing the patrons who came here to enjoy a children's show."

"Yes, I know," I strangle out breathlessly, "but I'm a paying customer too, and I have a right to be here, and so does my autistic son."

I appreciate that this is more feral, seemingly unjustified, but my reasons for staying are far more dignified than those of parents who dismissively ignore their screaming toddlers and disturb the peace without anyone batting an eye. I understand that this tantrum is frighteningly different, that decent people shouldn't be forced to witness the disturbing outburst.

"I'm sorry sir, I'm not trying to ram my son's autism down people's throats, they are free to walk away, it's just, I just have no choice when he gets this panicked so I have to see this through and get him into the show to understand. I'm sorry, but I have to . . . and it's my right."

Suddenly, from the far reaches of my mind, the legal jargon jettisons to the surface. What was that ADA language about the right of disabled people to access public facilities? That they have a right not be discriminated against because of their disability, a right to structural or other reasonable accommodations to access public venues and boldly go where everyone else has gone before? I didn't want this spectacle either. It's more excruciatingly painful than you can ever know, but my son is not legally required to enter the auditorium quietly. He's allowed to enter on his own disabled terms. I am Zack's disability ramp; I am his structural support; I am his reasonable accommodation.

Amazing how the complex statutory words from my former uninteresting career leapt into the scene just in time to allow me to articulate our rights when I need them most. They are the statutory shield which protects our right to stay rooted to the spot, regardless of public discomfort. My disabled son doesn't come to ordinary entertainment by conventional means. Gravely perplexed, but verbally defenseless, the manager shakes his head and slowly walks away, physically gesturing to the security officers to just let it be.

Okay, one more push and the curtain is within arm's reach. I quickly gesture with my hand to the kind woman guarding the entrance to please pull back that curtain so my son can finally see inside and glimpse the purpose behind the long, bitter altercation. I need her to act quickly, but instead she scrunches down on both knees and embarks in playful banter.

"You know little guy, all your friends are in there enjoying the show," she chirps.

"Miss, he has a disability," I reply tersely. "Please just pull back that curtain so he can see the show. He'll understand once he actually sees it." But she's determined to get through to him her way, oblivious to the venom and fury we just now experienced,

"C'mon, little guy, what's all that screaming for?" she cajoles while putting her face very close to his. He breaks away immediately to avoid the intensity of her glare as the ambitious woman foolishly persists. "Well, I'm sure not letting you in there until you behave like a gentleman! Don't you want to hear Elmo sing? I bet you know all the words to the songs."

"Miss!" I bark back. "My son has a serious disability. He's frantic and not focused on what you're saying, and he might bolt or bite me at any moment. So I really need you to lift that curtain right now!"

"Oh, but he needs to calm down first! Elmo certainly won't tolerate this kind of bad behavior. And what will all the other little boys and girls think if you go in there screaming like that, they might—"

"LADY, he's got AUTISM, he doesn't give a shit what the other little boys and girls think! Now will you please just pull back the damn curtain!"

Deeply insulted, she immediately resumes her upright posture and wordlessly pulls back the plush red velvet in a single swoop to reveal a bright red singing caricature on a large stage, clearly visible even from our long distance, as I quickly point Zack in his direction and exclaim, "There's ELMO! Elmo is singing! Look, Zack, it's Elmo!"

Zack's eyes catch hold of Elmo and suddenly he's too stunned to scream or speak, his hysteria abruptly interrupted by the sight of a familiar friend. Transfixed by the furry bounding creature, Zack sits very still and stares intently. I quickly move to slide him further along the floor, closer to the cushiony seating. Keep moving, keep sliding, closer to the action.

All the rigidness in Zack's entire body gives way as he palpably relaxes, a literal crossover to the other side. He is utterly silent, wholly transfixed by Elmo, and it's truly astonishing to behold the physical transition. Still seated beside him on the scrappy and filthy floor, I twist back toward Keith to gesture with my hands that he come. Keith ducks under the plush curtain and enters haltingly, steadily watchful and deadly serious, eyes locked on mine as he searches for a signal. He leans down and whispers stoically, "How's he doing now?"

"He's fantastic! He did it! He gets it completely. Look at him, he's totally calm now and focused on the show!"

Keith discharges a heavy sigh of relief as he scans me entirely. He can't help but notice that I'm completely saturated down to my damp scalp with sweat, soda, and God knows what else.

Zack is now so steady and even that Keith and I move in concert to lift him gently into a nearby cushion seat where the three of sit together, spellbound by Elmo and victorious at last. Zack is as smooth and malleable as liquid as he sits very upright at attention, almost unaware of his own physical existence and wholly locked in on Elmo. The past and future are of no consequence, for now there is only the present. The lyrics he has come to know so well from Sesame Street rise up to greet him, seemingly an act of divine intervention that of all the songs Elmo could be singing at this moment; he is singing the one Zack knows best—the alphabet song.

Zack nailed down the sequential rhyme years ago and now starts mouthing the letters right along with Elmo. As I look on I realize that, as large a role Sesame Street has played in the lives of generations of families, the producers may never know that for one extraordinary fan, Elmo's creators just built the bridge to the first truly inclusive experience my son has ever known. As I gaze around the auditorium at the flashing lights, coiffed bags of pastel cotton candy and stiffly inflated helium balloons, as I look back at him, Zack is recreationally indistinguishable from his peers. In these precious moments I can savor the reality that Zack has succeeded in the greatest challenge of his life—overriding his intense phobia of indoor spaces—long enough to access something beloved. He is visibly radiant and glowing as we make brief eye contact, before his eyes are hypnotized back on the show. As I lean back in the seat I imagine that on future ventures it may not take as long nor hurt as badly as this initial encounter. I lean over and ask Keith, "By the way, how long did that whole thing take? How long were we out there on the floor, an hour?"

Smilingly Keith replies, "It was thirty-six minutes and forty-four seconds exactly."

Keith's eyes meet mine and now finally here's the admiration that I needed so badly, and within the sparkle I detect flickers of triumph, relief, even gratitude. There's a silent discourse between two parents bonded over the unimaginable, partners who have been tested mightily over the years only to arrive in this moment where once again we realize that the two people married years ago who stood at the altar perhaps never really knew each other, and certainly not as well as we do now. As Keith basks in the victorious glow I lean over and whisper to my loyal life partner, "Thank you for standing by me and not interrupting, even when I could tell you so badly wanted to." He nods appreciatively. "Now go make yourself useful and buy us some pizza and ice cream."

I turn towards Zack and inform him we are even allowed to eat high quality cuisine in this cool palace where Elmo sings! I do still believe strongly in the power of positive reinforcement, especially when it comes to vanilla ice cream. When Zack eagerly spoons it into a direct route to his willing stomach, I look adoringly at my prince. I don't have the words to adequately thank him for making me, in this moment, the most satisfied mother on earth. It took thirty-six minutes and forty-five seconds—a brief stint in hell. And, yes, it was worth it.

LET'S MAKE A DEAL

When an uninstructed multitude attempts to see
with its eyes, it is exceedingly apt to be deceived.
When, however, it forms its judgment, as it usually
does, on the intuitions of its great and warm heart,
the conclusions thus attained are often so profound
and so unerring as to possess the character of
truth supernaturally revealed.

—THE SCARLET LETTER,
NATHANIEL HAWTHORNE

"HELLO, MOVIEGOERS!" I announce spiritedly to the mystified crowd at the movie opening of the newly released kids' feature "Happy Feet."

My name is Whitney and I have a precious son with autism. I'm not here to ask for anything but tolerance for about 20 minutes during the previews. My son is terrified of dark enclosed spaces and I want him to experience movies, so unfortunately, the only way to get him in and past his fears is to bring him forcibly, which makes you the lucky observers.

I'm not trying to ram autism down your throats. I'm sorry for what you're about to see, but there's no substitute for real life so there's no other way for me to do this. I'm asking that you let us ruin the previews, which we will completely, and if I can't calm him down by the time they end I promise we'll leave because I know you all paid to see a movie without distractions. So, if I can have your permission I'm going to bring him in. Please shield your young children so they're not afraid because he's terrified, so you're going to see things you'd rather not. But if you can just sit tight, I've done this before, we can ride this out—and then he'll watch the movie quietly and be able to see movies for the rest of his life. He'll never be this afraid again, so if you can give us twenty minutes, I'll be grateful to you forever because you will have made history in my son's life. How does that sound?

Crickets. Abject silence for what feels like the hundredth time in response to my intimate disclosure. Stunned disbelief yields to their collective understanding of the radical experiment I'm proposing. I'm taking a big risk and betting on compassion. We'll see.

There is no other way to conquer this particular venue because a movie theater is critically distinct from a huge concert auditorium in important ways. Zack's prior detonation took place first inside the wider auditorium corridors, like an alley with ample foxholes and exits for bystanders to avoid the calamity. Even when Zack initially entered the Elmo concert, audibly enraged, his volume was easily outweighed by Elmo's performance and the screaming fans. Distractions like music and helium balloons were vital to the clandestine operation of moving a loudly shrieking child into the space without disruption to others. But a movie theater is a still and quiet interior with only one means of egress, and a captive audience.

The spotlight will be squarely on a writhing and tormented Zack at center stage. Glancing around the crowd I see a surfeit of very young, innocent children who no doubt will be terrorized by the spectacle, and I silently beg the adults to explain or otherwise shield them, but time is quickly elapsing. Zack is just outside the door already ferociously protesting Keith's full-body clutch so I must act fast. Afraid and unsure, I must still forge ahead because this time I've alerted the captive crowd of a fundamental truth— that I can't do this without them.

As the lighting rapidly dims the crowd converges into a blurry and indiscernible mass, suddenly comments start flying fast.

"Hey, my son is bipolar! We're just getting him up on meds so he's doing much better!" calls out someone excited to share.

"That's great!" I respond energetically, relieved for the unusual ice-breaker. "Good for you for getting him where he needs to go!" The dam now burst, an outpouring floods me more quickly than I can get my head and words around.

"My cousin has Down's Syndrome. Will you work with him?"

"I used to cry at movies as a kid and I don't even have a disability! Go ahead, I get it!"

"Previews suck anyway, we'd rather watch you work!" *Yes I was counting on the penchant for live theater and I promise we'll deliver the drama better than any movie preview.*

The rapid unfurling of intimacies produces an unburdening of shameful secrets. The thread which binds us is authenticity, an emotional unburdening of the lie that everything is all right at home. Unable to speak, I respond with a grateful nod as I scurry out the door to seize Zack.

Though the movie screen is still placid, there's nothing serene about Zack's entrance as I drag him in, thrashing and biting like a fire-breathing dragon clamped down in a fierce metal trap. The crowd buzz halts immediately; no one was prepared for this level of violence, which is genuinely shocking and frightening. I'd wistfully hoped that Zack would carry the vestigial memories of his prior conquest and remain calm. But, no way. The screen is now lit, and so is my son, scratching and kicking with savagery at once again being forced against his will into another terrifying and unknown dark space, even smaller than the last one. You can hear a pin drop in the theater now frigid with fear, as young children dive and duck behind seat rows in total alarm. This feels very wrong; it's unfair to frighten small children as they cling urgently to adults with huge teary eyes. But I can't stop now; the damage is done.

I get Zack in lockdown fast as I pin him to the floor. Horrified but unable to look away from the live show unfolding before their eyes, wanting it to stop but too afraid to speak, the crowd is both captivated and held captive. As Zack keeps wailing in agony I feel people adjusting in their seats, wholly resentful and rethinking the wisdom of their former acquiescence to the scene which is far worse than any they had imagined.

Cue the physical corral and my simple refrain, this time purposely loud enough for all to hear. "Zack, there's nothing to fear. You did it, you're at the movies. You did it, just sit and watch, all done. You're doing it, Zack, you're done. You did it! All done, you did the movie!"

As previews flicker onscreen, Zack catches sight of the streaking images and musical flashes and, abruptly distracted, stops fighting long enough to stare. As his comprehension kicks in that these are merely flat images on the wide screen, he begins his palpable descent into calm. I'm quick to pivot my grip so I can point to familiar animals and actions onscreen, audibly enough to ensure the crowd itself is aware that the experiment is indeed working. Now lying on the floor, still prone, Zack absorbs my words and realizes that sitting and watching is all that's expected of him. There's nothing to fear—just sit and watch.

Zack's conspicuous crossover is unfolding in real time right before the eyes of the movie audience, which collectively exhales a sigh of relief. The emotional battering is over. It was hellish but brief, as Zack lies fully on the floor, his eyes glued to the impossibly wide screen. *Well done, Zack.* In keeping with his disability, Zack is wholly unselfconscious about the spectacle that just came before, and he sits upright for better viewing, impervious to background whispers. As I slowly loosen my grip and swing my head around to issue a quick thumbs-up to Keith in the back row, the crowd spontaneously erupt into raucous cheers for the exquisitely brave child.

"NOOOO!" Zack shrieks an auditory stab which rips through the darkness. Zack might have startled them with his entrance, but they just startled him right back. Far from appreciative of the ovation, Zack reacts badly to the sudden piercing applause and recoils in horror at the sharp sound in such tight confines. Realizing the misunderstanding, I leap to my feet and quickly address the crowd.

"Whoops! So sorry, but no clapping please! Zack's not used to being at the center of loud applause indoors. That just startled him, but his parents get it and appreciate you support, thank you!" As I drop back down to comfort a shaken Zack, I usher a sweeping wave to the gracious crowd to simply carry on. *Quietly, without cheering, please, but thank you dearly for that show of kindness.*

Zack is quickly reassured the cheers won't happen again and resumes his transfixed glare at the spectacularly wide visual landscape of the movie screen. Shaking off the jitters, I suddenly feel several pats on my shoulders. I look up to see outstretched hands in the aisles which reach over to clasp mine in unspoken celebration. The triumph of what we all just witnessed, feared might not happen, then stayed put long enough to make it happen. A few members actually kneel to give me strong hugs;

others pointedly ask me for my business card so I can work with their disabled children, cousins, grandchildren. Once again history has been made in the life of my child. Savor it.

The show must go on and as it does, Keith kneels and effortlessly sweeps Zack into his arms and plants him in the back row. Happily folding himself into the plush seat, Zack never takes his eyes off the screen, on which just opened an enchanted musical dance number to fully cement his total attention. "Hey Zack," I whisper. "They serve great food here, too, and we can eat pizza and popcorn while we watch. How cool is that?"

I turn to ask a smiling Keith for time stats and learn that Zack not only beat the previews reel, but bested his prior struggle by twenty minutes. Zack surprises me by suddenly looking very alert and upright, then he quickly rises to his little feet, his little *happy feet*. Transfixed by the music he begins twisting and pivoting, bouncing and swaying, and I realize he is trying to dance right along with the penguins onscreen. And why not? He's not blocking anyone's view. There's plenty of time to teach him the movie protocol of remaining seated. But for this moment it's fitting that he's so energized that he fully embrace the cinema by going along with the dancing. Looking around, I see a few other very young children are doing the same. So, I stand beside Zack to join him in supplying some much-needed rhythm. Keith wisely remains seated.

A once-petrified Zack now can't resist getting down to one of the greatest hits sung by one of the greatest music masters of all time. The song is "I Wish" by the legendary Stevie Wonder, fittingly sung for my son's very first movie experience. Not everyone knows that due to a very premature birth, Stevie Wonder was born with a medical condition called retinopathy which caused his blindness. But of course, we all know that his physical disability in no way derailed him from becoming a pioneer and innovator, a visionary who now serenades my own special-needs child. As Zack and I are literally dancing in the aisles, Mr. Wonder's lyrics play on.

You grow up and learn that kind of thing ain't right;
But while you were doing it, it sure felt outta sight . . .

MALE ROCKETTE

*The one thing you can do is to do nothing. Wait .
. . You will find that you survive humiliation and
that's an experience of incalculable value.*

—T.S. ELIOT

RIDING THE CREST of Zack's wave, I'm ready to return
to a previous venue to test my prediction that Zack will glide
readily into the auditorium he conquered. It's holiday season
and the New York City Rockettes have come to town, so it's
fitting that Zack be exposed to the splendor of the unrivaled
troupe. Our arena venue is that same gladiator stadium where
Zack first confronted Elmo. But as I'd hoped, our resistance time
has been bested with each new encounter, and having already
broken the terrifying association in Zack's mind for this venue,
I believe he'll stride in on confident feet. This is a crucial theory
to test, because overriding his personal protest must generate
more than temporary gain. I'm counting on lasting results in
navigating various venues not just in our town, but every town
going forward.

Taking the DC metro subway feels right. The rapid train tracks nicely with Zack's affinity for speed. Despite his autism, there are still many ways in which Zack is typical. His love of harrowingly steep roller coasters, spectator sports and Hollywood-style explosive action movies are testament to traditional gender leanings. Disparities between what he wants, needs and craves compared to his same-aged peers are not nearly as deep as I originally imagined. But so long as I'm still in charge of his social calendar, the cosmopolitan high-kick act is *my* preferred viewing, and Zack is a most gracious companion.

I'm increasingly discovering that there is no genre of music, movie, art, concert, sport, dance or any social activity to which he doesn't eagerly gravitate. His recreational appetite is huge and he adores exposure to everything. On the drive to the metro stop, I'm already choreographing transit details, calculating the steep escalator ride down to the ticket booth, letting Zack feed dollars to the machine, grasping the regurgitated ticket and inserting it correctly into the turnstile. I'll need to keep close watch of the train platform's edge while prompting Zack to carefully watch the distant dark tunnel through which the oncoming train arrives, with a single glaring headlight to visually alert him. Teaching Zack about mass transit is not merely entertaining; it's imperative training to ready Zack for a future which will depend on public transport. I'm not expecting him to drive independently, but I don't want him always reliant on others, either. Navigating the bus and metro system is well within his emerging skill set and crucial for his adulthood. With repeated exposure I'm certain he'll own it.

Zack's eyes are unblinking as he takes in the bustling panorama on our descent down the dark, grated escalator steps. I grip his hand tightly and point out all the banal details of the intersecting crowds, scaffolding for color-assigned trains, route directory, ticket booth and automated turnstile: no detail is unimportant to his hungry eyes. Details routinely overlooked by riders impatient to hit their destinations are met with keen scrutiny by my visual learner—lights flashing, trains rumbling above and below, screeching brakes. I'm reminded how lucky I am that Zack isn't overly sensitive to loud noise or chaos. As the pulsating sounds signal our oncoming train, Zack thrillingly bounces up and down on his heels. Laughingly, I squeeze his little shoulders. It's all I can do to hold him back from bursting into the train and ramming the exiting riders. Oblivious to protocol, Zack needs to be gently restrained and informed that exiting riders go first. Then we enter on bouncing feet, his body characteristically pushing back against my physical check, but this time my restraint is tender, merely guiding rather than trenchant.

Together we watch the energy of crossing bodies as they exit and enter, heady stuff for a first-time rider. Finally, the tone signals the abrupt door closure as I lean down to remind Zack that the train is leaving, that we're about to go fast forward. Hang onto that metal bar.

But as the train begins its propulsive trajectory, I'm jolted to see that Zack's far more anxious than I realized. He's just defecated himself badly. *Oh God, no! Not here, not now, please God no!* I begin panting in fear. I was so fixated on his return to the familiar venue I completely overlooked his potential reaction to the first-time speeding train. But the extent to which I overestimated his readiness is sprinting down his legs and heading for his winter boots. Putrid ooze and chunks quickly soak through his sweatpants. I'll never get it out of those furry-lined boots. *Oh God, can't wait for the next stop, have to stop this somehow and fast!*

As the stench radiates, nearby passengers begin angrily scanning the crowd perplexed at who would unleash such filth, and without any coat or accessories to disguise it we're in catastrophic territory. I don't want to alarm Zack, who's standing rigidly still and seems aware of the sudden crisis he's created as he looks down, helpless and petrified of my reaction.

"Okay Zack, we can fix this," I murmur inaudibly as I drop to my knees and flip Zack onto his back in a single gesture born of experience. Zack is cooperatively silent and cognizant of the urgency. Although he's still not expertly toilet trained, he's never soiled himself publicly, and seems to understand the gravity of where we're now caught. There's simply no choice; the real deal-making thrust upon us. Time is horribly brief before things get really and truly ugly, so with Zack leveled I quickly remove and set aside his boots, then begin stripping away his sweatpants and underwear that is now thickly layered in feces, part formed, part liquefied. I work triage-style to contain the contamination, but we're in so tight a space I'm stuck. Resting one heel gently on Zack's torso to cue him to remain flat, I stumble to my other leg and call out loudly,

"Hello everyone! Happy holidays! And boy, do I have a huge favor to ask of you this most charitable season! Okay, I have a young son with autism who is riding the metro for the first time and—" I glance down to see the filth spreading precariously towards the dingy floor, "I screwed up. He just had a major accident! I'm so sorry, but I can contain it and clean it fast if you give me a little space and all the tissues, wipes and plastic bags you have. Please! I'm so sorry. Help me, please!" I drop back to steady Zack because the train is lurching toward its stop and that stopping force will deliver another propulsive jolt that could jettison the feces straight to the floor and feet of nearby passengers. *Can't let that happen.*

No sooner do I kneel than a steady stream of long, soft, white cloth flurries downwards towards us on the ground, a virtual rope of quilted tissues, moist wipes, paper towels and even crinkly retail shopping bags. Not even a second to pause,

I begin grabbing at the fluffy, mercifully moist towelettes, and use broad sweeping gestures to grab and collect larger chunks first and quickly whip them away into the wrinkly bag. I barely even notice the stench I'm so busy, my hands expertly trained in black-belt competence of feces wipe, working in speedy coordinated synergy to smear, gather and catch migrating ooze just before it hits the floor. Wiping furiously and ducking soiled napkins into the bag, I generate a steady stream of gift tissues until, minutes later, Zack is remarkably clean, the final strokes with lavender wipes now just for fragrant measure. His fetid cascade is now squarely confined to the bag that I dexterously seal and sequester by tying the handles securely. Hazardous spill contained by professional FEMA-like efforts, made possible by the generous and quick perception of total strangers.

As I lift Zack calmly to his feet, I detect in him for the first time ever a distinct sense of self-consciousness. On previous endeavors he's swung so far to the extremes that he took no notice of surrounding people who had witnessed his every harrowing move. But he's undistracted now and so acutely aware that he's looking directly at them. And now, for perhaps the first time in his life, Zack appreciates that he himself is at the center of their attention. It's unclear whether he is reflecting on the coordinated undertaking on his behalf just now, but he's clearly registering the smiling, friendly faces as encouragement. He shyly smiles back.

As we emerge from the eventful ride, I hurriedly rush into the auditorium because snow flurries have begun to fall and it's frigidly cold outside. And now Zack indeed rises to my expectations of a smooth entry into a known space. Though, ironically, his demeanor is irrelevant because he's again courting confounded stares and startled looks, for an entirely different reason this time—he is naked from the waist down. Accompanied only by a short winter coat and shearling boots,

Zack floats through the ticket takers wholly unconcerned with his utter transparency. After all, there's a show to see behind that plush red curtain. I must confess that in this unique respect Zack's autism affords him a wickedly cool protective shield. I wouldn't dream of entering a packed public venue with full frontal nudity with anyone but Zack who is so aloof and wholly unpretentious. With not even a hint of false modesty, he's too busy scanning the curtain for cues of what lies behind to care a whit about the leering, horrified spectators. Good for him, though *I* do actually care.

Determined to navigate the auditorium with the same aplomb and shamelessness I displayed on our previous visit, I nudge Zack impatiently towards the Rockettes publicity shed which houses all range of overpriced memorabilia. Ignoring the vendor's quizzical stare, I slap down cash and ask them to hand over their most reasonably priced pair of sparkly tights. Forced to meet the stunned visage of the vendor, I reply quickly before he comments on my nudist companion. "Please don't ask! It's been an adventure that needs to end right now—with your best and least expensive pair of Rockettes' tights. Quickly please. The show's about to start and we don't want to miss the beginning."

As the vendor stares blinkingly at Zack he reaches under the counter and emerges with a perfect pair, which he kindly offers up at no charge. I smile gratefully, drop to my knees and pull off Zack's boots, then assiduously begin yanking the fuchsia glitter-infused fabric over Zack's feet and hiking it fully up his thighs. The crotch is bulging but still covers his groin. Good enough.

It's show time as I quickly usher Zack into the glittering auditorium to our seats very close to the stage. Beaming with excitement and wholly impervious to the occasional stares at his ripened bespectacled thighs, Zack begins bouncing vigorously on his toes yet again, visibly thrilled in anticipation. And as the ladies begin their very high, uncannily synchronized kicks, it isn't long before my son's hot pink legs are kicking in the air as well. He's a glorious sight, especially with the curling script spelling *I'm A Rockette* plastered in shimmering silver across his gorgeous little tush for all to behold and marvel how this little man made it into the show.

BITTERSWEET

It's like that old gypsy curse. May you get what
you want, and want what you get.

—13 CONVERSATIONS ABOUT ONE THING,
MOVIE QUOTE (2002)

MY GOD, DOES this child ever shut up? It's been an
exhausting day, it's late and I really need Cassie to do a quick
in and out of the bath and head straight to bed. But Cassie's
combative this evening and in the mood for a little linguistic
tango. Her remarkable speech is impressive, but less so at the
end of a long day. Impatient to get on with it, I'm biting down
hard to maintain my composure, silently keeping a vow I made
earlier this week not to lose my temper no matter how much
she provokes me. It's been two days of vow kept and it hasn't
been easy. Verbal fencing has become the only sport at which
she excels or shows any interest. She is so headstrong, jousting
across so many topics, I sometimes forget that as her mother I'm
supposed to be on her side.

"Okay, enough already, Cassie, let's just do this. I know you're
feeling playful, but I'm truly exhausted and not in the mood for

games tonight. So just for tonight, let's please make this quick."

"You know what, Mommy? You're not *even* my best friend!" she fires back with emphasis.

"Okay, I'm not your best friend," I echo calmly, "I'll adjust, now please get in the tub."

Undaunted, she continues. "And you know what, Mommy? You're not *even* my friend at all! From now until forever, I'm going to be friends with everyone *except* you!" She waits for my reaction, nothing. The resistance must forge on. "I don't *even* like your 'black-brown' hair; I don't *even* like your big brown eyes." She pauses again, allowing the atrocities to sink in. Still no reaction as I bite down hard and coach myself to breathe deeply.

"And I don't *even* like the way you dress!" Her voice is rising. "And you try, but you are not *even* funny!" Now I'm prepared to take issue with that insult. *Don't go there Cassie, no one is more fun than me.* But I must refuse to engage her in this battle of wills because I will lose—my temper, first and foremost, which I've repeatedly vowed not to do with my precocious little girl.

"That's fine," I acknowledge carefully. "You don't have to like my hair or my eyes or the way I dress. *Just get in the bath!*" Zack would have climbed into the tub at my first ask, compliant and grateful. He would have been fully bathed, clothed and nestled in bed by now, without deriding me with petulant insults. Then again, Zack listens. Cassie hears me but doesn't actually pay attention, so once again I find myself, maddeningly, repeating the simplest request on a loop while my frustration builds.

"NO! And you know what? Daddy is SO much more funner than you! And he's a better cook, and he's better at video games, and he looks better in his clothes than you do in yours and—"

"I agree, Cassie, I get all of that and I agree." The inner tremor is rising, the simmer rapidly heating to boil. "And I'll be more than happy for you to go play with your father—*after you get into that bathtub. I'm not kidding, I've had enough of this.*"

"And I don't *even—*"

"ENOUGH! ENOUGH OF THIS!" I explode, vow broken. Through clenched teeth I bite out, "I've had enough of this from you. Every single night is a battle, and I'm fed up and tired! Can you for once just do what I ask without arguing and having to get the last word in? *Get in the damn tub, now!*"

I'm sorry about the pact, truly, but this child provokes me in ways I didn't know possible, pushing and poking my most vulnerable and aggravated buttons to the point of overload. Zack never berates me or talks back. And never in his life did he deliberately provoke or disrespect me, because there's not a single cruel bone in his body. But Cassie seems actually to enjoy bringing me to the edge of derangement, and now I must dab the rabid froth from the edges of my mouth, my explosion thus validating her inevitable remark that she will be so much kinder to her own children.

Grudgingly, Cassie saunters over to tub, her limbs exaggeratedly swishing and jangling in defiant protest of my ruthlessly authoritarian parenting style. The tirade continues steadily under her breath.

"*God, you are SO mean!* Daddy is so much nicer than you. I should report you to the parent police because they would so arrest you right now!"

As the symphony of insults plays, my rigid shoulders, once taut with tension, suddenly collapse and I cannot help but bend over and start laughing uproariously at the bittersweet irony. *Oh, how desperately I wanted a verbal child!*

Cassie and I had a great stretch for a good long while. I look back on that time fondly, if disbelievingly. Prior to her turning three years old, I reveled in her unique blend of advanced and compassionate. Cassie was so sophisticated she quickly absorbed bits and pieces about the ways Zack was different, put them together and embraced him wholeheartedly. As the bitter freeze between them thawed over this past year, I was ecstatic to observe that since she was developmentally advanced and Zack delayed, their interests met in the middle. They jointly enjoyed the same movies, books and activities in ways that were truly stunning to behold.

Cassie became a *de facto* model for Zack, pushing him to imitate her speech and thereby acquire more words himself. A natural born ABA therapist, Cassie also loved being his boss, instructing him to do anything and everything under her command, including sitting patiently at her feet while she applied the last touches of rosy red lipstick and mascara to his bewildered face. I made a regular point of reminding her that Zack's tolerant and easygoing disposition made him an ideal companion, and that no one else would put up with her harassment. He was even sanguine when she decided to further his anatomy education by grabbing different colored Sharpies to label, in indelible ink, every single body part on his flesh itself, including privates, with cool drawings for reference.

But lately Cassie's tempestuous ways have become insufferable. In a complete role reversal, when once I scolded Zack for his mistreatment of her, he and I now exchange knowing looks and eye rolls about the pugilistic little princess she has become.

And it's precisely that quality I coveted for so many years in other children—*very verbal*—that is now my undoing. I honestly did not think it was possible. All that time I spent grieving over Zack's lack of speech, I'm now discovering a truth so unexpected it crept up behind me and reached up to smack me across the face. When exactly did I lose sight of the reality that if a child speaks fluently, it's only a matter of time before she cracks the verbal whip in your direction?

About the time Cassie's language really came flooding in, between ages two and three years old, so did her tilted worldview which cast me as the poorly dressed villain. From the moment Zack was born, and still to this day, it was clear from his adoring gaze that his appreciation for me was both emotional and aesthetic. It was unwavering even in the face of a missed shower or failure to wash my hair for days . . . he made me feel like the most beautiful mommy on earth, and I believe that, to him, I am. Not so with Cassie. She scolds me for my lazy sartorial style, admonishing me that if I wear my ugly, boxy athletic shorts one more time she will disown me as her mother. Her former pride about me has been replaced by observations that are bold, blunt and wholly unwelcome. Like a babbling brook, the criticisms flow freely about my boring "black/brown" hair, and about an outbreak of acne which she reminds me should not be happening at my age. *Thanks honey, and no, I'm not breaking out on purpose to try to look younger*. How relieved she is not to have inherited my loud, deep voice which frightens small children even when I'm not trying.

Astoundingly, I'm increasingly finding that Cassie is anxious about issues that never even registered on Zack's radar when he was her age. She's actually less independent than he was. I recall how easily Zack walked into his preschool class each day with nonchalant assurance and calm. Cassie has regular crises of confidence, sometimes so insecure and tearful that the teachers have to creatively cajole her to get her to set foot inside the room.

One key development is not even close. Toilet training came with relative ease to Zack, once he caught on visually to what was expected. Zack then generalized the habit easily to public restrooms, recognizing that one toilet functions pretty much like the next. But the concept itself is staggering for Cassie, whose ability to reason and negotiate over the topic of toilets is precisely what hinders her progress. Zack learned via imitation and repetition; Cassie is embattled by philosophical disputes about *why she should ever have to be toilet trained, and by which toilet.* So yet again I am hobbled on bended knees and hands for consecutive hours upon hours, begging her to release me and her urine from the austere grip. Unlike Zack, she finds absolutely nothing reinforcing enough to motivate her. In an act of sheer desperation after sitting on the grimy floor of a toy store bathroom for hours, I pledged to buy her any toy of her choice if she would pee. Instead, she took my hand and gently informed me, "Mommy, you should just give this up, you're only going to get hurt." Exhausted by my crippled posture and prolonged discourse, I threw in the towel countless times, sobbing in defeat.

So it dawns on me that despite his disability, Zack possesses certain personality traits and other strengths that Cassie lacks, and that Zack is in some ways easier to teach. While the sudden, forcible exposure methods used with Zack were painful, they proved far more efficient than my efforts with Cassie. His inability to verbally duel with me made him compliant and pliable in ways that she is not. Cassie's brilliance and corresponding tendency to overanalyze is actually inhibiting and maladaptive because she remains unpersuaded by facts. So she is not only having more difficulty conquering her fears, but her resistance is making them ever more steeply entrenched with each failed attempt. In the end, it took Zack a couple of dedicated months to get him fully toilet trained; Cassie is still a work in progress and it's been over a year of training. Purely as a matter of anthropology, the comparative analysis between the two is fascinating; but as matter of everyday functioning and pragmatism, Cassie's differences are excruciating.

Looking back on those early mournful days after Zack was diagnosed, my suffering was so intense and incurable I sometimes didn't want to rise from bed to meet another day. *I honestly would not have believed that a typically developing child could confound, exasperate and enrage me as much as my autistic child. I honestly did not believe Cassie could bring me to tears every bit as much as Zack, just for different reasons.*

No matter how many complaints I heard from friends about their kids, I privately thought the issues trivial, and friends selfish and greedy for not appreciating how relatively easy their kids were to raise. But my loving daughter has turned acidic at times, there will be plenty more to come in her teens, and the emotional stabs she inflicts are proving every bit as lacerating as Zack's physical ones were. Except when she defies me, it feels worse precisely because she isn't disabled and she knows better, or should. I expected better because surely, being gifted with a typical brain carries a corresponding responsibility to be grateful and behave respectfully. So I'm realizing how much I took for granted about typical children, presuming they are inherently easier and more rewarding—more skilled, less defiant, quicker to learn and easier to teach. While it's true our typical children don't present with the amplitude of lifelong challenges as our disabled children, even that assumption cannot be taken for granted since no one knows what the future holds for any child regardless of ability.

Unbelievably, the scales of enjoyment between my two children are tipping in a direction I had not thought possible. At times Cassie accuses me of loving Zack more than I love her, which is wholly untrue. But, do I prefer Zack's quiet and soothing company to her loquacious defiance? *Um, maybe . . . sometimes?* This will change, of course, tipping back and forth and ultimately always being even, but what's remarkable, given their different capabilities, is that it happens at all.

Most intriguingly to me, as a parent and once-dedicated career professional, is that my maternal instincts are in some ways more easily tapped into and drawn out by my disabled child. Something about Zack always did, and still does, bring out the best in me in terms of patience and commitment: his vulnerability, lack of guile or pretense, his abject purity regardless of his age. I can't seem to muster patience in a commensurate way in responding to my daughter's belligerence. Rather than rise to the challenge as I felt inspired to do with Zack, too often I descend to her level and engage in immature barbs. Zack also seems instinctively to trust me more than Cassie does. I know there are good reasons for that, but it has allowed me to guide him according to my best instincts for his personal welfare. Cassie is far more determined to make her own decisions, and mistakes, which is natural but admittedly more difficult to witness over and over. Separate from any consideration of disability, different features of my children's personalities provoke very real strengths and weaknesses in mine. I'm only now beginning to learn this.

But I really do need to slacken the reins on Cassie. I gave Zack lots of latitude when he was her age to allow him to be himself because he's disabled, so I must extend the same charity to her. No more unfavorable comparisons with Zack, that's just unfair. After all, it's not Cassie's fault she's normal, poor kid....

"YOU BAD, LiTTLE Z!"

Humans are so strongly wired to help one another—and enjoy such enormous social benefits from doing so—that people regularly risk their lives for complete strangers.

—*TRIBE*, SEBASTIAN JUNGER

ZACK AND I are far from home. It is sweltering outside and we are languishing in a very long ticket line awaiting entry into a huge waterpark we've never seen. It was my grand idea to abruptly cancel Zack's morning therapy session and whisk him off to a faraway adventure. Hours later we are standing still, irritated, and literally baking in the extreme heat. The massive layers of sunscreen feel like folly as streaming rivulets of sweat course down both of us, rinsing the sunscreen away from our arms and backs. But Zack is beyond excited and impatient as he tugs on me, each urgent yank telling me to just charge past these lines of crowds and race in.

Why are we standing here when the good stuff is in there? I want in. NOW. IN. NOW!

"No more waiting! All done waiting!" Zack announces loudly as several adults around us chuckle in agreement. Just beyond the ticket window awaits a huge collections of watery amusement and, like many children with autism, Zack adores water. He will drink only water, will lovingly watch as it trickles and trips over his fingers in the bath, and upon encountering a pool will enthusiastically leap in and sink slowly to the bottom where he nestles for as long as his little lungs allow. I am not surprised by this craving to be underwater, to suspend oneself where the body is weightless, and where no words are spoken.

Finally, we're in. Zack's eyes grow enormous with excitement as he takes in the panorama—the wave pool swelling with rhythmic thrashing tides, the massive tubular slides reverberating with happy screams. He gallops toward the attractions, ready to sample everything all at once. But I am struck by an entirely surprising fact: as far as the eye can see, there are only tough-looking young teens with angry tattoos, and some are provoking fights with each other.

Menacing-looking young men are travelling in packs, their bulging muscles swathed entirely in angry dark ink. One bicep boasts a sharp-edged-looking dagger cleaving a jagged heart in two, the blood drippings spewing forth as bulbous raindrops. Another inking simply shows *DEATH* scrawled in large gothic print across the broad back of a thick neck. Sneering teenage boys with sinewy limbs are draped possessively around their girlfriends, making out conspicuously, their tongues locked and roiling over each other in vulgar display, as if daring anyone to stop them. One thing is certain: no one here looks as quaint as Zack and me.

As I slowly scan the hundreds of bodies in motion around us, a sickening dread bubbles up in my throat that we are outnumbered by people who may react badly if Zack breaks into unpredictable behaviors. I look down at Zack but he is oblivious, his visual prism characteristically fixed on the splash park fixtures themselves, rather than the people frolicking all around them. I can already anticipate his explosive reaction to my suggestion, but still I must try to redirect him.

"Hey Z. Maybe we should head back to that big quiet pool from yesterday."

"NO!" he shouts abruptly. "NO LEAVE! NO BYE-BYE CAR!" *Dear God.* Coming here was a mistake, but now that Zack has laid eyes on these water features, leaving is clearly not an option. I can picture what will happen if I force it. Zack will collapse to the ground in a flashy spectacle, a defiant and ferocious dead weight, his entire body flailing in protest, me desperately struggling to drag him writhing and screaming across the grass and gravel toward the exit. He has grown much taller and he's heavier now, at least 70 pounds, and his furious strength will certainly overwhelm mine.

A sudden eeriness spreads over me as I realize I am actually afraid of my own son. I'm more afraid of his physical volatility than of these foreboding strangers who are already staring at him mockingly as he twists his fingers and flaps his hands and is bouncing rapidly on the balls of his feet.

"No leave! No more leave!" Zack declares again loudly. And so the decision has been made. I reach down and grip Zack's hand tightly in mine as we begin making our way more deeply into the park. As we pass throngs of people, it is not my imagination that we are being noticed. Low murmurs and jeering stares corroborate my fear that we do indeed stand out, and Zack and I are the only white people here. As we continue slowly walking towards the slides I purposely set my own eyes upon the water fixtures like Zack does, careful not to make eye contact with anyone scrutinizing or laughing at him. No one approaches us, for now they are only watching and wondering. But my heart pounds hard, my breath is shallow. I know I look frightened.

And still, we keep moving deeper and deeper into the park, farther and farther from a safe exit. As Zack keeps bounding he inadvertently steps on someone's foot, wholly oblivious, as I murmur a quick apology and push him forwards.

"That one, there!" Zack calls out sharply as he points to a mammoth vertical structure with a single plummeting slide.

"Are you nuts?" I snap testily. "That's not for you! No way! That's way too steep, not that one!"

"THAT! ONE!" he shouts back and my insides start churning as I recall the website description. *Take a plunge down our 10-story speed slide . . . "* so-named for its legendary capacity to jettison the body downwards at such terrific speed that when it slams into the reservoir pool at the bottom, a massive wave erupts and comes crashing down over the slider. It never dawned on me that Zack would even consider a vertical slide of this height and scale. Surely he sees how it ends as people slowly come to their feet in the reservoir pool, disoriented and struggling to regain balance.

I move quickly to distract him. "Okay, hold on. Let's check out that wave pool first. Look at those beach waves, that looks pretty rough, huh? Let's grab an inner tube and—"

"THAT. ONE. *THERE!*" he rallies back, topping off each word with an urgent point toward the giant slide, utterly frustrated at having already communicated so clearly. *We just had to teach this kid how to point so well!* My stomach tightens into a fist as I acquiesce and begin walking toward the tower of spiraling steps.

I console myself that the wait for this slide is eternal, so as we continue to melt in the blistering heat, Zack surely will grow impatient and lose interest. Not that he has ever in his life lost interest in something he wants.

Long minutes pass and we are silent as our skin ripens into a feverish tint, beads of sweat merging into tiny pools that form a steady trickle down our limbs. The collective herd inches forward,

slowly shoving upwards in an almost drunken stupor, as if we
have all forgotten what we're climbing towards. I'm judging we
won't get to the top for at least twenty-five minutes. Irritated, I
shield my eyes and look above for some merciful cloud to block the
sun's intensity for at least a few seconds. But the sky is cloudless,
the sun mocking us for so foolishly enduring its scorching rays in
exchange for a few thrilling moments of adventure.

I have time to examine my surroundings. Directly in front
of us is a very voluptuous young woman arguing with her
boyfriend, her taut bikini top barely containing her massive
breasts. Standing directly behind us are two very big, muscular
men. Their torsos are massive, flanked by thick, stacked
shoulders which form a ridge from which a rippling cascade
of muscles descend. One of the torsos twists sideways and I
witness the truly graphic artwork. Covering his entire back are
black clenched fists on either side, each fist tearing back portions
of mottled flesh to expose a bloodied skeletal spine. The visual
effect is grotesque and terrifying, yet I admit I cannot look away.

The crowd surges forward again and I realize we are nearing
the top, and I grasp that this is actually going to happen. A pulse
of anxiety shoots through me as I inspect others around us for
signs of stress, but see none. Just then, Zack's hands dart up
anxiously in front of his face and his fingers begin wildly twisting
and turning over themselves in a mad frenzy. He must be getting
nervous, too. He lets out a high pitched yelp and starts bouncing
vigorously. The sight of him sets off a flurry of random remarks
around us.

I remain silent as the realization slowly spreads over the
crowd that my kid isn't just playing or excited, that he must
have something seriously *off*. The tension mounting from the
spectacle feels unbearable.

"Um, hi, I'm Whitney!" I compulsively interrupt their
thoughts. "This is my son Zack, and he's only six, and I have to tell

you all that I'm just incredibly nervous about this slide thing for him. He's never done this before and he thinks he wants to, but I don't think he understands what's going to happen because—" I pause to draw breath, the center of bewildered attention from all sides, "well, because it's really hard to know how much he really understands because he has this disability, he has autism, so he probably doesn't understand what he thinks he wants or what's safe for him." The crowd remains silent, collectively hanging on my wildly mangled disclaimer in an earnest attempt to decipher what exactly is the problem here.

"So, um, I know it's a long climb back down, but if you could just let us by I'm going to walk him back down the stairs."

"He'll be all right," a barely audible voice murmurs nonchalantly from behind me.

"Well that's just it, I don't think he will be all right. Because he doesn't get how fast this thing is and I think he's just going to panic once he's flying down and then it's too late, and with his autism and all, he can't stand water splashing hard into his face."

I search their faces beseechingly for some shred of sympathy but am met with blank stares as I launch into another round. "So, I just think I should get him back down the stairs, if you can please move over a little and let us back down."

"LADY!" a young woman snaps suddenly. "You crazy! You got to just let him be! The boy knows what he wants; he's seen it and still climbed up here, right? He's got eyeballs, he ain't dumb, *LET THE BOY BE!*"

Yes, easy for you to say when you've never seen this kid in serious action.

Just then, that very low voice speaks again, as if under his breath, "I'll watch him, he'll be all right." One of the tattooed men behind us has spoken. Despite his implacable stare, our eyes manage a quick exchange during which he nods as a signal that this young boy is worthy of his protection and he will see to his safe ride. Maybe it's his very serious demeanor or the calm timbre of his voice, but I feel immediately comforted by him. I trust this stranger completely.

"Thank you," I whisper humbly, but it feels inadequate. I must repay his kindness with something more, so I turn to face him and offer up weakly, "Um, I really like that bloodied knife on your shoulder, it's very artistic and well-detailed."

"Oh yeah?" he asks slightly amused, then dismisses the compliment offhandedly. "Nah, that ain't nothin', just gang stuff." *Gang stuff. Great.*

We are at the very top looking down several stories below. I know I should cast my dread aside and take the plummet with my son, wrap my arms and legs around him in solidarity on this slide. That's what a good mother would do—she would not let him ride alone. But as I look down the vertical slope my stomach lurches. This is not just steep, this is a ten-story free fall and I cannot possibly survive the terror myself. I love my son, I would take a bullet for my son, but I ain't going down this beast.

A sour taste rises in my throat as I rationalize that it would be better, safer for Zack actually, if I descend hurriedly and wait at the bottom reservoir pool to be there for him after he's crashed down.

"Okay, here's what we're going to do!" I turn to the man and the group of lanky teens who appear to be interested in the saga unfolding. "I need to head down to the bottom so I'm there when he comes through that huge wave, because he's scared and may freak out! So I need you cool guys to please hold him steady at the top of the slide and get him on his back and lying down in the right position before you release him, and I'll wave from the bottom down there when he looks ready to let him go!" Stern conviction thickens my voice, as it must to conceal my obvious cowardice. But these kids aren't dumb and the jeers begin.

"You got to be kiddin', momma! You gonna just leave him here all alone? You goin' to let him do this scary-ass thing all by himself!?" *Yes, I am.* I immediately scurry down the stairs as the taunts keep flying along the race down and pray I don't get pelted in the head by something hard.

From the reservoir pool I look up and can see even from a distance how abandoned and anxious Zack just became. He's just now looked way down and realized what he signed up for and that there's no turning back, and even from my distance I recognize the fear in his gyrating hands. But the kind man seizes him firmly by the shoulders and sets him atop of the slide's watery entrance. Zack sits, but is struggling to align his body at the perch. It feels unnatural for him to lie back where he cannot use his visual cues to steer down the slide. He's not looking to be swept into a free-fall without watching. He keeps physically resisting, jerking his body back upright and unable to keep his limbs calmly at his sides as required before takeoff. Several of the teen boys grasp his arms on either side and clamp them down firmly by his sides, then a couple more reach down to uncoil his legs from underneath his body and lay them firmly flat and forcibly hold them down. Bless them.

C'mon baby, just trust them and lay back. Just let go and surrender and enjoy the ride.

Just then the towering man steps forward and waves all the teens back with a simple hand gesture as he wordlessly kneels down and extends a steady hand to Zack. And Zack, entirely unpolluted by prejudices that might have made another child recoil in fear from this stranger swathed in tattoos, grasps the outstretched hand with both of his as he stares up trustingly at the man's face. In a single fluid gesture the man sweeps Zack's little body into his air, cradles him in his huge arms, and gently lays Zack down on his back. He whispers something into his ears that seems to calm his body, then the man patiently nudges

Zack's body towards the cusp, all the while maintaining his firm grip on his limbs. It's an astonishingly coordinated feat as he whispers and holds Zack's entire being steady, an astonishing snapshot of compassion.

Zack has managed to captivate an entire crowd of strangers without ever speaking a word. It's the mystique of autism, the magnetic aura of purity and defenselessness, the wholly unguarded way that Zack accepts help from strangers who massage his world so that he can participate, too. Outstretched hands is all he has ever known, and so he has developed an ingrained expectation of kindness and support, even from strangers who he always interprets as being fully on his side. Which they are.

And then, without waiting for me cue, the man suddenly releases him.

For a few spellbinding moments we are all suspended together, fixated on my child. Water is spraying furiously on both sides of his body as he torpedoes down and I gasp at the force: it's as if he's literally flying, like a bullet shot out of a gun. Dozens of eyes are locked on Zack as he missiles downward at high speed. We are collectively holding our breath. *Will the kid do it? Will he manage or will he freak?*

A huge, raucous wave rears up at the bottom and yanks him under. He is engulfed and invisible for several seconds. I imagine the snarling waves smacking him in the face as he gasps for air. I don't see any part of him. He must be choking and disoriented. *Where is he and why on earth did I allow this?* I knew I shouldn't have let him do this. He's drowning and I can't even locate him beneath the tide.

As I'm searching frantically for the sight of even a limb, Zack's head pops up, his body more towards the end of the receiving pool than it first appeared when it hit. Slowly he lifts his head and shoulders, then limply elevates his torso and shakes his head quickly to expel the water from his eyes and ears. Looking all around him slightly dazed, he gets quickly to his feet and glances back up at the top of the slide.

"Okay, all done," he remarks happily and bounces once more on the balls of his feet at his accomplishment. "Bye-bye slide, all done!"

My lungs burst open from prolonged restraint as I exhale deeply, laugh and flash a big thumbs-up to the crowd above who is still holding their collective breath. Suddenly, I'm met with a huge eruption of cheers and thunderous clapping so loud it catches me off guard and knocks Zack to his knees in surprise. I'd clamped down on my breath so long that I am the one gasping and choking for air as I look upwards, and prickly joyous tears pool up and blur my vision. People are shouting seemingly from everywhere.

"You did it, boy!"

"You *BAD*, little man. You bad, little brother!"

"You GO boy! You a bad little mother-fucker man, brother Zack! That's right little man, you are one bad mother-fucker!"

I am astounded at the outpouring of generosity and loud cheering on my son's behalf we are all victorious in this moment. Total strangers, the people I feared most all this time, in a world I perceived as divided between *us* and *them*, a world I bitterly resigned to participating with my son only as an outsider, just united together to let us in. In a society seemingly constructed solely to accommodate its beloved normal children, the seas just parted gloriously to make way for my disabled child.

Zack, stunned by the cheers and unclear of their purpose, has already began sprinting towards the next water park challenge. But I'm determined not to let the precious moment pass unacknowledged by him because I am wise enough to know that being dubbed a "bad mother-fucker" is a distinction never to be taken lightly. Now I don't know exactly what type of positive reinforcements his elementary school teachers intend to provide for his achievements in class, but I'm fairly certain they will not cheer this. So, I chase Zack down and seize his little shoulders to pull him briefly back to the scene he created, turning him entirely facing the cheering crowd so he can fully absorb their enthusiasm for him.

"ZACK!" I instruct him jubilantly, "You did it! They all helped and you did it! You went down that huge slide! See everyone cheering up there? That's for you! Look at them cheering for you. You're "bad," Zack—which is good! You're a bad mother-fucker! Isn't that great?"

"Great," he echoes hazily trying to comprehend the moniker, then stares directly up as the crowd and begins to process that all this cheering and acclaim is truly about him. "Great . . . Great? *YES, GREAT!*" Zack shouts out as he looks up again at the screaming crowd and begins giggling hysterically. He collapses to the grassy floor in a hysterical fit of giggles, rolling back and forth gleefully wrapped in their approbation and fully understanding that it's all about him. As he takes a moment between giggles to look up at my beaming face and makes direct eye contact, there's a distinct glimmer in his eyes, as if has known all along that he's a bad dude.

Back home very late into the evening, I'm still turning over in my mind Zack's new moniker. I can't stop grinning, but I need to adopt a more somber tone for what I'm about to do. I've been debating for quite some time, but I'm ready. I retrieve the phone and brace myself for one last confrontation, and I call to inform Cara that her services are no longer needed.

ALCHEMY

*It is not the most intellectual or the strongest
species that survives, but the one that is able
to adapt to or adjust best to the changing
environment in which it finds itself.*

—CHARLES DARWIN

IN BOTH MY professional and personal life, I have always relied on a surfeit of words. But increasingly, Zack and I are finding nonverbal ways to communicate. Nonverbal cues are an essential and welcome relief from my compulsive need to speak aloud my every thought. How underused my hands, facial expressions and limbs have been! Only now can I see how vital they are in speaking to Zack in a language we both understand. He need only tune in to my facial expression to discern whether I'm angry or adoring, laughing or scowling, or downright confounded by something's he's done—like taste my new vanilla candle.

Long arms wrapped loosely around his little body connotes delight; a firmer grip means restraint or protection, even from himself and his occasional self-injurious bites. Interlacing of our fingers while walking sends a tactile shiver of love up my spine for the warm and deep interconnectedness between us that no words can describe. Looking back on my time at the DOJ, I recall the pity I felt for my deaf colleague with whom I signed, so uninformed was I about the power and clarity of hands. Whole populations speak fluently without ever uttering a word.

But the truest communication is still between our eyes. Zack's eye contact is usually fleeting with other people, but remains rock-solid with me. It's only when our eyes connect that I'm sure he is truly taking in all that I am saying.

Zack's own economy of words works to our mutual advantage—I talk too much, he too little. Somewhere between us lies a normal amount of speech. When I excitedly lapse into talking fits, Zack absorbs my enthusiasm without interruption. When I pause to ask, "Hey Z, do you get enough speaking time in our relationship?" he cracks up, totally receptive to his garrulous mom. "Yes!" he shouts, and there's nothing rote about it. I can confide in him without fear of repercussion or repeating to others. And when I have something truly serious to say, often after long walks when he's lying back lazily in the grass, I speak slowly and distinctly. In an always-fascinating gesture, he immediately sits upright so he can look me squarely the eyes, flickering down briefly to study the motions of my mouth, as he reads my lips and then looks at my eyes again. His head is cocked as he carefully processes the exact sequence of words, and I watch as the wheels grind and turn, unclear precisely how much of what I'm saying he deciphers, but knowing he clearly gets the gist. I don't just talk about us, I talk about him—he is brilliant, prescient, kind, funny, and has an uncanny sense of navigational direction which he regularly employs to help me find the car in crammed parking lots. He's physically strong and coordinated, an athlete. We must nurture and channel his physical strength into Special Olympics sports, he must eat healthily as an athlete. He seems to truly identify with that word. I also remind him that he is spectacularly handsome—I do not lie—and that with great magnetism comes great responsibility. As the George Clooney of autism, he must be gracious to all who pursue him.

Sometimes, it's as if we are meeting for the first time, and our similarities are striking. Turns out we have far more in common than I realized. A culinary preference for savory over sweet, reinforced by Zack's tendency to glance at my plate and swipe whatever food intrigues him. "Thank you," he declares presumptively while scooping my food hurriedly into his mouth, and his self-absorption is charming. The world, after all, belongs to those bold enough to take first and seek permission later. His historic affinity for sampling non-food items like wood chips and candles has afforded him rock-solid immunity from those germs that routinely sicken less hearty children. Zack can ingest a fistful of dirt, pass the contents easily, and then devour a pasta dinner without flinching. Am I proud of such intriguing intestinal achievement? You bet.

We share a love of long woodsy walks, stretching bike rides, action movies, every kind of music, deep massages, and most of all, splash parks with winding lazy rivers. In choosing our designated activity for the day, Zack seems to ingest my every word with his eyes, his fate hinging on the choice he makes. *To the pool or walk with music? Classical or filthy rap?* Zack's rare use of profanity seems to be mimicry, and while I certainly don't encourage it, I dare not reproach him because his articulation is flawless. The consonant cluster just makes certain words so much easier to pronounce, though for the life of me I cannot fathom how he discovered such inflammatory discourse.

Sometimes I sing while holding him gently suspended in my arms in deep waters, and his entire body palpably relaxes into utter limpness. He adores when I read to him, silent and fully absorbed, something I test by occasionally stopping mid-sentence when his head is turned away, just to see if he notices. Not only does he abruptly turn back to face me, he repeats verbatim the exact sequence of the last few words to prompt me to continue. It's interesting, when he deliberately turns away while I read, that it suddenly reminds me of something a lecturing adult with autism once described: that when someone in the audience asks him a question, he cannot take in the person's expression, voice and content at once as there are too many stimulating factors converging. So he instead bows his head and stares downward, thus enabling him to focus on one stimulus at a time. He just listens, processes the words, and then formulates his answer. Only then does he raise his head to make eye contact with the questioner and verbally respond. It seems Zack has a fascinatingly similar processing ritual since his receptive capabilities have always exceeded his expressive ones. He comprehends a great deal more than he can verbally demonstrate. As always, I'm unsure how much of what I'm reading is genuinely absorbed, but I don't care. He may understand every word, or he may just like the cadence of my animated voice. No matter, I'm not taking data.

My sense of humor, once cruelly crushed, has grown back in full with greater luster than ever before. Thinking back on the differential standards that applied to Zack versus typical kids, it was always Zack who was made to feel ashamed of meltdown behaviors identical to those of other kids. So I've adopted a cool double standard of my own. Zack loves the monumental height of the diving boards at our local pool, but if he dares begin the steep climb a moment before the child atop has leapt off, he's swiftly chastised by other parents for his rudeness. Should the child atop hesitate, I loudly heave an impatient sigh *Move it! My kid with autism is excited and he's waiting!* But once Zack's on the precarious ledge, should anyone dare urge him to hurry, I quickly snap back, "Hey! My kid has autism and he's nervous. Be patient!" And so they are.

I've adopted a more playful approach to being regularly informed that "his kind" does not belong in public spaces. Our local pool boasts several lap lanes, and though Zack's stroke is admittedly clumsy and uncoordinated, so is that of his elderly counterparts. But it's Zack who I'm briskly informed must exit the pool if he strays inches towards another swimmer. Both literally and politically, Zack must "stay in his lane." But this is a public facility, I reiterate time and again, which under Title II of the ADA means persons of all abilities are allowed to participate. Also lost on those who complain is that Zack will never learn to navigate the lanes if he's not allowed to occupy them. Never mind that other elderly swimmers also lack speed and precision: no one would ever contemplate asking them to vacate and swim elsewhere.

In response to Zack, one angry woman summons a young lifeguard who awkwardly backs my legal stand. She then announces loudly and with asperity, "If he has such special needs, maybe he needs somewhere special to swim! I don't see why we have to open up all the parts of the pool just to accommodate the 'special people.'"

Grinning, I reply, "Oh, but then where would *you* swim, dear?" for which I receive a sharp glare and rebuke. "Keep going, baby!" I cheer loudly and wave to Zack swimming as he continues to perfect his stroke, while I perfect mine.

Yes, Zack has breathed new life into me, and I into him. We are becoming known around town for our outrageous antics. Lit from within, crackling live wires, we make a formidable team. *We are on fire.*

Zack's ascent has been so glorious even Keith has been inspired to improve his striking distance. While at an inflatables gym, Keith, Zack and I are basking in the glow of how easily Zack darts and gallops with glee from one bouncy structure to the next, totally unafraid. As he rests quietly in the ball pit, turning a few balls over in his hands, I notice that a young boy around Zack's age has taken it upon himself to obnoxiously pelt Zack repeatedly in the head. Having first tried to verbally engage Zack without success, he's caught on to the fact that Zack is somehow disabled, and is deliberately taunting and provoking him with jeers and hits. Zack is confounded, uncertain why the striking balls are coming at him with such vitriol, as the boy grins wickedly enjoying Zack's inability to dexterously shield himself from the pelting. Although the balls themselves are relatively benign, his intent is not. "Hey, please could you stop hitting my son?" I demand briskly. "You're aiming straight for his head and you're hurting him, so knock it off!" The boy pauses momentarily, then abruptly turns his back on me to start shooting hoops in the basketball portion of the inflatable. Rude, but good enough.

Only five minutes later, having just returned from the bathroom, this boy is at it again with amplified speed and intensity. "Hey! My son is disabled, you need to stop it now!" I charge, forgetting that this child might not have been schooled in how to treat children with disabilities, or what exactly being disabled means. He must be taught.

I take a moment to scan for someone with supervisory authority, then give up and retrieve Keith as I explain angrily, pointing at the kid, that's he's deliberately hitting Zack despite my warnings and won't stop. Keith steps deliberately away from me and towards the boy, calling out congenially, "Hey there, how 'bout playing toss with me instead?" It's just like Keith to befriend the little demon when I wanted him excoriated, but then Keith has always been even-keeled in defending Zack. Still, I would have like to at least see him—what!?

A bloodcurdling scream comes from the ball pit, piercing the entire facility at such a pitch that people immediately gather. *Oh God, Zack!* I think reflexively, *he got hurt!* Frantically I scan the ball pit, but am stopped in my tracks to see the other boy laid out flat, choking and gasping for air, rolling side-to-side in a frenzy. Unbeknownst to me, Keith had furtively sneaked a Nerf-like football under his forearm during his casual remark to the boy, and then swiftly moved in to torpedo it straight to the kid's gut, knocking him squarely on his ass! "Keith!" I gasp, shocked by the sheer force of the hit—not to mention the surgical precision— as the boy, humiliated and enraged, begins wailing loudly and screaming for his mommy. Trying to gain his balance, the boy stands up briefly only to trip on the ball and tumble back down hard, landing on a much larger kid who ruthlessly thrusts him away as a "jerk." Disoriented and dazed, the boy fumbles to gain equilibrium but it's clear that all Keith did was knock the wind out of him to startle him into stopping his crusade against Zack.

But, oh, the beauty of watching the smiling assassin stumble to gain his grip, lose his footing to go back down again, shrieking in rage and defiance. I quickly pivot Keith's stance in the opposite direction, then take a moment to scan the crowd for signs of whether any of them can identify who exactly targeted this kid and delivered the blow. While the attorney in me has long laid dormant, the protective ghost knows when to rise, as I silently calculate a closing argument for Keith's trial: "*Your Honor, my husband had to act quickly in self-defense of an innocent child with autism . . . !*"

It's clear to all the kid isn't hurt, just embarrassed. There are no witnesses to the prelude of the incident. Keith ducks his head down low towards mine and mumbles sheepishly, "Holy crap, I actually didn't mean to throw it *that* hard . . . !" I burst out laughing, he and I quickly dissolving into hysterics as the boy is finally dragged off by his mother, still screaming in outrage that some old man hit him on purpose! Apparently acquainted with her son's tendency to bully, his mother absentmindedly nods, pats his head and keeps dragging.

"Oh, honey," I stare at him adoringly, barely able to speak between laughing spasms, *"I think I just fell in love with you all over again . . . !"*

MASTER THE KINGDOM

*We are not trying to entertain the critics. I'll take
my chances with the public.*

—WALT DISNEY

THERE IS ONE place we still must go. It's the place we
couldn't handle years ago, and it is the destination to which
we must now return—Disney World. I recall from years ago
the catastrophic flight to Miami when Zack nearly landed the
plane with his terrified reaction to being suspended in air,
uncomprehending the nature of air travel with no visual cues in
sight. Now he's a frequent flyer, jovially looking out the windows
to narrate loudly that the plane is now "GOING UP!" and met
with appreciative smiles as I mouth silently, "*autism.*"

The first time we went, I was devastated by Zack's inability
to enjoy the park, and I had lapsed into fantasies about how our
experience should have been if Zack were a normal child. Feeling
robbed, I checked Zack's behavior moment-to-moment against
that of his typical peers around the park so often that I became

unable to shake the alternate reality. I couldn't remain present with my own son. It seemed yet another cruel hoax of fate that the enchanted park, which I grew up loving as a child, the one I'd always envisioned sharing with my own child, had become a place of torment and exclusion. My memories crystallized of forcibly holding Zack down as we gently rode boats through dark interiors, his terrorized screams reverberating off the walls and frightening the other children. Collapsing in defeat, I dragged him by his knees out of the park and vowed never to return. And I don't intend to re-enact defeat today. We have traveled many miles by plane, car and monorail to get here and I'm hopeful of an entirely different outcome.

I've just learned that Disney World has a glorious invention called a *disability pass* whereby persons with special needs go directly to the front of every line for every ride, the political equivalent of a *fast pass*. I'm getting one, not because Zack can't tolerate long waits—that's actually a strength of his—but because I choose not to. We've been through enough. But the habitually sunny guest services staff is surprisingly rude, insisting on documented medical proof of Zack's autism. I readily hand it over and politely inform her we'll be visiting the Magic Kingdom for four days straight. Dripping with snark, she retorts, "So do you actually intend to use the pass for all four days?"

My response is equally vinegary: "Well, I expect my son to have autism for all four days. But of course if it clears up overnight I'll be sure hand it back in." And with a wink and a nod we are off, strutting our way through the Magic Kingdom where everything is magical and the kingdom belongs to Zack.

We saunter, we gallop, we bounce, we flap. So much easier to cover massive ground this way, being first in line—everywhere. As we sprint gleefully from ride to ride, the crowds part to make way for master Zack, disabled VIP. Step aside please, autism does have its privileges.

We'll be able to ride three times over at the rate we're going, and ready in plenty of time to dine with Mickey and take in the spectacular light parade and fireworks. Snow White, Haunted House and Peter Pan, oh my! But most especially I want us to visit "It's a Small World," with the exquisite inner landscape and singing from children worldwide. As the music beckons us on friendly waters, Zack is leaning so far forward in excitement that my only fear is keeping him in the boat. I watch as Zack's eyes widen in total wonder that anything on earth could be this visually splendid.

I suddenly recall a developmental milestone described to me by the doctor who initially diagnosed Zack with autism at nineteen months. With the concept of *joint attention,* a child directs the parent towards a desired object by pointing, or laughs with the parent over something funny, thus joining parent and child with shared intent and mutual understanding. Once lacking in Zack—thus a defining marker of his autism—*joint attention* is beamingly present now as he excitedly engages me. We laugh together in concert, like the synchronized swimmers we have become. Our bond has deepened immeasurably, and there's another shared truth he's telling me—how grateful he is to be out of that therapy room and truly immersed in the world.

His eyes lock on mine: *Thank you Mommy! This is the best!* Yes, it is. I'm so deliriously happy right now that, I swear, this eclipses all the pain that came before, which made Zack eligible for the disability pass in the first place. Our joy is as limitless as the Kingdom itself, and my satisfaction a million times greater than if he had conquered the park as a typical child. Thank you, my beloved.

"WHY DOES ZACK EAT PLAYDOH?"

When a child asks you something, answer him, for goodness sake. But don't make a production of it. Children are children, but they can spot an evasion faster than adults, and evasion simply muddles 'em.

—*TO KILL A MOCKINGBIRD*, HARPER LEE

I'VE ENROLLED ZACK in our neighborhood public elementary school where he'll be fully mainstreamed with peers in first grade, with no private shadow. He'll be included for the majority of the day, pulled out for special needs instruction where the curriculum will be modified for his learning level. This balance feels correct for now with Zack, age 7, immersed in typical peers but still functioning on a level commensurate with his needs. Mainstream inclusion tracks Zack for a high school diploma, though down the road I may opt for a more restrictive placement in special education. The recent trend towards inclusion of children with disabilities regardless of severity is noble but has many exceptions. The prestige of being fully mainstreamed is empty if the child is so overwhelmed and outmatched that he's incapable of absorbing the lessons. As a parent who traffics in function, I'll keep Zack mainstreamed only as long as it's worthwhile to him.

There are limits to Zack's cognitive retention, so if academic choices must be made I'll eschew curriculum details about US presidents and capitals of states in favor of life skills that teach Zack how to grocery shop independently. Zack's time is too valuable for me to get distracted by the pedigree of a high school diploma if it's at the expense of salient skills he needs to navigate his community. We'll see.

It won't take long for his first grade compatriots to pick up on Zack's differences, especially since he's the only disabled student in the class. While other children with learning disabilities are likely to assimilate socially, I have no illusions for Zack. In the time it takes classmates to initiate a conversation, participate in circle time or engage during recess, they will quickly gauge how dramatically Zack's behavior deviates. Absent explanation, they'll lack the proper context to interpret his differences. Once again, I stand at the crossroads of disclosure versus privacy, weighing Zack's autonomy against larger issues of what it means to be meaningfully included. To my mind, the noble goal posts of inclusion are within reach only if his peers truly know who Zack is and why he behaves as he does.

In broaching this topic at school I'm met with unexpected resistance. Intriguingly, parents of more mildly impacted autistic students vehemently object to any description of autism that risks outing their own children to their classmates. Given that their children are capable of the kind of self-advocacy that allows them to express their discomfort with being identified, I completely respect their wishes. But these parents insist that my lecture be confined to a description of autism symptoms without using the "*A* word" itself. I refuse this adjustment because concealment of Zack's diagnosis suggests shame, and my purpose is to educate, not obfuscate. School officials object to a lecture on policy grounds, arguing that the defining ingredient of inclusion is precisely *not* to single out a child based on his disability. I acknowledge that, but in Zack's case this venerable objection misses the point. The reality is that Zack stands out, and that gulf will continue to widen over time, whether we spotlight him or not. Explaining his disability is a form of self-definition which doesn't undermine his belonging, but rather affords peers the requisite background to accommodate his uniqueness. Unknowing peers who Zack routinely ignores or offends will draw false conclusions, thus exposing him to ridicule and alienation far greater than if I come clean about the reasons for Zack's aloofness. Darkness is a breeding ground for misunderstanding and secrecy is Zack's undoing.

In a series of conferences with parents and the school principal, my reasoning ultimately prevails, but with important restrictions. I'm permitted to give lectures about autism generally, and about Zack specifically, to all children grades K-5, provided I exclude those classrooms which also have spectrum students. Total candor is permitted, provided the school counselor first reviews and collaborates with me on wording the lecture. This is fair, so I draft my lecture on Zack. Then, I hit another ethical quandary about whether Zack should remain in the room or be escorted out. Since I'm unable to secure Zack's consent to the lecture, both options feel like a betrayal of his autonomy— deciding whether to disclose his disability, yet another in a long line of choices I make for Zack, just like overriding his vehement protest to get him into venues. These decisions are not frivolous, but earnestly calculated to ensure that Zack is given access to succeed in as many realms as possible. Once again, the ethical balance tips in favor of candor.

The evening before the lecture, I soften my decision as best I can by explaining to Zack what I intend to say so I can educate his classmates to fully understand him. As always, Zack's eyes lock unblinkingly on mine, his head slightly cocked—behavioral indicators that he is listening intently to every word. That he does not cry out "NO!" is the closest I can come to permission, and I take solace only in the fact that our shared history proves that I would never do anything I did not believe to be in Zack's best interest.

As I arrive at Zack's first grade class, a paraeducator dutifully escorts a bemused Zack out of the room. As the children scurry quickly to the carpet to sit cross-legged at my feet, I scan their curious faces and begin:

- Look around and notice all the differences among you. Some of you have dark skin, some of you have blue eyes—not one of us is exactly the same as the other. And that's a good thing! Imagine how boring it would be if we all looked the same, talked the same, acted the same. It's our differences that make us interesting.

- Some children have challenges with certain parts of their body. Some of the students at school are in wheelchairs and walkers because they have difficulty using their legs, and need help. The part of Zack's body that is different than all of yours is a part you can't see—his brain. Zack has a disability called autism, and it's a condition that affects his brain. His brain isn't better or worse than yours, it's just different.

- There are three things to know about Zack and other kids who have autism: (1) they have trouble getting words out; (2) they sometimes don't know when to put the *brakes* on their thoughts; and (3) even if they don't act like it, they really do like you and want to be included with you. Zack has so much to say but the way his brain is wired makes it very hard for him to find the words and say them out loud, so if he doesn't talk as much as all of you, that's why. But he's always thinking his thoughts and the funny thing is, sometimes that's what he does talk about out loud. Even if it's not part of your conversation, Zack doesn't always know how to brake or not say some of his thoughts out loud, just so you know.

- But this point about autism is actually the most important of all: even though Zack doesn't always smile or say "Hi" back to you, even if he doesn't come over to play with you, it's not because he doesn't like you. It's because the way his brain works. It makes it very hard for him to show you exactly how much he really does like you, which can be very sad and frustrating for him. So, please trust me as his mom to tell you that each and every one of you matters to Zack. He is looking to you to learn how to talk, how to play, and how to become your friend. Think of yourselves as his most special teachers; grab him and bring him into your games, go ahead and talk to him even if he doesn't answer, because now you know why. Now we can all work together to help him.

- I'm sure some of you are a little nervous and wondering if you can catch autism by playing with Zack, but don't worry, you can't. Autism is one of those things that you are born with or you're not, and if you are born with it you will have it forever, but if not you, will never get it. So Zack will always have autism: it's a part of him just as much as his brown eyes and dark hair; he will never outgrow it; even as a grown-up, his brain will still work differently than yours. That's why as his mom I think it's so important to explain that to you all so you can become friends with him now, and hopefully stay friends. Zack learns differently than you do. He needs lots and lots of repetition, but he does learn. He also learns best from watching all of you, he learns things he sees over and over every day, so you all are his best example of how to behave.

- Zack's life will always be a little different from yours because his brain is wired differently, so he feels and sees things differently. Sometimes that's very frustrating for him, so if he gets angry I try to be patient and understand how hard it is to live in a world where your brain works differently than so many other people. Zack will always need extra help for his whole life, but he can still make friends, learn in school, get a job and have just as wonderful and happy a life as each of you. But his life will be so much happier if you all try to be in it.

- As Zack's mother, what matters to me is not that he be just like all of you, he can't be, that isn't how he was born. What's most important to me is that Zack becomes the very best person he can become, and that all of you understand his autism and accept him for who he is. That would be the very best gift you could give him—your understanding and friendship. So if you have anything at all you want to ask, anything on your minds about Zack, don't be afraid to ask me, I want to answer it. I want to hear everything that is confusing or that you want to know more about. And Zack wants that, too.

These children are absorbed and sit very silently. There's not been a break in attention, not even a squirm. As I open the door to questions, I detect a sudden apprehension from the teacher, and quickly signal her that nothing is off limits. More than anything I've just asked of Zack's peers, what I want most is to know what's streaking across their busy little minds. Questions begin impulsively erupting with gusto as the teacher reminds them they must wait to be called on, which triggers a collective salute of arms thrust hard into the air, rigid and impatient, each straining to be heard. The remarks are as prescient as they are blunt.

"So if a person with autism dies, does the autism die with them or is it reincarnated into another soul?" *That's a tough one, though in Zack's case here on earth autism sticks for life.*

"If a mom has twins and one baby has autism, does that mean the other one automatically does, too?" *If they are identical twins, yes, well-reasoned you.*

"I think I know how Zack feels. I moved here from Japan last year and I had so much trouble learning English. I got frustrated, too, when I tried to ask something. I think for Zack it must be like that, like everyone around him is speaking a better language so he gets mad . . . " *Precisely! There's no better explanation than a strong analogy so thanks for that.*

"I understand why he gets mad. Sometimes when I have something really good to say and I have my hand up for a long time and the teacher doesn't call on me, I get really mad so I start to bite my hand! I don't know why, I just have to do something so I start biting . . . " *I couldn't have explained Zack's frustration any better, and am so glad I didn't keep you waiting too long!*

The more hands I release from their tension, the larger the conversation grows, and the urgency for answers does not ease as we dive into deeper waters, more personal matters. The teacher shifts anxiously again, but I shake my head against her instinct to steer the dialogue away, because only uninhibited expressions of thought can be met with equal frankness. Children are naturally uncensored, their straight-line questions don't disappoint.

"Were you sad when you found out Zack had autism?"

"Yes, I was very sad." I reply truthfully. "At first I wanted him to be just like all of you, I wanted him to be typical so life would be easier for him—and for me. But once I realized that he could still be happy and do so many things—" there's mounting suspense as I quickly reach into my bag and flash a photo of Zack on the famed *Claw* amusement park ride, which requires no further explanation beyond its name. The photo dutifully elicits a collective "Whoooaaa!" at the sight of Zack upside down on the twisting, hurling wonder.

"Is Zack ever going to be normal? Like even for an hour, or a weekend, or ever when he grows up?" I detect a hint of mournful regret as the gravity of Zack's incurable condition truly seeps in to the young crowd.

"No, Zack will never be normal. But that's okay, don't let that be a sad end of the story for him, because as long as his friends accept him and his autism, Zack will be just fine. And as his mother, nothing in this world would make me happier."

There's time only for one more as I select an uncommonly pensive girl who asks very shyly, "Does Zack *mind* that he has autism?"

I'm walloped, speechless from this deceptively simple question, a question I never thought to ask in that way. I've spent so much of Zack's life in reactive stance, so fixed on others' opinions of Zack, I confess to her that her question has me considering it from his angle for the first time. I'm well acquainted with my own narrative arc, how my relationship with autism has bent over time. But over the years—even as I tried to get into Zack's mind, his visual speak, talk back to his muted fears—never did I ask precisely how Zack experiences his own disability. *Does Zack mind that he has autism?* I honestly don't know. So I tell her what I do know, that this is one of the most sensitive and intelligent questions I've ever been asked. That no matter how hard it's been, and at times it's been incredibly hard, Zack's autism is totally worth it for me. And to the kernel of her larger question, I know that Zack is happy and values his life despite his limitations. It is indeed frustrating to be Zack, to struggle to find the words and be heard, but his life is still joyous and deeply satisfying. I don't waver because on that point I know his answer.

In the days and weeks that follow, a stark new problem arises. Zack is being literally assaulted by peers, not with cruelty but exaggerated expressions of kindness and instruction. Children all across the school are physically accosting him at every turn, in the halls, at lunch time and recess, stopping purposely to pat his head, give him a high-five, hug and kiss him, sometimes just place a face right next to his to further examine him. The children have taken their roles to heart, instructing him as best they can, like the meticulous little teachers and models they have suddenly become.

"Zack, look at me, no, directly into my eyes, good boy."

"Come with me, Zack, I'm going to teach you how to play basketball."

"Okay, I'm going to hug you now and then you are going to hug me right back!"

Zack is immediately the target of so many affectionate missiles it's confounding to him, I'm told, but the kids aren't letting up. I imagine him mentally retracing his steps. *So, I went to lunch while Mommy spoke to my friends, then I came back to a world gone mad! What on earth did she do this time? Poor Mommy seems to need so much real-world validation.* Okay, maybe not that last thought, but it's clear the children take their mission quite seriously and Zack is at the epicenter. Touchingly, one new friend found just the words to discuss his newfound erudition by composing a poem which he dedicated to Zack and was shared with me.

DIFFERENCES

Why are we so different?
I do not know why.
Some have blond hair, some have brown hair.
Some have autism, some have Down Syndrome.
Some are blind.
As you can see differences are everywhere.
You should be happy!

-- *Jaden Wallach*
First Grade

Zack now goes bounding on well-adjusted feet into Ms. Meyers' first grade class. Every day I walk him into the towering building, his little hand clasped in mine, every day the electric jolt to my heart as I surrender him to events that will not be recounted at the end of the day because he can't recount them. But just now, in a cruel twist of defiance, he ruthlessly cut the cord and pushed back just outside the school entrance with a simple declarative, "Goodbye Mommy! Goodbye!" He then marches into the building alone. Independent. And what about this assertive milestone had I imagined would be so sweetly redolent of hard-fought trials? Instead, this feels like a bitter pill jammed down my throat.

Standing here, aghast and embarrassed for all the right reasons, I take a moment to collect myself in the abrupt aftermath of Zack's brutish rejection. In these bittersweet seconds it makes absolutely no difference that Zack is about to enter a mainstream class where he is unlike everyone else. Nor does it matter that he is, technically speaking, the lowest functioning child in his class and will likely score lowest on every standardized test. Nor is it relevant that, as one little girl informed me, "I think other kids at this school have autism too, but Zack has it the most."

BURDEN-SHIFTING

Many of us spend our whole lives running from feeling with the mistaken belief that you cannot bear the pain. But you have already borne the pain. What you have not done is feel all you are beyond that pain.

—KAHLIL GIBRAN

SOMETHING PERMANENT HAS crossed over in Zack; it has crossed over in me as well. We are in a very different place than before, in relationship both to the world and each other. With each new conquest, no matter how disastrously it began, we have gained crucial ground and unearthed newfound mutual respect. Despite the fierce opposition of his screaming and thrashing, Zack now comprehends the purpose behind the forcible pushes. In the far reaches of his mind he now understands that I push him because I love him, because I want something more for him than he might have imagined for himself. Somehow he grasps that if I am going to such great physical lengths to override his fears and even his will, it must be in furtherance of something larger, something tremendously rewarding that I know he can access because I am deeply confident in his abilities. Beneath the initial betrayal now lies a sturdy bedrock of trust he can reference, having realized that his interest and mine are inextricably related. When we come out the other side, it is both our lives which are being rescued.

What motivated this ordeal was a fundamental truth—that I cannot be happy if my son cannot function competently in his community. We have been through battle together, he and I, and we are infinitely stronger for having done so. And in the end it's why I believe he forgives me all my transgressions against him, just as I forgive his. We have jointly massaged the world into a more predictable place, and his tantrums are virtually nonexistent. In a word, my son is *living*.

Along with his stunning physical growth, Zack's self-esteem has grown in, lush and abundant. It's not simply that Zack is steadily conquering his fears, *but that he understands that he is conquering them*. And what's ripened inside me is a level of abject patience I never knew existed because I've never been pushed to my own limitations in this capacity—a reservoir of hours upon hours working tirelessly in pursuit of someone else's progress besides my own. I'm not just a better parent, I'm a better person because of what Zack has unearthed in me. Having struggled with bouts of anxiety long before Zack arrived, I'm at my calmest when guiding him through an outburst and away from his own acute distress. His urgent needs displace mine, his abject fears are a productive catalyst which forces me to surrender any egotistical impulses in order to manage his very real emergency. Zack's needs are a remarkable diversion from my own ruminating mind, and my once-internalized radar, carefully calibrated to detect my own erratic fears, is externalized to focus on someone in greater need. His autism has unexpectedly calmed me down.

I've channeled Zack's raging passions toward more productive ends; he's unexpectedly done the same for me. Zack's inability to speak for himself has ignited advocacy from me more earnest and eloquent than anything I ever uttered in the courtroom. His continued capacity to astonish me at the very moment I'm losing hope has inspired an unwavering persistence in me to never stop pushing him to ever higher levels. Now, finally, I am an advocate of the most unexpected sort, someone who regularly engages in public disclosures and educational lectures from which I would have recoiled in those early diagnostic days and felt incapable of back when I was actually working at the DOJ on behalf of people like my son. Now finally, I'm an expert in a chosen field.

I've come to believe that, as parents, there is no better means of advocating for our autistic children than by educating a crowd in the heat of a public tantrum. But it's not through angry discourse, it's through plain-spoken identification of the child's diagnosis that places the behavior in proper context. There should be no apologizing for who our children are, but instead who we need the general public to be—compatriots in the mission of genuine inclusion of our disabled children for the common good. The metaphor, for me, is legal burden shifting. As parents, we assume initial burden of disclosure to cement lifelong functional skills, no matter how uncomfortable it may be for bystanders to witness a tantrum. Once informed, the public now carries the burden to exhibit compassion, and if they are courageous, then assistance. A judicious balance must be struck. The daily experience of autism cannot be fully understood by those who have not lived it; but one need not personally identify with the struggle to show compassion for it. *The duty to educate arises from tolerance towards those who haven't lived it, the same tolerance that we seek for our children.*

If we expect our children's behaviors to be accommodated and for them to be meaningfully included in our communities, we must provide an excuse to those who don't automatically understand the startling behaviors. If we do not want our children painted with a broad diminutive brush, we must likewise not categorically dismiss or accuse others of insensitivity to the huge challenge about which they are not yet informed. We don't underestimate our own children's capacity to evolve and learn; we must not denigrate the public's capacity to grow and learn, too.

Even in this most helpless of worlds, we have a choice. We can *choose* to be humiliated by our children's behavior, or we can *refuse* to be. We can choose to submit to a brief stint in hell or resign ourselves to a lifetime of it. We can choose to boldly educate those around us, or we can remain isolated and ashamed. It is indeed painful to withstand the glares when you take your child out in public places and he suddenly erupts in unconventional behaviors. Do it anyway! It's excruciating to withstand the initial judgment and condemnation that attends a public tantrum. Withstand it anyway! And as you do so, try to inform concisely and with no more verbiage than "My child has autism, I am working with him."

Do not let prejudice or shame define your parameters for where your child can go; you are the one charged with his future, and no one else. You are entitled by law and common sense to take calculated risks on his behalf. As parents, we must do our best to carve out a life for ourselves and our children in spite of the constraints of autism, or we surely surrender to its power to destroy our lives. So often it seems we have no choices, but in fact we have many.

Whenever I'm out in the community, I'm amazed I don't regularly witness a child with autism having a full-blown tantrum. Given autism's epidemic numbers, this should be occurring hourly. And yet, it is not surprising at all, because too often our children are hidden away at home, their behaviors shielded from view so that we may all be spared the trauma. I wonder how many parents are going through the ritualistic retreat even at this very second. Whether or not they admit it to themselves, their world is rapidly shrinking. Secretly devastated and imprisoned by shame, they retreat home after a swift kick in the teeth, just another cruel consequence of having a child with autism. And with that resignation, they quietly surrender another piece of their soul. And try as I might, I honestly cannot conceive of anyone who benefits from the confinement and concealment of our children, though I can imagine millions who are suffering from it.

I do not believe I was divinely anointed to have a disabled child. I am an ordinary woman who, in profound desperation and despair, carved a risky path out of the darkness. I have always believed that what unites us as humans is not our common fortune—there's nothing common about fortune. But we do share common misfortune, because misfortune is the rod that touches each and every one of us at different times in our lives.

Since taking up the mantle of public disclosure of Zack's autism, I've been consistently awed by strangers' ability, in the searing heat of the moment, to immediately grasp that autism has touched my life, and it could have just as easily touched theirs. Whenever I have disclosed Zack's autism and need for tolerance, I have received a great deal more in return. Strangers have gone to extraordinary lengths to accommodate and assist us across all venues. People who characteristically won't tolerate for long the screams of a tantrum in a closed indoor space, have proven willing to withstand twenty minutes of intense screaming from an autistic child if they understand that by doing so they are making history in that child's life. Compassion exists in far greater quantities than we may realize. I have seen the proverbial waters part to make way for my son. Zack is the human prism through which my cynicism about strangers has been refracted into a more charitable spectrum.

Do I still feel pangs of grief at times? Yes, but they are briefly lived and much more easily put in perspective against the backdrop of other human suffering. A young man once gave me sorely needed perspective without realizing what he'd done. Max was a gifted and talented teen, and was featured among the top ten most extraordinary teens in a local publication. Max was assigned to shadow Zack through a spectacularly inclusive summer camp routinely filled with both disabled and typical peers.

When I first met Max, and every morning I turned Zack over to him, I couldn't help but be struck by the lopsided genetic imbalance between the two. This young man was at once a divinely gifted artist, drummer, literary thinker, academic, and he was handsome to boot. The bundling of Max and Zack did at times strike an excruciating note as I watched Max, the genius, reach out to Zack, the impaired. Max's daily-logged briefings on Zack were so thorough and inspired, it couldn't escape my attention that in some alternate universe, this remarkable young man could have been my son, with everything I wanted in a child.

One day Max made a personal disclosure. Just prior to working with Zack he had experienced a trauma which left him starting his summer "shadow" job in despair, and insecure of his abilities to steer Zack. He confided that it was the very experience of working side by side every day with Zack that helped heal the wounds. He then recounted how closely he'd been observing and decoding Zack. It struck me as generous for Max to share with me, nothing more, until one day Max seized upon Zack's peculiar way of holding himself when trying to concentrate.

"You know that way Zack sits with a sort of a blank stare and cocks his head?" *Very well,* I thought as I stiffened to ready myself for the inevitable pity. "Well, to be really honest, when I see Zack like that I can't help feeling—jealous of him. It's like he's so at peace with himself and the world, so serene, I'd just love to know what that feels like to him."

I'm floored. *Jealous, of Zack?* As Max went on to explain, layered into his genius mind are darker corners, haunting inspirations that he would gladly shed to become a less complicated artist. He hints at depression, despair and austere medications to counteract the highs and lows. Life is not nearly as easy for this virtuoso as appearances would lead one to believe; he longs for the equanimity that Zack exhibits. I was too dumbfounded at the time to respond. Never in a million years would I have imagined a person so gifted would feel envious of my disabled son, though the way he described it, it made perfect sense. His disclosure has reverberated many times, it provided insight I never forgot when comparing the quality of Zack's life to others'.

Zack is my child and I know he will never recover from autism as I had once desperately hoped. To my mind, success for a person with autism should not be defined by *recovery* or passing for normal, but instead by whether that person can become a meaningful contributor to society, capable of recreation, and able to form attachments to others. I am not a clinical expert, not a doctor or a scientist, so I do not know what's possible for our children if we allow them to be themselves while we provide a loving push. But I would very much like to find out, because in the end, it is not my son who has recovered, it is me.

RE-ENTRY

*I don't care what anything was designed to do. I care about what it **can** do.*

—*"APOLLO 13"* GENE KRANZ, ASTRONAUT

I AM RE-ENTERING the legal biosphere, picking up the pieces from almost seven years ago and finding them surprisingly easy to reassemble. With Zack nestled in first grade and Cassie beginning preschool, it's time to get back to what I was meant for. It's remarkable that my prior diligence as an adoption attorney carved a groove in my former boutique law firm into which, so many years after I departed, I'm now able to slide. Contemplating whether to work part-or full-time, I walk into my tiny old unfurnished cubicle and am instantly flooded with details from past cases including the smooth and joyous adoptions, but also those acrimonious contests to determine the best interest of the child who was both blessed and cursed to be at the center of possessive controversy. I know something of the vitriol born of a broken heart. I shall use my experience wisely to shepherd my clients through the vicissitudes of uncertainty inherent in the adoption process. Although many of the legal players at my firm have shifted—some resigned, some still here—the laudable mission remains unchanged. It's finally time for me to mitigate the intellectual losses from my derailment years ago. I have arrived, once again.

It's going to take a while to catch up on the particulars of the law, which varies state to state, but I'm determined to study every bit as hard as I did in law school to achieve mastery. So today I'm all suited up—granted the zipper of my skirt didn't quite close at the top—and ready to become a virtual sponge at this annual adoption law conference in DC. The timing couldn't be better for me to reclaim my continuing legal education. My body is tingling to my fingertips as, lined legal pad in hand, I prepare to scribble each and every word. In walks the panel of presenting attorneys and each introduces his or her personal biography. It's interesting how many of them entered the field on the heels of their own failed adoption which motivated them to alter the *status quo* in favor of adoptive parents.

The room is packed to the doors with attorneys and prospective adoptive parents desperate to begin the journey and come out the other end, wholly fulfilled. As the first lawyer begins his lecture I'm struck by his theme—persistence. There can be false starts, devastating pitfalls, changes of heart and revocation of consent. It's clear that unwavering persistence is needed in pursuit of a beloved child. My dedication to these parents just redoubled. I know something of persistence and resilience in the face of despair. Yes, my experience will serve me well.

Except suddenly, I feel ice cold as a wave of unexpected dislocation crashes over me. I try desperately to shake off this profound sense of isolation from the herd, but it's gaining momentum throughout my body. My once-nimble fingers are trembling badly, and now I'm having trouble writing, even concentrating, on the words. *What on earth is going on?*

Furiously, I scold myself to get a grip, but it's entirely unpersuasive. Something inside of me is unraveling at a frantic pace. As so often happens in moments of acute panic, I disassociate. The professional voices dim to become ambient background noise as I spiral off into space, into my own surreal world, in utter disbelief that this could possibly be happening to me, yet again, in the place I least expect.

Zack is nowhere in sight, there are no tantrums to defuse and no scorching crisis. I finally have my legal bearings and professional trajectory, so why now am I consumed by senseless anxiety? Disturbing thoughts are rising swiftly to the surface as I furiously clamp down to suppress them, but it's of no use. They demand to be heard. *I don't belong here.*

I'm feeling wildly outpaced by these talking heads. There's so much new information to absorb from seasoned professionals who recite it glibly off the top of their heads, and it's second nature for those who've been immersed for years. I'm not used to feeling so seriously overmatched. Breaking out into a cold sweat, I realize I can't possibly catch up. What was I thinking to imagine I could contribute, much less compete? Why would any of these desperate clients choose me to represent them over the dozens of infinitely more qualified lawyers? *So you'll get there*, I coach myself. *It's natural to feel panicky when you've been out of the game for so long.* But the drumbeat is sounding louder, the rebels are restive, roiling and turning against me in an angry insistence to be heard.

Oh God, I don't belong here. I can't catch up, these parents don't need me. Others are way more qualified to do this, desperate clients don't need a desperately inexperienced lawyer, I am of no use to them.

Rationally, I calculate that if I study hard and bring all resources to bear I can be competent, but not indispensable. Personal experience with adoption is not a prerequisite, but it certainly helps in forging an intimate connection with clients in pain. I'm all about life experience as teacher. Although my face registers blank, my gut could not be more certain. I am a foreigner in this room because my people are not in this room. They are out there, roaming the streets in shock and disbelief, locked down in their houses to avoid the trauma of public explosions. The parents in here don't need me, but I have a feeling parents out there might.

I exhale breathlessly and release the tight grip on my ballpoint pen as it tumbles to the floor. Zack has done it again. He has disrupted everything I thought I knew about myself, flung it ruthlessly into outer space, leaving me to reassemble the pieces in line with an irrepressible truth. I have been irreversibly changed by Zack and our journey. I'm no longer the person I once was, and my life's purpose must shift along with who I've become. *I am autism and it is me; I live and breathe it, fully intoxicated: it's in my marrow.* And most unexpectedly, it gives me profound joy and sense of purpose to acknowledge it.

It doesn't matter that I was trained to be an attorney. I'm meant to be something more feral, more hands-on, more intimate and immediate. After a decade spent wandering the wilderness as a *little attorney lost,* possessing raging zeal with no clearly identifiable group to ignite it, I have come home.

Slowly and discreetly, I stand up and quietly make my way out of the conference room. I won't be missed. Even before I reach my car my eager fingers are tugging to release the pressure of my skirt zipper from its onerous task of constricting the flesh. I never did like the inflexible fabric of these uptight suits. Still dazed but very much awake, I now know what I have to do.

MEET THE AMBASSADORS

I'm on your side, when times get rough,
And friends just can't be found...
I'll take your part when darkness comes
And pain is all around
Like a bridge over troubled water
I will lay me down.
Like a bridge over troubled water
I will lay me down.

—"BRIDGE OVER TROUBLED WATER,"
LYRICS BY PAUL SIMON

I STARTED THIS journey with Zack, determined not to let his autism derail me personally or professionally. The plan was to intervene swiftly and with intensity and recover my son, then resume my life. But, like Zack, somewhere along the way I experienced an interior shift from which there's been no turning back. I can even mark the moment it happened— that Elmo show when we yanked back the curtain and Zack triumphantly overcame his fear. I came home that day so elated and feverishly sent out an email to everyone I knew jubilantly recounting the details. As we plowed forward conquering venue after venue, as I forcibly pushed Zack into movies and subways, and he alternately shoved me down that ferocious vertical slide, something indescribable was building. It redefined my staid notions of what it meant to be productive, successful, satisfied— what it meant to change a life. Unbeknownst to me, I was becoming gratified by a most unexpected client who ignited in me a healthy obsession with discovering what an autistic child could achieve when pushed beyond his comfort zone. I have come to embrace the unconventionality of autism, as well as its authenticity and total lack of pretense, even the enormous challenge itself. It is the particulars of autism that serenade my heart and mind, and quench my own thirst for nonconformity.

I no longer practice law, but I now know that a law degree is merely a professional license to advocate—not a prerequisite. Hungry for more creative ways to channel my energy, I founded a charitable venture called *Autism Ambassadors*—Ambassadors because I consider people with autism, and those who care for them, to be the noblest, most intriguing and industrious people walking the planet. But Ambassadors need "a room of their own," an exclusive retreat away from the public glare. They need to be surrounded by others who get it. Autism is both leveler and equalizer of all persons touched, and if I have my way, a unifier too.

The mission of Autism Ambassadors is simple: to provide exclusive recreational events for children, teens and adults of all ages across the spectrum. Ambassador families attend my events monthly in a variety of venues rented out exclusively for our use—movie theaters, indoor and outdoor pools and splash parks, gymnastic facilities, inflatables gyms, dance studios and, when I can nail them down, live theater productions. Events are restricted to families impacted by autism not because I wish to exclude others, but because our numbers are epidemic. At events our children communicate in an unspoken language; the buzz of acceptance crackles in the air and infects parents and siblings, too. Diagnostic distinctions such as high or low functioning are not needed. All who reside on the mighty spectrum are welcome. Gourmet pizza is served, because a party isn't a party without food, and I always over order at least ten pies each time, just in case. No Ambassador shall go hungry or uninspired in my presence.

I have only one strict policy: no apologies for behaviors. Parents, check your anxieties at the door. We're all about fun here and on our own autistic terms, which are as follows:

- If you as a parent feel lost, alone and need a safe space to allow your child to be himself among others being themselves

- If you're afraid to take your child to public venues because of potential judgment, odd behaviors or full-blown tantrums

- If your child yelps or talks loudly at movies, roams the perimeter of the theater, flaps incessantly, screams, twirls, bounces

- If you fear that even in this most safe space, your child still can't come because you are convinced his behaviors are worse or more humiliating than those of the pack

- If you are this parent, then you had better come right now. These events are especially for you.

The events began years ago with only fifteen families because those were the only people I knew then who were impacted by autism; now they have grown to more than 600 families. We are each other's bedrock, therapists, financial advisors and reservoir of professional resources. Parents cast off the crippling tension that weighs them down day and night; siblings, who often evolve into *de facto* therapists, are included to make sure they know they are not navigating the autistic seas alone. Virtually every week new members join, parents of newly diagnosed children reach out, genuinely petrified and in desperate need of the warm tribal embrace. Some Ambassadors have stayed since the beginning; others outgrow the protective exclusivity and integrate into public recreation, having used the events as their transitional tool. So it is that overall attendance at events remains steady via constant influx and defection, exactly as it should be.

I look forward to the events as much—if not more—than the children. Deflated as soon as an event ends, I comfort some children crying in the corner to commiserate, then begin furiously planning for the next. That's how I know how truly satisfied I am, that's how I know how lost I would feel without the Ambassadors.

One chronic similarity among autism parents is disturbingly but amazingly consistent—the *toxic womb* of self-blame. Lest I wonder if I was alone in my private grief and shame, I now have massive data on the shared agony so many mothers bear silently. They pull me aside to confess their sins, each wholly convinced she alone did something terrible to deserve her fate. "I'm afraid to tell you why I think this happened," is the too-common refrain. The range of *sins* is as vast as the spectrum itself, and includes everything from adultery to depression to a sip of alcohol during gestation. While the sins differ widely, the unabated grief does not. That so many mothers fall victim to this myth proves not only its potency, but also the innate compulsion to assign blame and affix cause for random events over which we actually have no control.

The myth feeds on the fallacy that if something is wrong with the child, the vessel must be to blame. It's that same fiction that fueled Dr. Leo Kanner's debunked *refrigerator moms* which still has glowing embers today. The tragic irony is that the loathing should reside with the person who often provides the greatest care and makes the deepest sacrifices. Every mother I know would do anything in her capacity to help her child, which is exactly the sort of noble responsibility such myths pervert.

At first I just listen. Sometimes the fathers have confessions, too. I understand only too well how real the punishment feels following the unexpected discovery of autism. The confessions are eerily reminiscent—those seeds of destruction and self-loathing lie within each and every one of us. How easily they are sown. How little water it takes for them to thrive! Seeds sit dormant until injustice strikes, and then are activated as the parent frantically searches for clues. The misfortune surely must lie in past misdeeds, but in parents' profound shame I see the opposite: nobility. It's to their credit—not scorn—that parents assume blame. Their self-blame is in direct measure to the depth of their loyalty to their beloved children for whom they are willing to sacrifice, for whom they are willing to suffer indescribable pain. There is profound dignity to these primary caretakers, but none in the shame. I make sure they understand, because I buried that toxic myth long ago.

At the splash park today I spy one mother who just caught my eye, a frightened newcomer to the events, looking wildly around in awe and fear. Frazzled and cowering, she stares anxiously at the flowing fountains as I walk over to introduce myself. She responds to my hug by clinging tightly; she can't let go, I can feel her trembling. She disengages long enough to point out her young son who is sitting beneath a bursting mushroom fountain, but absolutely still.

"I just . . . I just thought he'd run around and play like the other kids," she cries mournfully. "I just want him to do what the others are doing!"

"Yes, I know," I say, "but the key is, he's here. He's tolerating the chaos and commotion, and he's doing well. For some of our children, simply passing under the awning entrance is terrifying."

"It's just . . . he just does so many things." Her voice cracks, the dam about to break. I gently hug her to release the tightly restrained waters. "I'm so sorry," she sobs, "this is my first event and I'm so new to this and—"

I stroke her back soothingly as I whisper, "I know, believe me, I know. But you've only just begun and there's reason to be hopeful, it can get so much better."

She abruptly pulls herself back, embarrassed by her impulsive loss of control. "I'm so sorry to fall apart, I know you're busy, you don't have time for this. It's just, you just seem so positive, so strong, upbeat, and I'm just not like you." She gulps miserably.

I'm aware of the calm strength I project to my Ambassadors, and their corresponding illusion that I must be one of those rare parents who heartily accepts what comes my way with assurance that I can handle it. Soon they will know my true story and how I got here.

"Come, my new friend," I say smiling as I protectively drape my arm around her shoulders and lead her to a quiet patch of shade where we can talk freely. "Come and let me tell you a story . . ."

EPILOGUE

And there may be times where it is right to be
angry and defiant . . . But if you're so invested
in the anger that you don't see when somebody
is putting out their hand in a sincere gesture of
friendship, then you've now become your own
jailer. It's not just someone else jailing you.

—PRESIDENT BARACK OBAMA, *THE ATLANTIC*,
INTERVIEW BY TA-NEHISI COATES,
(DECEMBER 20, 2016)

I NO LONGER look back in anger. I understand that I, and everyone working with Zack over the years, did the very best we could operating on the best information. Countless parents worldwide are at this very moment doing the same. I don't seek to pass broad judgment on medical and behavioral interventions. My story and observations are restricted to my own experience with Zack. Autism is so inscrutable, each child so distinct, it makes sense for parents to pursue whichever treatments they suspect might be productive for their child.

My only urging, from far down the intervention road, is that parents remember to trust their own instincts about their own child. No medical opinion, no matter how competent or research-based, can supplant a parent's intuition based on careful observation. The autism diagnosis is marked by a shared constellation of symptoms, but that's where the similarities end. Predicting which interventions will have most impact, or how much progress any child will make, is exceedingly difficult. But therein lies the capacity for realistic hope. No matter where your child resides on the spectrum, no matter how severe the behaviors, your child has the same potential as any other to make serious functional progress.

Dear readers, thank you for listening to my uncensored voice. While I hope *Autism Uncensored* speaks to you, it's still only one woman's insights. I pulled back the curtain on my own interior life with the hope that the understanding and discoveries I gained along my journey might spare others pain and provide new perspectives on the very real challenges. While I worship and admire those impacted, I don't pretend that coping with autism is easy for anyone involved. Having expertise in a given field has always been something I've needed for my own self-esteem. Not since I left my legal career so many years ago did I fully fill the professional vacancy. I've always known that the only way I would, my only path back to being me, was to do something tangible in a given field. So I wrote a book about autism. In many ways the field chose me, and now I feel whole. I am more grateful to you for reading my story than you can know, and in doing so you are now officially a part of it. The chapters keep writing themselves.

Although my main messages are self-evident in the narrative, here's some final wisdom for fellow travelers on autism's path.

GIVE EVERY MEDICAL OR BEHAVIORAL
INTERVENTION TIME, BUT NOT TOO MUCH.

It takes at least six to eight months before you should draw any conclusions about its efficacy. But don't wait longer than a year to re-examine or discard practices which don't appear to provide perceptible benefit. Today, there are interventions that didn't exist when Zack was diagnosed. While ongoing research and new treatments are welcome, allow common sense to govern your intervention choices. To date, there is still no uniform treatment that cures autism or guarantees meaningful progress across the wide spectrum. For this reason, the litmus test I use in observing an intervention asks the following questions:

- Is each new skill or word or behavior truly acquired, owned and applied by the child across a variety of settings? Does the child use it consistently in the classroom, or while watching movies, and in the community? Or is the skill demonstrated largely or exclusively during the intervention session itself, like only when prompted or in exchange for positive reinforcements?

- Is the skill retained by the child over several months, even as he acquires new information, or is it discarded and displaced by the child in order to make room for more recent information?

- Is the skill used independently or is it prompt-reliant? Does he initiate it on his own for functional use, or does he require a specific verbal prompt or therapist thoroughly conversant with its use? If the latter, can the skill reasonably become independent down the road in the absence of specific prompts or aids? If dependent, is the child prepared to apply the skills with persons unacquainted with him? Is he flexible about who administers prompts or assists in executing the skill?

- Is the skill functional and pragmatic for his community? True functionality is entirely separate from rote memorization, though the two can co-exist. But if epistemic choices must be made to supply the child with the most information he can retain, err on the side of teaching skills he can truly use—personal hygiene, financial transactions, ordering off a menu. Does the skill assist him in social interactions, enhance his ability to forge attachments to others, allow him to protect himself or make him more qualified for certain employment?

Irrespective of the intervention, I still believe that the child's natural environment is both the best instructor and motivator for cementing real-world skills. It is those critical functional skills that better allow the child to be meaningfully included in social operations—recreational, employment—with or without supports, as our children fully deserve to be.

DON'T OVERREACT TO EMERGING BEHAVIORS OR SEEK TO QUASH THEM IMMEDIATELY.

If aggressive or serious self-injurious behaviors emerge, they must indeed be dealt with swiftly insofar as they pose a danger to the child or others. However, when it comes to myriad self-stimulating behaviors—flapping, twirling, yelping, fixating on objects, holding one's groin in public (yes, Zack has done all of these)—remember, it may be a brief phase through which the child passes. Too often we forget that our autistic children develop normally in many ways, and like all children they will experiment creatively with their minds and body parts. Parents traumatized by autism will naturally and reflexively seek to suffocate new and unusual behaviors, but it's possible that in four to six months the child may outgrow and abandon it entirely on his own.

As our children mature and change, many behaviors emerge and then fade whether you actively intervene or do nothing at all. This observation has become a guiding principle and welcome relief in resisting my own impulse to police Zack's ever-evolving behaviors to this day.

DON'T WAIT TOO LONG TO SOCIALIZE.

This principle applies to parents and children. Autism has no borders—it cuts across every race, ethnicity, religion, status— and it strips parents of any pretenses. So don't pretend. Seek out other parents with children on the spectrum, and they may become the deepest friendships you'll ever make. Our children need to socialize, too, as early and often as possible and regardless of whether they have verbal expression. Young children have their own means of communicating and bonding with one another, and they are often nonverbal and unconcerned with respective differences. Expose your child to preferred activities on a repeated basis—playgrounds, sports, pools, movies, dancing. Do not eschew play dates because you presume your child isn't verbal or engaging enough; even if the play is more parallel than interactive, children are naturally tolerant and forgiving. Your child senses the difference between unscripted play versus intensive therapy in isolation from peers.

BEWARE OF TOO MUCH POLITICAL CORRECTNESS.

It cannot have escaped readers' attention that I consistently use the words "normal," "typically developing" and "typical" in my writing. This is not a value judgment. I use the words literally to mean that which is statistically average, or the norm. I believe we need more tolerance for well-intended words. I applaud candid discourse on autism and, while I favor sensitivity, I'm not in favor of calculated parsing of words or verbally slapping down a speaker whose intent is good despite using antiquated terms.

When we punish those who use the wrong words, we obfuscate the truth of their intent. I can't summon the courage of people unacquainted with autism to ask the questions really on their minds if I judgmentally censor the way they ask them. If the cost of asking honest questions with imprecise words is a smack-down, people will predictably choose not to speak at all. Silencing curiosity alienates others and undercuts our cause, issues of greatest value to our children, particularly those issues we need the general public to absorb.

In my own lifetime, the terms used to address persons with disabilities have changed radically over the years; terms that were once considered descriptively accurate are now construed by many as deeply offensive. Politically correct language is an ever-moving target, so I recommend we all consider focusing our energy on the intent of the speaker in the overall context.

PARENTS WHO DON'T HAVE A CHILD WITH AUTISM ARE FRIENDS, NOT FOES.

Misfortune is the rod which touches each and every one of us at different times. Years after my house was running smoothly, lightning struck one of my closest friends. Heather, my wise and compassionate friend throughout my ordeal, has four glorious children. One day, while vacationing with them at the beach, she learned suddenly that one of them who'd been struggling with a persistent fever for weeks actually had leukemia. Within twenty-four hours, Heather and her child were rushed by ambulance from a tranquil vacation to a large city children's hospital, where they immediately took up residence in the pediatric oncology ward for thirty days straight.

Words fail to capture the true experience of walking down the long corridor of pediatric oncology where children must ingest poison, which sickens and weakens them in body and soul, in order to combat something more toxic threatening their lives. Heather's child is well now, and I was informed long after Heather's prolonged ordeal that along the way I had made countless missteps in my desperation to comfort her. As we sit side by side today, both survivors, I feel enormously grateful that Heather never allowed me to cut her off when Zack was diagnosed, as I considered doing in my painful state.

We would be wise not to punish or alienate loved ones trying to help. They may succeed now, or down the arduous road, in ways we never imagined. And, when they in turn call upon us in times of desperate need, we are reminded that no one is spared pain. We, too, may struggle to find the correct words, and will be grateful to be forgiven our mistakes.

REMEMBER THAT TIMES, THEY ARE A CHANGING.

Society is always playing catch up with reality, often lagging a step behind what's breaking this very moment. When it comes to autism, I believe we're now moving fast in the right direction, and in fact there's never been a better time in social history to be *different* or *other*. A social exfoliation is sloughing off crusty, stale and outdated notions of what it means to be authentically oneself and still belong.

The national non-profit organization, Autism Speaks, announced that it abandoned its founding principle of finding a cure in favor of funding services for persons on the spectrum. The time-honored children's educational program, *Sesame Street*, just welcomed a beautiful new puppet named Julia, the first-ever character with autism. In the wise and prescient words of Julia's creator, "in time Julia will cease being a character with autism and will simply be Julia, a remarkable little girl who fits neatly into the spectrum of humanity."

New York City's Broadway theater productions of "The Lion King," "Mary Poppins," and more, now offer "sensory-friendly" performances that allow our children to experience live theater on their own terms. Regal Cinemas nationwide are offering sensory-friendly showings of movies for our children to enjoy. Savvy entrepreneurs like SAP are purposely hiring adults with autism for strategic business reasons. Our children bring unique abilities to the table. Sensory-friendly zoos, airplane practice rides, cruises, movies, splash parks now abound nationwide. I expect these trends to continue exploding worldwide.

As for me, the Autism Ambassador events will continue indefinitely. In the meantime, dedicated research on autism's causes and treatments will continue forge on. But as has been the case throughout history, the most critical developments, breakthroughs and innovations, will continue to come from parents, siblings and persons coping with the mighty spectrum. As parents and caretakers, we remain the angriest, most courageous, and most ferociously resourceful advocates our beloved children will ever know. Always.

FiNALLY, MY MESSAGE FOR ZACK.

Today you can read simple books with clear comprehension, so I fully expect that one day you will read this book, perhaps long after I am gone. So, to you I make this wish: if you develop an awareness about your disability enough to articulate your experience, speak of it publicly and proudly. Wear your autism as a badge of honor to further the social enlightenment you have already made possible. If you do this, you will not only improve lives, but add yet another chapter of accomplishment to a life marked by achievement.

I am forever in your and your sister's debt. I can never repay you for what you both have contributed to my life. And until my last breath, I will continue my nightly ritual of gazing up at the constellations of stars and thank the universe for bringing you both into my life. Our story is now uncensored, but it's also unfinished, with new chapters being written every day. In the words of the poet Kahlil Gibran, "One day you will ask me which is more important: my life or yours? I will say mine, and you will walk away, not knowing that you are my life."

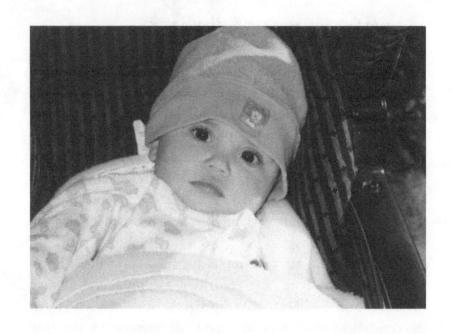

12/19/2006

12/19/2006

APR 3 2010

WiTH GRATiTUDE

Keith Reuben, whose quiet heroism has made the Autism Ambassadors possible; the partner who inspires my strength and eccentricity, and whose innate goodness and equanimity make him the only person with whom I could ever have weathered the storm of parenting.

Cassie Reuben, my daughter and soul mate who has only ever known life with autism, and whose natural gifts of justice and joy have made her the best friend that Zack, Keith and I will ever know.

Jay Ellenby, my extraordinary father who taught me the true meaning of unconditional love.

Carole, Jesse and Stacey Reuben, Karen and Melissa Ellenby, Janet and Jay Detzel, whose love and ongoing support over the years of Zack's life has been the bedrock of my ability to function and run my Ambassador events, and whose support kept me afloat when I was drowning.

Todd Hayes Reuben, whose loving memory we honored by naming our daughter Cassandra Todd Reuben, and whose loss we feel every day, knowing that Todd would have been one of

Zack's strongest allies and friends, and who Zack would have adored in kind.

Cynthia Del Rosario (CC), living proof that angels exist, whose relentless optimism and dedication to Zack before, during and after Zack's diagnosis shone light into my very darkest hours, and who helped me with my own special needs.

Roni Bianco, the most wonderful and authentic friend a person struggling with life could be lucky enough to know; resourceful, wise and willing to do anything and everything in her power to help a friend in need.

Heather, my beloved friend who accompanied me on my tumultuous journey from the beginning, whose wise counsel kept me steady in demoralizing times, and who offered compassion without ever slipping over into pity.

Anne, Arielle, Eva, Cindy, Ali, Fabiana, Marci, Jackie, Jenn, Susan H, Susan I., Marjorie, Karen, Jillian, Melissa Bracamonte, Joy Barwick, and Stefanie Missner, my real-world editors who delicately remind me that I do not need to publish my every thought, and who, like the sturdiest of ropes, intertwined to create a safety net into which I can fall, even when their own rope is fraying.

Jamie Raskin, an unconquerable statesman who stands strong and unfailingly for all that is decent, compassionate and just, and who entered my life at just the right moment to provide much-needed scaffolding during the vicissitudes of writing my story.

Dr. Steven Polakoff and Regina Ottaviani, physicians and rightful experts in their field who helped me get through dark tunnels of emotional pain, helped me to stand upright once more, and without whose invaluable help this book might never have been written.

Donna Meyer, Linnea Powery and Amanda Reynolds, the extraordinary teachers who helped shape Zack into the person he is today, who ignited in me the desire to write this book, and who are living examples of what special education is, and should be.

Carolyn Dorn, Freddie Rosenfeld, Martha Stobs, John Camp and Hiram Goza, my beloved and mighty teachers from middle and high school, who accepted and shaped my eccentricities into literary expression at an early age when I was too unformed to know what life had in store. They will be proud to see that my adult writing, including rare use of profanity, is spelled correctly and uses flawless grammar.

Ron Suskind, a brilliant storyteller who channeled his personal pain into enlightenment about natural preferences of persons with autism, and who generously extended a hand to an unknown, fledging writer on a similar mission.

John Koehler and Joe Coccaro, my "unicorns" in the publishing world who I feared might not exist. Men of clarity, compassion and wisdom who immediately intuited what I set out to accomplish, who opened the door to a first-time author, and whose generosity will help light the match that sets ablaze the conventional expectations about what our children with autism can achieve. And to John, who taught me that the most critical component in any relationship, even with oneself, is forgiveness.

The Autism Ambassadors, my beloved and mighty spectrum of children, parents and caregivers upon whom my very happiness depends.

ABOUT THE AUTHOR

WHITNEY ELLENBY is a former US Department of Justice, Disability Rights attorney whose writings have been published in *The Washington Post*, a law review periodical, and the U.S. DOJ website. She is the author of "Divinity vs. Discrimination: Curtailing the Divine Reach of Church Authority," *Golden Gate University Law Review* (1996)), as well as an amicus brief on behalf of the U.S. DOJ Disability Rights Division regarding discrimination against mobility-impaired individuals in violation of the Americans with Disabilities Act (ADA). She is the proud parent of a son with Autism and founder of "Autism Ambassadors," a charitable venture through which she runs exclusive recreational events for over 600 families impacted by Autism in the Washington, DC/Maryland area, including a Sensory-Friendly showing of the world-famous "Gazillion Bubbles Show." She is an expert on Autism and has testified before the Maryland Senate on disability-related issues, is a member of the Developmental Disabilities Advisory Council for Montgomery County, MD and serves on the University of Maryland Autism Spectrum Disorder Advisory Board. Whitney's expertise is steeped in her extensive disability law background, personal experience with her own son, and over 10 years of serving children, teens and adults with Autism of all ages through her "Autism Ambassador" events. Her monthly "Ambassador events" have been featured in local t.v. news, *The Washington Post, Bethesda Magazine,* and *The Bethesda Gazette*. Whitney was most recently honored with an "Autism Awareness Proclamation" and "Community Leader" award for her advocacy and dedication to the disability community of Maryland. She has what she describes as a "healthy obsession" with all things Autism.